ADVANCE PRAISE FOR
SICKNESS AND WEALTH

"A timely, radical, and accessible tool for understanding the corporate attack on health care as a right. An exceptional mix of activist and scholarly voices makes *Sickness and Wealth* stand apart. This book is indispensable to those interested in health and social justice."

—Sarah Shannon,
Hesperian Foundation

"*Sickness and Wealth* arrives none too soon. This important book is published as a growing unease spreads among those who have access to books, whether published in English or any other language. The reading classes are learning what the world's bottom billion have long been forced to know: that global economic and social arrangements are increasingly inegalitarian and are bad for our health. Militarization, privatization, and unfair trade policies are in fact tightly linked to diseases such as malaria, cholera, and AIDS; current policies have sapped the movement for primary health care for all. *Sickness and Wealth* exposes the mechanisms of these connections.

" 'Knowledge is power' now sounds like a silly piety in large part because the vast preponderance of knowledge long available buttresses the central theses of this book. Power is power. But *Sickness and Wealth* gives teachers and activists and other concerned citizens of a sickly planet a new tool—one designed to do more than merely annoy the powerful architects of the unhealthy policies that move the globe, and help us fight preventable sickness and disease."

—Paul Farmer,
Partners in Health

"The essays in this volume demonstrate in so many ways how the achievement of health for all is not just a matter of providing more clinics and more medicine. With passion and eloquence, they show that ending human rights violations that deprive people of access to health care and the conditions for leading healthy lives is central to that struggle."

—Leonard S. Rubenstein,
Physicians for Human Rights

"This exciting book drives home connections on local and global levels, making it abundantly clear that perverse incentives should be eliminated and new financial resources created to start—and sustain—equitable development and health for all."

—Paul R. Epstein,
Center for Health and the Global Environment

Praise for Health Alliance International

"Over the last ten years, Health Alliance International has demonstrated that progressive health professionals can still effectively combine political analysis, advocacy, and activism with on-the-ground health practice in this era of relentless attacks on equity-oriented health service delivery. Their potent blend of pragmatism and principled commitment to public sector health care has made them extraordinarily effective at both promoting equity-oriented policy and strengthening the actual provision of sustainable local services."

—James Pfeiffer,
Case Western University

SICKNESS AND WEALTH

SICKNESS AND WEALTH

THE CORPORATE ASSAULT ON GLOBAL HEALTH

edited by
Meredith Fort,
Mary Anne Mercer,
and Oscar Gish

South End Press
Cambridge, Massachusetts

BP45

Cover design by Ellen P. Shapiro
Cover photograph by Hartmut Schwarzbach, with permission from Peter Arnold, Inc.

Page design and production by the South End Press collective
Printed on acid-free, recycled paper
Printed by union labor

Library of Congress Cataloging-in-Publication Data

Sickness and wealth : the corporate assault on global health / edited by Meredith Fort, Mary Anne Mercer, and Oscar Gish.
    p. ; cm.
  Includes bibliographical references and index.
  ISBN 0-89608-717-4 (cloth : alk. paper) — ISBN 0-89608-716-6 (pbk. : alk. paper)
  1. Public health—Economic aspects—Developing countries. 2. Public health—Political aspects—Developing countries. 3. Globalization—Health aspects. 4. World health.
  [DNLM: 1. World Health. 2. Developing Countries. 3. Health Policy. 4. Socioeconomic Factors. WA 530.1 S566 2004] I. Fort, Meredith P. II. Mercer, Mary Anne. III. Gish, Oscar.
  RA441.5.S53 2004
  338.4'33621'091724—dc22
                    2004014498

South End Press, 7 Brookline Street #1, Cambridge, MA 02139-4146
www.southendpress.org
    08 07 06 05 04   1 2 3 4 5

® GCIU 196

12/3/04

CONTENTS

Acknowledgments   xi

Preface
DIAGNOSING GLOBAL INJUSTICE   xiii
    JOIA MUKHERJEE

Introduction
GLOBALIZATION AND HEALTH   1
    MEREDITH FORT

Section ONE
BRIEF HISTORY OF HEALTH
AND DEVELOPMENT STRATEGIES   9

Chapter 1
THE LETHAL DIVIDE:
HOW ECONOMIC INEQUALITY AFFECTS HEALTH   11
    STEPHEN BEZRUCHKA AND MARY ANNE MERCER

Chapter 2
THE LEGACY OF COLONIAL MEDICINE   19
    OSCAR GISH

Chapter 3
THE PRIMARY HEALTH CARE MOVEMENT
MEETS THE FREE MARKET   27
    EVELYNE HONG

Chapter 4
SAPPING THE POOR:
THE IMPACT OF STRUCTURAL ADJUSTMENT PROGRAMS   43
    STEVE GLOYD

Section TWO
EXPANSION OF THE NEOLIBERAL MODEL   55

Chapter 5
THE FAILURES OF NEOLIBERALISM:
HEALTH SECTOR REFORM IN GUATEMALA   57
    JUAN CARLOS VERDUGO

Chapter 6
HMO'S ABROAD:
MANAGED CARE IN LATIN AMERICA   69
    CELIA IRIART, HOWARD WAITZKIN, AND EMERSON MERHY

Chapter 7
TRADE AND HEALTH CARE:
CORPORATIZING VITAL HUMAN SERVICES   79
    ELLEN SHAFFER AND JOSEPH BRENNER

Chapter 8
MILITARISM AND THE SOCIAL PRODUCTION OF DISEASE   95
    SEIJI YAMADA

Section THREE
HOW ECONOMIC GLOBALIZATION POLICIES
AFFECT HEALTH   105

Chapter 9
STOLEN HARVEST:
THE HIJACKING OF THE GLOBAL FOOD SUPPLY   107
    VANDANA SHIVA

Chapter 10
THE POLITICAL ROOTS
OF SOUTH AFRICA'S CHOLERA EPIDEMIC   119
 PATRICK BOND

Chapter 11
THE REGLOBALIZATION OF MALARIA   131
 TIMOTHY HOLTZ AND S. PATRICK KACHUR

Chapter 12
THE BATTLE AGAINST GLOBAL AIDS   145
 PAUL DAVIS AND MEREDITH FORT

Section FOUR

MOBILIZING FOR HEALTH   159

Chapter 13
THE STRUGGLE FOR PEOPLE'S HEALTH   161
 ALEJANDRO CERÓN, ABHIJIT DAS, AND MEREDITH FORT

Conclusion
SHALL WE LEAVE IT TO THE EXPERTS?   167
 MARY ANNE MERCER

Glossary: Terms and Organizations   173
Resource Guide   177
Contributors   193
Endnotes   199
Index   223
About South End Press   238

Dedicated to Oscar Gish, who fought the good fight.
Teacher, friend, husband, father.
1929-2004

ACKNOWLEDGMENTS

For their encouragement and support for the initial idea, we would like to thank Kevin Danaher, Steve Gloyd, Todd Jailer, and Sarah Shannon. Writers who dare to tell a different story have inspired us—especially those involved in *Dying for Growth: Global Inequality and the Health of the Poor*, as well as Arundhati Roy, Noam Chomsky, and Eduardo Galeano. Health activists, including the Health GAP Coalition, Health Alliance International staff in Mozambique, and many others mentioned in the book have helped to keep us focused on what is really important and motivated us to never stop trying.

Many people contributed to the book from beginning to end. First and foremost, we salute the many wonderful authors for the time and effort they invested in these chapters, and for their enduring dedication to social change.

The Equality Network Foundation financed the book proposal and initial work on the book. We appreciate Cecile De Sweemer for her generous assistance in conceptualizing and drafting sections, and Jennifer Meyer and Tim Struna for their editorial help. Beth Peterman and Kenneth Sherr helped with early research. The staff at HAI, including Loreen Lee, Julie Beschta, Tom Martin, Paula Brentlinger, Peggy Riehle, and Andrea Chateaubriand, provided creative ideas and general support. Andrew Bryant at HAI and Megan Morrissey at South End Press were particularly helpful with factchecking and endnote editing.

A number of readers helped to review chapters and gave valuable feedback, including Erik Jensen, Ashok Ready, Sharon Garret, Roberta Greenwood, and Michael Right.

Special appreciation to our family members whose patience and encouragement was essential, including: Stephen Bezruchka and Maia Mercer; Liz, Adam, and Alex Gish; Susan and David Fort; Sarah and Bill Fort; and Alejandro Cerón, who also helped review chapters.

We also want to thank Jill Petty, our editor at South End Press, for her help in shaping the book, as well as her attention to accessible language, clarity, and saliency.

Most importantly, we want to recognize our colleague Oscar Gish for his support in editing *Sickness and Wealth.* Unfortunately, Professor Gish, who made numerous contributions to the field of public health, died as this book was going to press. His experience as a health sector planner with the WHO and country governments, as well as a practiced researcher and writer, brought a profound understanding of the discipline to the book.

Trained as a health economist, Oscar had the opportunity to work in numerous countries, including Tanzania, where he helped to design a primary health care model with the Nyerere government. As he saw postcolonial social development programs replaced by neoliberal policies, Oscar never hesitated to criticize the limited, vertical projects that are most common in "international health" today. Over the years, he has been one of the strongest voices in the industrialized world to speak against the practice of providing poor services to the poor.

In the International Health Program at the University of Washington, we knew Oscar as a supportive colleague and mentor to many. At times students and others new to the field were eager for rapid public health "solutions," but Oscar never let us off easy. He always made it clear that poor health in the Third World was not "an act of nature," but rather the direct result of colonialism and neoliberal policies. And as he exposed the sometimes discouraging politics of health, he never forgot to provide hope and encouragement for the larger, difficult struggle.

We are lucky to have known and worked with Oscar on this book, and on other efforts in the International Health Program and Health Alliance International. Although Oscar will not be with us to see the day when "health for all" is realized, we will honor him by working that much harder.

DIAGNOSING GLOBAL INJUSTICE

JOIA MUKHERJEE

In 2003, I met Dr. Steve Gloyd, one of the contributors to this fine book, at a meeting about implementing HIV treatment in resource poor settings. The meeting was held at a Partners in Health-run hospital in rural Haiti, and attended by AIDS experts from many developed countries. While many well-meaning European and North American medical academics—very new to the health landscape in the developing world—debated the merits of one HIV treatment regimen over another, Steve and I bemoaned the profound and entrenched poverty that underlies the fragile existence of the poor, and the abysmal state of the public health sector that is charged with caring for them.

At this well-attended meeting, only the small group of us who regularly face the stark contrasts between the developed and developing worlds continually linked these important clinical discussions about HIV treatment to the international agents and policies that foment poor health: the corporate interests and neoliberal "reforms" that force some governments to decrease their public service budgets and allow the "first world" unfettered access to their economies.

No doubt, some of our clinical and scientific colleagues from places like the US, France, and England thought that such policy arguments should be vetted elsewhere—after all, hadn't we come to Haiti to talk about scaling up access to HIV care? Certainly, they supposed, there must be groups better positioned to address the thorny issues of international finance.

But for the doctors, nurses, activists, and others who help to bring needed medical care to the world's most vulnerable groups, the paltry health budgets (usually less than US $5 per person per year) allotted to the very countries where health is poorest serve as a cruel and formidable barrier against substantive improvement in global health. In Haiti, the government health budget is just $1.75 per person per year. At this level of health funding, even infant vaccination cannot be sustained. In Haitian Kreyol the word for poverty is *mize*, misery. Indeed, our work in poor countries demonstrates not the life of the "happy peasant," but lives of misery borne by the poor, who have little or no access to food, shelter, education, or health care.

We are taught in medical school that 90 percent of diagnoses are revealed by listening, taking a careful accounting of the symptoms present, and understanding the history of the illness. Worldwide problems such as AIDS, tuberculosis, maternal mortality, and infant death are only the symptoms of a larger global pathology. So it seems obvious that we must tend to the symptoms of our sick body politic to the best of our ability—prevent diseases which are preventable and treat people who live with AIDS, tuberculosis, typhoid, malaria, and all the other diseases that have been relegated, increasingly, to the category "diseases of poverty."

But to properly diagnosis the sickness that affects the body politic we must also ask, "What is the history of this problem? What is the cause of this sickness?" Our collective diagnosis, and the one outlined so well in this book, is that the cause of this global sickness *is* poverty, misery. Its history is rooted in the deliberately inequitable distribution of wealth. By dissecting the body and examining the pathology within it, this book, *Sickness and Wealth: The Corporate Assault On Global Heath,* attempts to give us an honest diagnosis with which to work.

The first and most important part of making the right diagnosis is to understand the history of this seemingly intractable poverty. Much of the current global inequality is a direct result of colonialism, subjugation, and the slave trade. Colonized countries from Brazil to Uganda, rich in natural resources, were not developed for the people of these lands. Rather, colonies were used solely to extract resources to support the empires of England, France, Spain, Portugal, Holland, and others.

History is replete with examples of this exploitation—from the Congolese slaves who worked for the Belgian rubber trade in their own land, to slaves were sold by the English to the French and Spanish to farm sugar cane in Hispaniola. Not a penny of reparations has been paid to affected countries by the colonial powers who carried out this awful rape of peoples and lands, despite the fact that they profited enormously.

In fact, rather than reparations for damage done to the people, land, and psyches of these deliberately undeveloped countries, this exploitation continued once independence was won in the 1950s and 1960s. The same colonial interests were given a capitalist face, and were underwritten by a new

American superpower. The work force is nearly the same, slavery barely hidden by the pretense of paying laborers meager wages. Some countries tried to reclaim their resources or nationalize them, as Zambia did with the nationalization of copper mines. However, with little in the way of infrastructure to develop, poor countries became rapidly dependent on loans from the countries that had historically exploited their land and people. These loans come with harsh restrictions or structural adjustment policies. The policies demand that governments "open markets" and privatize public services such as health, education, and water—services upon which the poor are even more dependent than the wealthy.

This book outlines some of the consequences of these policies, implemented in a massive global experiment to export the "free market" to the already exploited poor world. Ironically, once forced into free market economies, the poorest countries have hardly been allowed to trade freely on the global stage. Subsidies that protect farmers from financial ruin in wealthy countries are considered "bad economics" when granted to the world's poorest farmers. Protective tariffs in rich countries ensure that agricultural goods such as sugar, cotton and beef will not be exported from the poor world to the rich. Moreover, the processing that adds value to a raw material or crop is protected by trade barriers and corporate interests. The coffee grown in East Africa, for example, cannot be roasted there. The difference between the price for the unprocessed coffee beans harvested by the poor and roasted beans sold in wealthy countries is ten fold, making an eight billion dollar coffee harvest, and $80 billion revenue generating venture for corporations.

What in the world does this financial cycle have to do with health—with infant vaccinations, water quality, or AIDS treatment? Unfortunately, this carefully crafted structural violence under which the poor suffer and die has everything to do with the colonial past and the neoliberal corporate present. There is no attention paid to the health and welfare of the poorest people in either the colonial or corporate models. While it is said that the rising economic tide expected by market reforms will "lift all boats," the poor have no boat, and are drowning in this tsunami of corporate profit.

Human rights serve as a life boat, a safety net against the exploitation of the vulnerable. Yet not since 1978, when the Alma-Ata Declaration called for "health for all by the year 2000," have we heard a rights-based call for access to health care. The rights-based goals of Alma-Ata were modest; 90 percent of children should have weight for age that corresponds to reference values, every family should be within a 15-minute walk of potable water, and women should have access to medically trained attendants for childbirth. There was unanimous agreement that these goals could not be achieved or sustained by the world's poorest governments without increased international aid. However, the proposed right to universal basic health care was attacked by international experts as naive, too expensive, and not "sustainable."

In the years since, its become devastatingly clear that revitalizing the public health infrastructure and improving the delivery of essentials—such as vaccination, sanitation, and clean water—is an essential step in addressing the social injustice that underlies disease. Governments, of course, must set rational, stable, and rights-based policies that guarantee health care for even the most poor and vulnerable citizens. But, while this responsibility rests with the governments of the world's poorest countries, "health for all" is only possible with large scale and ongoing international assistance, and with the elimination of onerous debts. Our advocacy work as health activists must recognize that more money is needed for health now, and for decades to come. Recent calls for debt relief are rooted in the notion that if governments spent less money paying back debt, there will be more money to invest in health and education. Additionally, novel strategies to more adequately support global health have been initiated in the last few years, including the Global Fund to Fight AIDS, Tuberculosis, and Malaria, the largest multilateral public health fund. The Fund and the international movement for debt relief are reflect a growing understanding that fulfilling the right to health care is a responsibility that all of us must share.

The deep roots of health inequality assure us that, until systemic change takes place, the misery will continue. Without money to train human resources, build real health infrastructure, procure medicines and diagnostics, successful health projects will remain pilots and large scale initiatives to improve health will seem naive. But the past and present can help us diagnosis the sickness we find globally and it is only if we understand the pathology that we can imagine a healthier future. *Sickness and Wealth: The Corporate Assault On Global Heath* gives us the diagnosis, and suggests that the team to cure the sickness is the collective of those who care about the lives of the poor and are willing to address the real causes of inequality to truly improve global health.

GLOBALIZATION AND HEALTH

MEREDITH FORT

Although the term "globalization" has come into popular use only in the last 20 years, it is not a new phenomenon. Its principles were fundamental to the mercantile system of imperial Europe and to colonialism. From the days of Columbus's contact with Taino natives in Hispaniola to the industrial revolution, globalization has evolved and adapted, always maximizing the accumulation of wealth by the wealthy.

Contemporary globalization differs, in a number of ways, from its predecessors. For example, corporate middle men, such as food and agricultural multinationals, have created large markets for themselves by setting prices at both ends; today, the price that farmers receive for their product has no relationship to the price consumers pay for the final product. In reality, most of the exchange that occurs is carried out through computerized transactions rather than through the trade of actual goods, with futures markets, energy trading, and speculation being extreme versions of this phenomenon. Nevertheless, the wealthy still dominate the process and the poor are expected to give up their resources and participate as cheap labor and willing consumers, while waiting patiently for the benefits to trickle down.

Not surprisingly, countries in the South are obliged to play the globalization game by a different set of rules than those in the North. Most acquired freedom and independence by the 1960s but have been unable to fundamentally reorient their economies to this new reality. By the 1980s, most poor countries were heavily indebted to commercial banks, as well as the International Monetary Fund (IMF) and the World Bank. Then, Third World countries were told they had to implement structural adjustment programs (SAPs) to deal with their debts and ensure regular payments. More recently, as a condition for participation in the global economy, countries in the South have been pressured to sign onto unbalanced free trade agreements that make their economies even more dependent on the export of low-priced goods, and more vulnerable to exploitation by multinational corporations. Roberto Bissio, global coordinator of Social Watch in Uruguay, describes this dilemma in relation to agricultural subsidies: "With European subsidies it would be possible to send every European cow around the world on a business class ticket." But under World Trade Organization (WTO) rules, countries in the developing world are being told that they cannot subsidize *their* farmers, who, on average earn less than half of what a US or European cow is allotted.[1]

The basis for many WTO, IMF, and World Bank–sponsored policies is neoliberal economic theory. Supporters of neoliberalism view the public sector as a force which inhibits the market; therefore, governments must be downsized to promote free trade. Neoliberal policy makers consider the maintenance of common goods—like clean air and clean water—an impediment to economic growth, and agree that other public safeguards—like tax-based health care—should be limited or eliminated.

How does this theory translate into real effects on people's health? Almost everywhere in the Third World, publicly distributed water is not clean or safe for drinking, but Coca-Cola and Pepsi are almost universally accessible because the market—and marketing—demand it.

In places like Sri Lanka and India, peasant farmers are literally committing suicide with pesticides because they cannot compete with agroindustry.[2] And in terms of access to medical care, in many poor countries patients must pay before any services are provided, even in emergencies. In some places, patients who cannot pay for their hospital are "held hostage" until they or their families can scrape together funds to pay the medical costs.[3]

Finally, fifteen years after the introduction of life-extending treatment, more than 95 percent of the people living with HIV/AIDS do not have access to antiretroviral drugs because they cannot afford them.[4]

The consequences for the environment and living conditions are also severe. Humans, plants, animals, and entire ecosystems suffer from the contamination of water, soil, and air, as well as from the overuse of natural resources. In the name of efficiency and economic development, forests are felled; mangrove ecosystems (some of the most efficient in the world) are replaced with shrimp farms, and massive dams have been built in places like China and India, flooding out farmland and homes. The poor and people of color are most affected because their communities are more likely to become dumping grounds for the by-products of uncontrolled economic growth; shiploads of industrial waste and truckloads of rich people's trash are dumped near their homes with no regard for the long-term health effects. And since resources are scarce, the poor use whatever they can find in their immediate environments to meet the needs of their family. Health and hygiene quickly become secondary to immediate, daily needs, as the photo on this book's cover shows—the Nepali woman in Kathmandu uses water from one of the most polluted rivers in the world to wash her dishes.[5]

"Development" and Injustice

In the past decade, millions of people around the world have responded to the injustice and hypocrisy of the global economic system. The "Battle of Seattle" at the 1999 WTO ministerial meeting was one of the first times that activists in the industrialized world mobilized on a large scale to demonstrate against economic globalization. There have also been many sizable street demonstrations in countries such as South Africa, Bolivia, Mexico, Argentina, Malaysia, Thailand, Italy, the UK, and Canada, which have effectively disrupted similar meetings and attracted media attention and the public's eye. In addition to the critics in the streets, public figures and well-known representatives in the so-called development field are increasingly questioning the effects of globalization from the inside.

For many years, globalization policies have been scrutinized by representatives of the United Nations and other development agencies. In 1972, the UN adopted a new set of guidelines, by Amartya Sen, for adopting development projects. Sen's revisionist approach to development was people-centered and emphasized the importance of health and social development, as well as economic growth. Consequently, every year the United Nations Development Program (UNDP) publishes a report chronicling each nation's progress or decline in human development. In 1987, UNICEF published a critique of structural adjustment called *Adjustment with a Human Face*, which called for the protection of vulnerable populations and drew attention to the increase in malnutrition and disease that had taken place in the early 1980s.

More recently, even some in the international financial institutions have begun to show signs that the criticisms are warranted. Joseph Stiglitz, former chief economist at the World Bank, who resigned after clashes with the IMF, including one touched off by the IMF's bungling of the East Asian economic crisis, has publicly spoken out about the need to change development strategies. Branko Milanovic, the World Bank's top economic researcher on matters involving poverty, has compiled reports that question the benefits of globalization and free trade. In one study he demonstrates that income distribution has become more inequitable in poor countries, contradicting the belief that the poor benefit from globalization and free trade as much as the rich.[6] In another, Milanovic writes that the current view of globalization as an automatic and benign force systematically ignores its "malignant side," and that "the record of the last two decades (1978–1998) is shown to be almost uniformly worse than the previous two (1960–78)." [7]

In February 2001, the retiring head of the IMF, Michel Camdessus, gave a speech that was surprisingly similar to the claims of protestors in the streets. He said: "The widening gaps between rich and poor within nations, and the gulf between the affluent and the most impoverished nations, are morally outrageous, economically wasteful, and potentially socially explosive."[8]

The US: A Model, or a Threat to Global Health?

The United States, the wealthiest country in the world, spends far more per capita on health care than any other country (more than five thousand dollars per year). Nevertheless, more than 40 million people go without health insurance, one fourth of whom are children.[9] Nearly one in three non-elderly Americans are without health insurance when those who receive insurance for only part of the year, but not the whole year, are counted.[10]

The reality is that private managed care organizations, insurance companies, and the pharmaceutical industry run the country's health industry—an industry taking in record-high profits despite growing concerns about the cost, quality, and efficiency of managed care. More importantly, the profit motive driving the US health care system is at odds with health care as a basic human right. Not surprisingly, under the current regime the most vulnerable —the poor, chronically ill, racial and ethnic minorities, children, and the elderly—are suffering the most.

In addition to being profit-driven, the US system is based on the dominant biomedical model, which has traditionally neglected the tremendous potential of healing practices from around the world. Furthermore, this curative orientation does not address the underlying social problems that can create illness. As a result, the US is plagued by diseases of leisure, overfeeding, and poor diet, such as obesity, alcoholism, and heart disease. Physical manifestations of inequity, like chronic anxiety, substance abuse and violence, are also common.

Despite these limitations, countries in the developing world are adopting the corporate health model. Often they are compelled to do so by the IMF, the World Bank, other regional development banks, or the WTO through participation in mandated health sector reforms, structural adjustment programs, or trade agreements. And the policies that are being foisted on to these governments—reducing social services, privatization, and regressive taxation—have already had unfavorable results for health in the US.

Sickness and Wealth

The examples from this book are meant to give an historical context for both globalization and health, as well as a glimpse at the problems faced by health activists around the world. These essays show how globalization has negatively affected the health and well-being of the majority of the world's citizens, bringing on more misery and despair for the poor.

In the first section of this book, the authors demonstrate how global poverty and inequality—the major barriers to achieving health—have become more intractable over the last 20 years. While increases in inequality result in poorer health across the board, we can improve health by reducing the income gap between the rich and poor, the clear message offered by public health activists Stephen Bezruchka and Mary Anne Mercer in Chapter One.

In Chapter Two, health economist Oscar Gish outlines how colonialism deprived many poor countries of relevant, effective or equitable health services, as well as the capacity to develop these resources. Independence for former colonies in Africa and Asia brought, primarily, a replication of the irrelevant and inefficient health systems that had been developed by their ruling powers.

For a brief period there was a global effort to provide "health for all," as spelled out in the declaration of Alma-Ata, and described by Evelyne Hong—a member of Third World Network, an international network involved in trade, development, and Third World issues—in Chapter Three. She shows how this attempt to address the social, economic and cultural aspects of health was quickly overtaken by a disease-specific approach, however, which persists more or less to this day.

In Chapter Four, physician, activist and Health Alliance International founder Steve Gloyd explores the debt burden of poor countries, which is largely a result of economic policies enforced by industrialized countries and international financial institutions in the 1970s and early 1980s. When these countries became unable to repay loans for expensive development projects, they were pressured to accept structural adjustment programs. SAPs mandated major restructuring of government functions and austerity provisions, which deepened poverty and reduced social services.

In Section Two, the authors document how the US model of health and development is being exported to the rest of the world. Health policies that have had disastrous results elsewhere are now being implemented in Latin America and other settings. These changes are resulting in disjointed, piecemeal systems in which private agencies—many North American or European—take over public services. In Chapter Five, Juan Carlos Verdugo, a Guatemalan physician and cofounder of the grassroots group Instancia Nacional de Salud (National Health Advocacy Platform) exposes the limitations and dangers of neoliberal policymaking in Guatemala's health sector. In Chapter Six, social medicine teachers and professionals Celia Iriart, Howard Waitzkin, and Emerson Merhy turn a critical eye to the proliferation of companies peddling HMOs in Latin America.

In Chapter Seven, health policy analysts Ellen Shaffer and Joseph Brenner present another dark side of globalization—trade laws that may transform all services, including health care, into commercial products and turn public health protections into "trade barriers."

In Chapter Eight, physician and activist Seiji Yamada reminds us that militarism remains an awesome threat to the well-being of humankind. The example of the Marshall Islands illustrates several effects of militarization on vulnerable people.

Section Three presents some of the consequences of globalization policies on health. Vandana Shiva reveals how food security in India, as elsewhere, is threatened by policies that favor the well-being of corporate interests over those of farmers and consumers in Chapter Nine. Shiva documents how centuries-old seeds are being patented and withdrawn from public use, stripping peasant farmers of their livelihood and further promoting dependence on agribusiness.

In a similar vein, public health researcher and activist Patrick Bond explores the impact of water privatization in Chapter Ten. He tells the underreported story of how more than 150,000 South Africans fell ill with cholera when water was priced beyond their means.

Chapter Eleven presents an example of an ancient scourge—malaria—that appears to be "reglobalizing," as epidemiologists Timothy Holtz and Patrick Kachur write. This mosquito-borne parasitic disease, still kills more than a million persons—most of them children—every year.

In Chapter Twelve, Paul Davis of the US-based AIDS activist group—Health GAP (Global Access Project)—and Meredith Fort look at how AIDS has spread through the developing world in the last 20 years—as corporate-centered globalization became more entrenched—while rich countries made modest efforts, at best, to contain it. Davis and Fort examine the role pharmaceutical companies have played in the pandemic, as well as the response by activists to greedy corporations and stingy first world governments.

Finally, in Chapter Thirteen, the authors explore what is needed to sustain a global movement for health and social justice. Public health practitioners Alejandro Cerón, Abhijit Das and Meredith Fort present examples of groups from all over the world—many struggling against great odds—who are informing and inspiring people who want to be a part this necessary effort.

Similarly, the purpose of *Sickness and Wealth* is to inform and to inspire. While we are being coaxed by politicians, policymakers, and the mainstream media to accept corporate-centered globalization as an inevitable process, the majority of the world's population is being alienated and discriminated against by these policies. By globalizing the struggle, we can all construct a different world on terms that guarantee health, well-being, and dignity.

BRIEF HISTORY OF HEALTH
AND DEVELOPMENT STRATEGIES

Section One provides background and an overview of public health and development strategies. Chapter One focuses on the factors that keep populations healthy. What does the growing gap between the rich and the poor, made worse by current policies, mean for people's health? Although "health" is often equated with "health care," the level of equity in a society plays a key role in determining people's health.

Millions become sick and die each year from preventable diseases because their basic needs—food, safe water, and shelter—are not met. Even in industrialized countries, where more people have access to these basic resources, economic hierarchy has strong and measurable effects on people's health.

Yet the health-wealth gap that we see today has not always existed. Chapter Two describes how colonialism underdeveloped today's developing countries and created dysfunctional heath care systems. Not only were natural resources and labor extracted from Africa, Latin America, and Asia—which allowed industrialized countries to become wealthy—colonial health care systems were established in the colonies to serve the urban elite, and they excluded the majority of people.

The 1978 World Health Organization (WHO) meeting in Alma-Ata marked an turning point in public health history. It demonstrated the hopeful thinking of the time and distilled the wisdom of two decades of the struggle for health for the common man. All 134 countries that attended the conference signed on to the Alma-Ata Declaration, which recognized that health would be achieved through a shift in power and control of resources and through the implementation of a comprehensive approach to health known as Primary Health Care.

Chapters Three and Four show how, since Alma-Ata, economic globalization and the policies put forth by the Bretton Woods institutions have diminished the hope of achieving "Health for All by the Year 2000." If we return to our original reflection in Chapter One of the importance of equity in determining people's health, today's view of health care services as consumer goods shows us just how far we have strayed.

Chapter Three shows how the role of national governments and the WHO in determining health sector policies have declined in relation to the World Bank and regional development banks, with an ideological shift toward privately provided health care. Bank-imposed health sector reform and World Bank globalization dogma have led public health off track.

Neoliberal economic policies such as structural adjustment programs (SAPs) described in Chapter Four have driven people deeper into poverty and have made them more vulnerable to illness. SAPs have squeezed governments of resources, especially affecting the health and social sectors, and have reshaped developing countries' economies to focus on export-oriented trade.

Chapter 1

THE LETHAL DIVIDE: HOW ECONOMIC INEQUALITY AFFECTS HEALTH

STEPHEN BEZRUCHKA AND MARY ANNE MERCER

What are the connections between globalization, growing inequality, and the health of populations? This chapter asserts that inequality is the fundamental cause of poor health and premature death. Global inequality has produced a world where millions die of preventable causes every year. Globalization, as described in the introduction, appears to increase inequality both among and within countries.[1] Thus, although a multiplicity of factors affect health, we posit that corporate-centered globalization alone will have a profoundly negative impact on international health in the twenty-first century.

Measuring the health of a group of people is different from looking at the health of individuals. We can assess various indicators of poor health—signs of illness, disability, subjective well-being—in individuals. But the measures used to gauge the health of a population typically involve comparisons of mortality-related rates such as life expectancy (average number of years lived at current mortality rates) or infant mortality (proportion of babies born that die in their first year of life).

All rich countries and a number of poor countries track births and deaths and publish rates annually, which makes comparisons easy. In poorer countries where vital statistics are not collected, surveys estimate infant mortality and other health measures with some precision. And since death is often the end result of long-term health problems, they are intuitively a useful indicator of patterns of illness and injury. This chapter uses lower infant mortality rates and longer life expectancy as indicators of better health.

What Produces Good Health?

Many discussions about human welfare do not attempt to identify the most basic determinants of health and well-being. Yet it's clear that the fundamental prerequisites for a healthy society are access to the basic necessities of life, such as adequate food, clothing, sanitation, housing, and health care. Much of the world today lacks the ability to provide those necessities, with an estimated 3 billion people living on less than two dollars a day.[2] Even worse, for many the situation is deteriorating: At least 100 countries underwent serious economic decline during the 1970s, 1980s, and 1990s.[3]

This kind of deprivation takes a terrible toll on the health of people living in developing countries. The immense health gap between people living in the poorest countries and those in wealthier countries is dramatically illustrated by comparing women's risk of dying from childbearing-related causes. In the industrialized countries that risk is approximately 1 in 2800, while in sub-Saharan Africa the risk is 1 in 16.[4] Infant mortality is as much as 15 times higher in much of Africa than in the developed world.[5]

Such global inequities are a legacy of colonialism, but they also reflect in large part a global economic order that maintains the advantage of the rich countries at the expense of the poor. And the desire of rich countries to maintain their advantage, while all the time espousing a desire to improve human welfare, is not new. A US State Department policy planning study in 1948 explicitly spelled out the task,

> The US has about 50 percent of the world's wealth but only 6.3 percent of its population. This situation cannot fail to be the object of envy and resentment. Our real task . . . is to devise a pattern of relationships which will permit us to maintain this position of disparity without positive detriment to our national security.[6]

Even in wealthier countries, we see a wide range in average life expectancy. For example, Japanese live 4.6 years longer than people in the US.[7] Clearly, spending on health care alone does not produce good health: The US accounts for close to half of the world's spending on health, and it ranks behind 25 other wealthy countries in life expectancy.[8]

Another prescription for good health in the developed world stresses individual behavior: Eating a healthy diet, getting regular exercise, avoiding smoking, and other "preventive" measures. However, when taken to the population level such reasoning often does not hold. The country with the highest life expectancy in the world, Japan, has the greatest proportion of smokers of all rich countries—Japanese men smoke at twice the rate of American men.[9] Even among smokers, mortality associated with this behavior appears to be much lower in Japanese men than in American men.[10] Similar paradoxes can be found related to low-fat or other special diets, exercise, and other "healthy" individual behaviors. While we are not advocating that governments and employers cut back on measures that support preventive health care, the relative importance of individual behavior must be understood in relation to more basic determinants of population health.

In an effort to identify other factors, a number of research studies have focused on the relationship between a country's income distribution and its infant mortality and life expectancy rates. These studies found strong and consistent relationships between income distribution and health: A greater difference between the incomes of the rich and the poor within a country meant worse overall health.[11] The strength of this effect is maintained even after epidemiological correction for average incomes, rates of smoking, poverty, and other factors that might be expected to explain the relationship.[12] More recently, studies in the US show that wider gaps between the incomes of rich and poor people are associated with increased mortality rates, a greater number of teen pregnancies, violent crime, poor educational outcomes, and obesity.[13] After basic needs are met, people who live in settings with smaller income differences appear to be healthier.[14] With further research we may come to agree with Nobel Prize–winning economist Amartya Sen, who said, "I believe that virtually all the problems in the world come from inequality of one kind or another."[15]

Opinion is divided on the mechanisms that produce these effects, although most explanations are not mutually exclusive. A neo-materialist view suggests that a larger gap indicates there are more poor people who are less able to purchase material goods needed to maintain their health. This undoubtedly is at least part of the problem in very low-income countries. In contrast, a psychosocial interpretation posits that social anxiety and shame, which are created by living in a hierarchical social system, eventually produce poor health; in industrialized countries, this interpretation of the equity-health relationship is gaining currency. Central to the psychosocial interpretation is the concept of hierarchy or social stratification—which considers factors such as net worth, job status, lifestyle, income, possessions, dress, ethnicity, and language. In most societies, these markers ascribe value and worth to individuals.

Although hierarchy is not easily measured, income—a measure of economic stratification—is often used as a proxy for the social stratification that hierarchy represents. Yet however it is measured, in both rich and poor settings, the association between inequality and health status is remarkably strong and consistent.

Growing Inequalities

What is the evidence that inequality is growing, and that it is related to what we call globalization? The extent of global economic disparities today is stark: per capita gross national incomes reported in 2003 for the 50 least developed countries in the world, containing nearly 700 million people, was $295, compared with $28,210 in the industrialized countries—nearly a 100-fold difference.[16] The growth of inequality since the 1970s, thought of as the period of globalization, is well documented in today's economic literature. The gap in incomes between the richest 20 percent and the poorest 20 percent of the world's population was 30 to 1 in 1960; 60 to 1 in 1990; and 74 to 1 in 1997.[17] By 1997, the richest 20 percent of the world's population shared 86 percent of the world's gross domestic product, while the poorest 20 percent had only 1 percent.[18] Conversely, between 1980 and 1993, a billion people saw their real incomes fall.[19] For example, the average African household consumed 20 percent less in 2000 than it did in 1975.[20] This trend of growing inequality also holds within countries, including many industrialized countries. In the US, the top 1 percent owned 22 percent of household wealth in 1976; by 1998, they owned 38 percent.[21]

Is there a strong link between the growing inequality and globalization? There are ample reasons to assume that there is. As explained in the introduction, we refer to globalization simply as the system of global capitalism as it has evolved since the 1970s. Underlying the current world order is an explicit requirement for growth of national economies, and an implicit requirement for the expanded role of multinational corporations in promoting that growth, while increasing their own profit margins. Trade is seen as the key to economic growth. And today's de facto trade rules effectively require markets in poor countries to be free or unregulated, while maintaining state subsidies for key industries in the industrialized countries. Those subsidies overwhelmingly benefit large corporations at the expense of smaller entities, even within the rich countries, and they wreak devastation on the poor. (More detail on the effects of trade agreements is provided in Chapter Seven.)

Although globalization and the growth of economic inequality occurred simultaneously, a causal association between the two phenomena is not easy to prove. However, a landmark trade agreement took place in 1993 that to many symbolizes the strategies and results of the "free trade" movement. The

North American Free Trade Agreement, or NAFTA, provides 10 years of evidence on the effects of the neoliberal approach to economic growth on inequality in Canada, Mexico, and the US. NAFTA promised to produce both jobs and prosperity in all three countries. Ten years later, analyses of the economic effects of NAFTA range from cautiously positive (by its proponents) to strongly critical.[22]

In Mexico, the NAFTA decade was a decidedly difficult one for farmers and workers. In the first five years, the purchasing power of the minimum wage dropped by 20 percent.[23] Farmers growing corn, the Mexican staple food, find themselves undercut by heavily subsidized American corn: Mexican farmers faced price reductions of up to 60 percent within the first five years of the agreement.[24] Economic growth in Mexico averaged an anemic 1 percent per capita annually for the NAFTA decade—a stark comparison with that of other countries such as Korea, which averaged 4.3 percent, or China, at 7 percent.[25]

In the US, NAFTA is documented to be directly responsible for a net loss of nearly 900,000 jobs between 1993 and 2002.[26] Although that number was small as a proportion of the national workforce, many more jobs were transformed from the relatively higher-paying manufacturing sector to the much lower-paid service sector. This change contributed to a growing income inequality within the US.[27] Not surprisingly, the benefits of NAFTA appear to have accrued primarily to the corporate entities that were its supporters in the first place. Despite growing evidence of NAFTA's failures, the US is currently negotiating similar trade agreements similar to NAFTA with countries around the world.

Globalization Harms Health

Some who support corporate-centered globalization claim that it has improved health in poor countries.[28] And health, measured by infant mortality and life expectancy rates, has steadily improved throughout most of the world during the 19th and 20th centuries.[29] Yet one way to measure how globalization has contributed to that improvement is by comparing health statistics in the 1980s and 1990s, when the current model of economic globalization became firmly entrenched, with statistics from the 1960s and 1970s. Improvements in life expectancy were significantly higher for most countries in the earlier period than in the later years.[30] Similarly, infant and young child mortality improved more quickly in the 1960s and 1970s compared with the following two decades.[31] Even national economic growth, an important measure of economic success for supporters of corporate globalization, was higher for most countries in the two decades before 1980 than since then.[32]

More evidence linking globalization with declining health in poor countries comes from a study of infant mortality and the debt burdens of countries in sub-Saharan Africa between 1970 and 1997. In 1970, there was essentially no relationship between the severity of a country's national debt and its infant mortality. However, as the structural adjustment policies of the international lending agencies were put into place in the 1980s in response to staggering debt loads (see Chapter Four), the association between debt and infant mortality grew.[33] Structural adjustment led to higher prices for food and other necessities, such as education and health care, with well-documented effects on health. By 1997, countries with proportionately greater debt had significantly higher infant mortality than countries with lower debt.[34] Researchers estimated that without debt burden in this period, infant mortality would have been reduced by 15 deaths per 1,000 births, or 80 out of 1,000 instead of 95 per 1,000.[35]

In the Soviet Union, the quick switch to a capitalist economy, advised by US experts and national elites, led directly to declines in health. Between 1990 and 1994, life expectancy dropped significantly in nearly all of the countries in the former Soviet Union.[36] The declines were stunning, such as a life expectancy reduction of nine years for men and four for women in Russia.[37] Explanations for the declines were widely debated, but massive increases in inequality seemed to have played a major role. Even today the declines have not stabilized: In Russia, life expectancy for men continues to decline.[38] To date, the toll on human lives from this experiment certainly exceeds 10 million and may be closer to 20 million for the whole region.[39] This staggering number of deaths, which has received comparatively little attention, is comparable to the Soviet famines of the 1930s under Stalin.

Encouraging Examples

In a handful of developing countries, a commitment to equity has produced healthy populations. For example, the state of Kerala in India, as well as Cuba, Sri Lanka, and Costa Rica and some of the formerly communist states of Eastern Europe, have significantly lower infant and child mortality rates than other poor countries.[40] Equity-oriented policies in Kerala, one of the poorest states in India, include subsidized food distribution, effective land redistribution, a focus on universal primary education and health care services, and, finally, a vibrant public political consciousness that elects socialist governments and rarely re-elects the incumbent.[41] Health policy in

Kerala, which supports health and nutrition services equally across the entire population, contrasts sharply with that of other states in India where the wealthier population benefits proportionately more from state services than the poor. As a result, the infant death rate in Kerala is close to that of the US.[42]

A few developed countries also provide examples of successful equity-oriented health-promoting policies. Although the income gap has widened in Canada since the mid-1980s, taxation has helped to level the differences. Income redistribution takes the form of improved models of unemployment insurance and social assistance, and universal access to health care and education. These equity-promoting policies allow Canada to have one of the highest life expectancies in the world.[43] Sweden and other Scandinavian countries are even better at using fiscal policies to limit poverty. Various private, universal, and social transfers—as well as taxes and social assistance—reduce poverty rates by 19 percent in the US, 40 percent in Canada, and almost 82 percent in Sweden.[44]

Before World War II, Japan—now the country with the longest life expectancy and lowest infant mortality rates in the world—ranked poorly in these areas.[45] After World War II, Japan was compelled by American occupiers to demilitarize, democratize, and decentralize wealth and power. The army was abolished and spending on the military was drastically reduced. Corporate conglomerates were also broken up. (American politicians decided that these conglomerates, which dominated three quarters of Japan's industrial and commercial activities, were the architects of Japan's irresponsible government and they had to be dismantled.)[46] The Japanese government also instituted a successful land reform program. Landlords, who had been village elites, were replaced by a broad class of independent farmers.

Finally, the constitution was revised to give more power to citizens, separate Shintoism and the state, and include a very meaningful peace clause requiring that "the Japanese people forever renounce war as a sovereign right of the nation and the threat or use of force as a means of settling international disputes." More progressive than the American constitution, the Japanese constitution provided for free universal education, the promotion of public health and social security, the right of workers to organize and bargain collectively, and the right of everyone "to maintain the minimum standards of wholesome and cultured living."[47]

Obviously, Japan is a major economic power today, and shares the interests of other wealthy countries. However, the history of the country's reconstruction may be provocative, if not encouraging, to those seeking to improve global health through political and economic policies.

Conclusion

Unbridled economic growth and trade (or corporate-centered globalization) has contributed to economic inequality, and as we have seen, inequality suppresses the health and well-being of poor people all over the world. If improved human health in this globalizing world is a goal, then we must create and support economic and social policies that will positively affect health. When he received his Nobel Peace Prize in 2002, Jimmy Carter said,

> I was asked to discuss…the greatest challenge that the world faces. I decided that the most serious and universal problem is the growing chasm between the richest and poorest people on earth. The results of this disparity are root causes of most of the world's unresolved problems, including starvation, illiteracy, environmental degradation, violent conflict and unnecessary illnesses that range from Guinea worm to HIV/AIDS.[48]

As long as these extreme disparities persist, inequities in health outcomes, such as life expectancy and infant mortality, will persist. Clearly, achieving equity in health requires us to work well beyond the borders of the health care sector and secure safe food and water, decent housing, education, and reliable and reasonable incomes for the most vulnerable. These goals will only be accomplished through major social changes that will decrease inequality. Besides bringing those at the bottom up, it will also require those at the top to share wealth, resources, and power.

Chapter 2

THE LEGACY OF COLONIAL MEDICINE

OSCAR GISH

The relative wealth and health of the North is generally assumed to be an enduring reality, and one unrelated to the poverty and ill health of the South. While there is poverty in the North, and considerable wealth in the South, the economic gap between the hemispheres continues to grow. For example, in 1949, as the colonial era was coming to an end, the gross national product per capita in high income countries was less than 20 times that of low income countries (roughly $900 to $50).[1] As stated in Chapter 1, comparable numbers today show a ratio of almost 100 to 1: $28,000 to $300.[2]

Of course, many factors are contributing to the growing wealth gap between richer and poorer countries. One factor often overlooked is the contribution made by poor countries to the economic development of the North—as colonizing powers, they extract much of their wealth from the South. Perhaps the best known example is the extraction of human capital from Africa during the slave trade. The native people living in the "colonies" were not seen as equals by the colonial powers; often whites didn't even consider them to be human. There's no need to guess about these attitudes; they were well-documented by the colonizers themselves. A late-nineteenth-century report from a British civil servant in Basutoland, now called Lesotho, states:

> Though for its size and population Basutoland produces a comparatively enormous amount of grain, it has industry of great economic value to South Africa, viz., the output of native labor. It supplies the sinews of agriculture in the Orange Free State; to a large extent it keeps going railway works, coal mining, the diamond mines at Jagesfontein and Kimberly, the gold mines of the Transvaal and furnishes, in addition, a large amount of domestic services in surrounding territories. The number of men who received passes for labor during the year under review amounted to 37,371. These factors are the best rejoinder to those who argue that Basutoland is a useless native reserve. To others, who urge higher education of the natives, it may be pointed out that to educate them above labor would be a great mistake. Primarily the

native labor industry supplies a dominion want, and secondly it tends to fertilize native territories with cash which is at once diffused for English goods.[3]

Today, globalization reinforces the basic exploitive relationship between North and South; transnational corporations seek out countries where they will find the highest return, namely, where labor and natural resources are cheapest, and where restrictions on working conditions and environmental destruction are minimized. The huge flows of wealth out of Asia, Africa, and the Americas not only constitute a massive contribution to the growth and development of Europe, but poor countries have been (and are still being) stripped of tools and resources they might use for their own development.

There are many examples of the impact of colonization on health and development. For example, colonial powers depleted colonies of their food resources, and in some places per capita food consumption fell considerably during the colonial years. In Algeria, per capita food consumption was between five and six times higher in 1863 than it was in 1954.[4] Under colonial rule, those in power took land from peasants who had used it to meet local consumption needs (such as through the production of cereal grains) and shifted land use to production for export to the North.

Yet, just as today's industrialized countries have not always been rich, they have not always been healthy. For example, in New York City in 1900, near the end of the industrial revolution, the infant mortality rate was 137 per 1000 live births. By 1940, it had dropped to 40 per 1000 live births.[5] It is noteworthy that this decline took place before the advent of antibiotics or vaccines for the common diseases of early childhood, such as pneumonia. While science was moving slowly, populist movements, led by social progressives, labor and civil rights activists, brought about improved conditions. In Europe and the US, the right to vote was extended to women, the labor movement grew in size and strength, education and literacy campaigns were expanded, water and sanitation systems were significantly improved, and other specific public health interventions were made. Such developments were squashed by colonizing powers in the countries of the South.

Medical Care under Colonialism

All societies develop strategies to fight illness. In fact, it may still be the case that more people in the world are in regular contact with "traditional" practitioners of the healing arts than with allopathic healers. The systems to which these traditional practitioners belong vary widely in both their content and effectiveness. Until the 20th century, traditional medicine in countries like

China and India probably rested upon a greater body of knowledge than the western allopathic system. Even less scientifically developed systems in other parts of the world may have been as effective as the western medicine practiced in rural parts of Europe or North America.

Yet, the conquest of Asia, Africa, and the Americas by Europe led to virtually worldwide domination by European forms of organization and scientific systems.[6] In the colonies, western medicine, like all other things European, received official support while traditional systems were consciously suppressed or marginalized. In addition, the transfer of wealth from the colonies to Europe and the US funded the rapid development of scientific and medical institutions, enabling western medical and scientific structures to outstrip those in the South.

To shore up their ability to rule, the colonial powers introduced their own medical systems into their overseas territories.[7] In many cases these early services were developed and managed by military personnel. Typically, "modern" medicine in the colonies—whether in Africa, the Caribbean, Asia, or Latin America—comprised three major components: the urban hospital, the rural dispensary, which was often related to the Christian church, and the hygiene or public health system. In essence, this inadequate and top-heavy structure has persisted in poor countries right up to the present day.

The colonial urban hospital dates as far back as the 1800s in some former colonies. It was first built to meet the needs of nonnative administrators and their families and other Europeans residing in the colony. At times, there were relatively minor inpatient provisions for non-Europeans.[8] These hospitals were found primarily in the major cities, which boasted the greatest concentrations of nonnative populations. The church missions also started to build hospitals early. The government hospital was a major institution in colonial life and, along with the barracks, it was essential to colonial rule. In some places, in fact, the colonial medical department was a direct extension of the military.

The rural dispensary, like the hospital, was mainly a curative institution, a place where drugs were dispensed to sick ambulatory patients. Dispensaries fulfilled the role played by pharmacies (and apothecaries) in Europe or North America at an earlier time—and sometimes still do. Simple illnesses are diagnosed without charge, and patients are then sold remedies to match the diagnoses. The dispensaries were sometimes government run, in which case they might be free, but more commonly they were private institutions, usually run by a Christian church body, and charged a fee. Many dispensaries included a few maternity or inpatient beds, but their limitations were great.

The third essential element of colonial medicine was the hygiene or public health system, which dealt with larger health issues such as illness outbreaks and sanitation. With regard to health and health care, the colonial administrator faced two major problems. First, he had to work to keep Europeans healthy and alive in the hostile environments of Asia and Africa;[9] and second, he needed to do his part to ensure the smooth flow of primary products—such as tea, cocoa, jute, and sisal—from his territory to the ships waiting at the coastal ports. The first health problem was partly met by the urban hospital, and the second was met by the plantation dispensary, which treated acute and disabling illnesses among the workers.

An additional measure was the introduction of the sanitary inspector, an import from Victorian Europe, into the colonial town. (The colonial town was itself often a new addition to the older "native" city.) The sanitary inspector, or scout, was responsible in some countries for ensuring that schools and restaurants met cleanliness standards and that latrines were built and kept clean, and for keeping watch for vectors. The European administration attempted to separate from the prevailing environment and to create a different and cleaner one for itself. This entailed not only ensuring sanitary conditions in their own living areas but very often creating a sanitary cordon between itself and the surrounding native quarters. Similar hygienic efforts were made in the most important areas of primary production, and estates and plantations were eventually to become more protected environments than their surroundings.

The Years After Independence

Colonial medical structures persisted into the 20th century, but the two decades following the Second World War saw successful independence movements take hold. In the late 1940s and 1950s, many countries in Asia, such as India, Sri Lanka, and Burma (now Myanmar) declared their sovereignty. In the 1960s and 1970s, many countries in Africa and the Caribbean, including Nigeria, Kenya, Tanzania, Jamaica, and Trinidad and Tobago, did the same. (Most countries in the Americas had achieved independence more than a century earlier.) Most countries came to political independence under leadership that envisioned orderly democratic development (in the conventional western sense). These independence movements were significantly informed by social democratic movements, often within the framework of particular forms of African (in Ghana and Kenya), Arab (in Egypt), or Indian socialisms.

The end of the formal colonial era was an historic event of tremendous significance, and for the first 10 to 15 years after independence, many of the newly independent countries made serious attempts to develop governing structures and policies that would benefit their populations. However, most postcolonial governments have not succeeded in significantly reducing hunger, illiteracy, and the extremes of ill health among their citizenries. A fundamental reason for the lack of progress is that the South remains profoundly vulnerable to and dependent upon economic and political decisions made by European and North American interests and powers—a powerful obstacle to achieving stable and equitable societies. As a result, small economic and social groups at home and former colonial interests abroad are continuing to grow rich while the majority of the population, after experiencing some initial improvements after independence, now see few, if any, such positive changes.

Most newly independent countries began to introduce medium- and long-term health development plans. Governments usually proposed the rapid extension of the health services in their existing forms. They sometimes introduced such new elements as primary health centers or community participation into the health services but did not question the basic focus of the western model. If these plans were in their formulation primarily only "more of the same," in application they became, at best, a replication of an inherently flawed health care delivery system, with primary weaknesses in their emphasis on curative care instead of public health, inaccessibility to most of the population, and limited community participation. At worst, these expanded systems allocated health sector resources even more sharply toward elite and/or urban groups and populations than had been the case before national independence.

Often, leaders of newly independent countries, and, more particularly, the medical leadership, did not question the essential character of the health services they had inherited. Instead, they aspired to spread these services to the whole of the population. The new services were to be "high standard," as defined by the medical elite, and at the same time serve the needs of the whole population. More often than not though, it was the prestigious hospital plan that was approved and built, and not the health centers, rural clinics, or preventive programs.

The postindependence period, then, often saw a continuation of the same kind of health care system which operated during colonial rule—a system in which the rural poor was provided limited care and services only after the needs of the urban elite was attended to. Of course, it was an expanded system staffed by nationals at all levels rather than foreigners, and was more readily accessible to a somewhat larger proportion of the entire population. Nonetheless, the system could not be characterized as different in any way from the colonial systems that preceded, except for geographic reach.

Indeed, external models have heavily influenced the development of health care systems in poor countries. They were influential at least partly because they fit well with already existing internal social and class interests. One obvious example of external influence on the development of Third World health services is the British or American type of medical school and related teaching hospital. Many of these schools followed the centers-of-excellence models developed by institutions such as The Rockefeller Foundation. Many became centers of research for American and other universities. As with the teaching, the research is "excellent," even if it produces little positive effect on Third World populations. And this orientation has contributed to the emigration of doctors—the "brain drain"—from the Third World to industrialized countries.

Massive eradication campaigns targeting infectious diseases like smallpox, malaria, polio, and schistosomiasis have also been developed in response to external influences, with program funding made available by the industrialized countries, often through the World Health Organization (WHO). In keeping with this funding, it was possible for donors to encourage, if not insist upon, the creation of separate, vertical organizations for—most notably—the smallpox and malaria campaigns in the 1960s and 1970s. Donors felt the need for a separate, more managerially efficient, and better-monitored structure than was generally to be found in the national ministry of health, so most aid funded a specific project or program instead of general health services.

However, this efficiency comes at great cost in terms of absolute monetary expenditures and, more important, the overall balance of health care activities within the country. In effect, relatively small sums of external assistance often become the tail wagging the dog. Although recent years have seen a declining interest by donors in specific disease eradication programs,[10] the same approach is now being liberally applied to reproductive health activities. The central lesson of the vertical campaign does not seem to have been learned, namely, that given the underdeveloped state of national health services and their consequent inability to carry out health sector programs, the only special campaigns likely to succeed are those that require only a single application, as was the case with smallpox.

These special, externally supported activities also generate pressures that have contributed to the breakdown of one of the better legacies of British colonialism—a structured public sector responsibility, primarily through the ministry of health. The problem is almost always exacerbated when the external support or intervention comes from US institutions; historically, American health services have been provided primarily by the private sector. (The exportation of the US managed care model to Latin America presented in Chapter Six is a recent example of the dismantling of health care systems). So rather than strengthening health systems, American government intervention mainly takes the form of "special programs." Given the present incoherence of the American health delivery system,[11] the special-program approach may be the most effective at this time in the US, but it has a negative impact on other countries that have had more comprehensive systems.

Conclusion

Corporate globalization seems to be worsening the situation for many poor countries. This crisis is characterized by static or worsening conditions for the majority of the population, while a relative few appropriate the wealth of the nation to themselves. This process goes forward in the context of very rapidly growing and increasingly polluted urban environments, the impoverishment of subsistence farmers and other small peasants and farmers, high unemployment, and underemployment of unprecedented proportions. These problems are coupled with the importation of inappropriate, capital-intensive technologies, high rates of illiteracy that remain constant, and very rapid population growth flowing out of continuing poverty. In the meantime, militant and revolutionary reactions grow. Just as inevitably, unrepresentative and repressive regimes continue to appear, as the privileged struggle to protect their interests.

It is becoming increasingly clear that improving health in poor countries is not a matter of implementing medical systems. Those interested in advocating for global health must first address the specifics of underdevelopment. As long as it remains impossible to seriously deal with existing social and property relations, it will remain impossible to significantly alter the health status of the world's poorest people.

Fears are growing in the richer parts of the world, and among many of the better off in poor countries, over continued underdevelopment, population growth, the degradation of the environment, and the survival of the planet. This sharpening awareness of an impending calamity makes it more remarkable that the issues of inequality and oppression—the basic causes of the growing world crisis—are repeatedly put aside.

Although the poor have always lived in ecological crisis, their increasing numbers are now bringing that crisis to the better off, whether in the wealthy suburbs of Manila or in Los Angeles. The weakness that supposedly characterizes most developing countries is not to be found when it comes to the defense of privilege. Perhaps it need not be so, but history teaches that the powerful never give up anything without being forced to.

Chapter 3

THE PRIMARY HEALTH CARE MOVEMENT MEETS THE FREE MARKET

EVELYNE HONG

In the wake of the freedom struggles against colonialism and repressive regimes, many societies in the Third World attempted to create self-reliant, people-centered models of development. As described in Chapter Two, the legacy of colonial health systems persisted in most former colonies. However, some governments did view more accessible health care as their responsibility and made remarkable advances in expanding services and reaching the population.

During its Cultural Revolution, China made a major contribution with the "barefoot doctor" program based on community-led health initiatives and the integration of traditional Chinese health systems into basic services. The Chinese success in eradicating schistosomiasis through mass mobilization was an inspiring example for other countries.

Cuba, Vietnam, Sri Lanka and Tanzania adopted equity-oriented approaches which emphasized the socioeconomic bases of disease and health.[1] Pioneering work in community-based health initiatives was also carried out by NGOs, church- or university-related agencies, and sometimes even by individual health and community workers at the grassroots level.

In the 1960s and 1970s, these grassroots programs, which were based on participation and awareness-raising approaches, grew in India, South Africa, Bangladesh, the Philippines, Mexico, and parts of Central America.[2] In India, significant achievements were made through a combination of volunteer and auxiliary development, community health efforts, research, public health services, and the integration of indigenous care into health care services. India's pioneering and successful work on tuberculosis research had a major impact on TB programs all over the world, including in the North.[3]

Despite their successes, however, many of these enlightened health systems and movements were short-lived, falling victim to changing international priorities. This chapter briefly examines the genesis of the Primary Health Care movement, and the successive redefinitions of health priorities that have followed it. Today, the struggle to assure that health systems serve the needs of people, and not of powerful interests in search of profits, continues.

The Alma-Ata Declaration

During the 1960s and 1970s, there was a window of opportunity for new health and development strategies in the Third World. Countries mobilized to shape a new international economic order to complete their liberation from colonialism and external domination, and in response to cold war politics, a nonaligned movement emerged.

Under the leadership of World Health Organization director-general Halfdan Mahler of Denmark (1973-88), the value of some the experiments in health care in the Third World were promoted, and the goal of "Health for All" was proposed. This goal was formally put forth in the 1978 WHO-UNICEF Alma-Ata Declaration.[4] Alma-Ata was the culmination of a potentially radical approach to health and health policies. Those attending the conference recognized that improving health called for a comprehensive approach, which is encompassed in the definition of Primary Health Care. PHC was seen as "the key to achieving an acceptable level of health throughout the world in the foreseeable future as a part of social development and in the spirit of social justice."[5]

In short, Alma-Ata affirmed health as a fundamental human right and called for a transformation of conventional health care systems and for broad, intersectoral collaboration and community organizing. The declaration sought to address the underlying social, economic, and political causes of illness and disease, as well as press for comprehensive health care. The community-based health initiatives which form the basis of primary health care were intended to support a larger struggle by the marginalized for their well-being and rights. The emphasis on addressing the root causes of poor health and the efforts to put health in the hands of the people, however, posed a threat to entrenched interests, namely the medical and nursing establishment, the elites, and governments that claimed a monopoly on knowledge and the power of healing.[6]

In some countries community health workers were harassed or arrested; in Latin America, some health care providers in possession of David Werner's pathbreaking book, *Where There Is No Doctor*, were arrested and dealt with brutally. The Alma-Ata document posed a direct challenge to the economic and political thinking of the day. It was only a matter of time before a full-scale attack against its principles was launched.

Using the minimum definition of PHC, Alma-Ata advised that governments implement *at least* the following basic components: (1) education about diseases, health problems, and their control; (2) promotion of food and proper nutrition; (3) safe water and basic sanitation; (4) maternal and child care, including family planning; (5) immunization against major infectious diseases; (6) prevention and control of locally endemic diseases; (7) appropriate treatment of common diseases and injuries; and (8) provision of essential drugs.

Even though these elements represent the *minimum* definition of what should be carried out, only rarely have they been implemented. Dr. David Tejada de Rivero of Peru, deputy director-general of WHO when Alma-Ata was passed in 1978, wrote in a recent article about the conference,

> Perhaps because of what might be called professional deformation, it was not really understood that health is a social phenomenon whose determinants cannot be separated from other social and economic determinants. Nor can it be assigned solely to one bureaucratic-administrative sector of the state. Nor was it understood sufficiently—though it was spelled out clearly—that health is, above all, a complex social and political process that requires political decision-making not only at the sectoral level but also by the state, so that these decisions are binding upon all sectors without exception.[7]

Some international public health "experts" associated with wealthy donors and institutions openly criticized the Primary Health Care approach, arguing that was not feasible. The first salvo was fired when the concept of Selective Primary Health Care (SPHC) was proposed. Led by the Rockefeller Foundation, the Ford Foundation, and the Population Council, supporters of SPHC proposed a limited number of technical interventions intended to reduce mortality from common ailments until more comprehensive services could be put in place.

They considered PHC to be too costly and complex and justified SPHC by claiming that high-risk groups needed to be targeted with "selective cost effective interventions" that were less ambitious.[8] The SPHC strategy reduced the broad social changes envisioned at Alma-Ata to a few high-priority technological interventions and justified the elimination of certain basic services, such as water and sanitation. The original comprehensive approach to health was stripped of its strongest components and the emphasis on socioeconomic development was removed.[9] Priorities would be determined by health experts, based not on the community's priorities but on the cost-effectiveness of interventions. In this way, the centrality of community involvement in the planning, implementation, and control of PHC was challenged.

Primary Health Care was never really given a chance to succeed in most of the Third World. Many countries adopted the new language from the Alma-Ata conference, but in reality their work persisted more or less as it had before. A few countries that had not previously provided Primary Health Care, like Nicaragua and Mozambique, did carry out some elements of the Alma-Ata mold in the 1980s; they showed impressive progress on malaria control and extensive immunization against common diseases. However, these successes were short-lived, destabilized by governments in the US and South Africa.

The Reagan and Thatcher governments created a conservative climate which also contributed to undermining Primary Health Care. In the early 1980s, US foreign aid agencies took on a pro-private health sector stance, opposing spending for public sector curative care and hospitals, in particular, as set out in a health sector policy paper released soon after Reagan took office.[10] At the same time, government health budgets in the Third World were hard hit by structural adjustment programs (described in Chapter Four), which, given the need to pay off crushing debts, made selective, limited interventions appear to be the only possible option.

The Advent of "Selective" Primary Health Care

In 1983 UNICEF, following the SPHC model, adopted a new "child survival" strategy of health interventions called GOBI (growth monitoring, oral rehydration therapy, breastfeeding and immunization). This was later expanded to include family planning, food supplements for malnourished, and female education (FFF). GOBI was an instant hit with donors because of its relatively limited scope and technology-based focus, and money poured in from the World Bank, USAID, the Vatican, and many NGOs.

By the 1980s, almost all Third World countries were promoting GOBI, but even implementation of this narrow approach was sometimes limited. Many countries reduced their child survival campaigns to oral rehydration therapy and immunization, which UNICEF called the twin engines of the "child survival revolution." In India, GOBI was reduced to the distribution of oral rehydration solution packets and immunization; the focus of family planning was antenatal care, namely registering pregnancies, and nutrition was converted to the distribution of iodized salt, iron and Vitamin A supplements.[11]

UNICEF's endorsement of SPHC through GOBI was a shift back to the vertical programs that it had previously supported. According to some activists, SPHC and GOBI corrupted the ideals of Alma-Ata and "was a way for governments and health professionals to avoid dealing with the social and political causes of poor health and thus preserve the inequities of the status quo. . . .UNICEF's policy was tantamount to accepting inequity and poverty as unalterable facts of life."[12]

Some experts claimed these "vertical" or "top-down" programs were as good as the comprehensive local service model promoted under Primary Health Care, but some critics, mostly academics and political activists, argued that they were in fact little more than "old wine in new bottles."[13] One cannot oppose the specific activities of SPHC, as it is quite reasonable to invest in growth monitoring, oral rehydration, etc., but the overall approach of SPHC —building up slowly through vertical programs—has, in many places, diverted resources from health systems and degraded government services. Instead of local communities determining their own health priorities, with SPHC they are determined by distant medical bureaucracies or funding agencies. Thus if a region has a particular health problem of importance to the local population, such as hepatitis or snakebite, SPHC is limited in its capacity to respond.

By the 1980s WHO, UNICEF, aid agencies such as USAID, and the World Bank launched additional global initiatives for SPHC focusing on immunization, HIV/AIDS and TB. But the global initiative programs were inconsistent, contradictory, and scientifically flawed. These prefabricated programs usually did not take into account the extreme variations among and within Third World countries.[14]

World Health Organization Faces Corporate Attacks

In addition to facing criticism by health experts and donors on "Health for All" primary health care goals, WHO was attacked by corporations with financial interests in specific health technologies or approaches, making it difficult for the organization to carry out its job as a global health adviser.

WHO is governed by 192 Member States through the World Health Assembly (WHA), which approves WHO programs, budget, and major policy questions. In 1978, WHO introduced an Action Program on Essential Drugs followed by passage of the International Code of Marketing of Breastmilk Substitutes by the WHA meeting in 1981. Both acts aimed to promote greater responsibility on the part of pharmaceutical and infant formula manufacturers. For example, the Code forbids unscrupulous marketing practices, like the provision of free formula to mothers who deliver in hospitals, which may encourage their subsequent reliance on formula they cannot afford. It also forbids widespread advertising of formula feeding as "modern," and thus, desirable.

Not surprisingly, the Code faced fierce opposition from the food and drug industries; pharmaceutical and infant formula companies campaigned vigorously against these actions. The code was passed, despite the fact the US was the single country to oppose it, on the grounds that it would interfere with free trade.[15] But even though WHO's "Baby-friendly Initiative" aims to restrict certain practices, regular violations of the Code continue to be documented.[16]

These violations can have grave consequences. In 1992, it was estimated that the use of infant formula was responsible for the deaths of three to four thousand infants in developing countries every day.[17] The deaths occur because in some poor households the formula is either prepared improperly—for example, in a too-diluted mixture, resulting in a baby's failure to thrive—or it is contaminated by unclean water. Consequently, there is an increased risk of diarrhea, dehydration, and of acute infections that are usually prevented by natural antibodies in breast milk.

Furthermore, because health problems are so prevalent in poor countries and only scant information is available to the average householder and the health practitioner, drug companies intensively market many drugs. As a result, many poor nations spend as much as half of their health budgets on pharmaceuticals—as many as 70 percent of which have been found to be 'non-essential' —that is, unnecessary or ineffective.[18] Worse yet, many of the drugs sold are known to be harmful, or even outlawed in the industrialized countries. The Action Program on Essential Drugs aimed to promote the rational use of a relatively small number of known effective drugs at national levels. Yet the WHO has never been able to enforce it, limited by the open support for the rights of pharmaceuticals by the US government (which provides 25 percent of the WHO's operating budget).[19]

In 1996, the World Health Assembly confronted the tobacco industry by initiating the Framework Convention on Tobacco Control (FCTC), guidelines for international governance on tobacco control. In 2000, a WHO committee released a report entitled *Tobacco Company Strategies to Undermine Tobacco Control Activities at the World Health Organization.* The report detailed deliberate ploys by tobacco companies to "contain . . . and re-orient" their products through control activities.[20] While more than 100 countries signed and a handful ratified the FCTC in 2003, signaling a victory for WHO and advocates working on the cause, industry continues to closely watch the organization.

For example, in 2003 the US sugar industry tried to undermine WHO by co-authoring a report with the Food and Agriculture Organization called *The Expert Consultation on Diet, Nutrition and the Prevention of Chronic Diseases.* It recommended that intake of added sugars be no more than 10 percent of a healthy diet.[21] A trade group called the Sugar Association asked members of the US Congress to challenge the US $406 million in contributions to WHO and also demanded that WHO remove an early draft of the report from its Web site. Under this pressure, the US Department of Health and Human Services wrote a 28-page critique of the report focusing on the lack of transparency in the scientific and peer review process.[22] To date, WHO has held to its proposed strategy on diet.

Enter the World Bank

In 1987, partially in response to growing criticism of the deleterious effects of structural adjustment programs—namely the precipitous decline in living standards and the resulting social conflicts—the World Bank released *Financing Health Services in Developing Countries: An Agenda for Reform.*[23] (See Chapters Four and Five on the effects of SAPs.) With this publication, the World Bank gave notice that it intended to play a prominent role in global health sector reform by promoting the role of the market in financing health care services. The World Bank's world development report for 1993, *Investing in Health,* defined the neoliberal logic underlying health sector reform. (See Chapter Five for a more thorough discussion of health sector reform and the role of lending agencies in Guatemala.)

Investing in Health recognizes that poverty is a threat to health. The report states that economic growth is a condition for good health, that is, economic growth will fuel good health and better health will result in more secure economic growth.[24] But it does not address the issue of *economic inequality* and poor health. Nor does it begin to tackle the health consequences of unbridled economic growth, which has led to greater income disparities and wider health differentials within countries. (See Chapter One.) In fact, under the guise of promoting cost-effective, decentralized and country-appropriate health systems, the report's key recommendations seem to be derived from previous policies (like structural adjustment policies) which have worsened poverty and lowered levels of health.

Furthermore, *Investing in Health* explicitly defines health in terms of the global burden of disease measured in disability adjusted life years (DALYs). DALYs incorporate questionable assumptions about the value of life. With DALYs , the Bank assigns different values to years of life lost at different ages. The value for each year of life lost rises from zero at birth to peak at 25 years and then declines with increasing age. The assumption is that the very young, the elderly and disabled people are less likely to contribute to society in economic terms and are thus less valuable. Fewer DALYs will be saved by health interventions which address their ills. This logic might lead one to conclude that public money should not be "wasted" on interventions for these groups, a concept that is not consistent with the deeply held beliefs and values of many societies. (See Chapter Six for a more thorough discussion of health sector reform and the role of lending agencies in the case of Guatemala.)

Privatization and Profits

Like the 1987 report, *Financing Health Services in Developing Countries: An Agenda for Reform, Investing in Health* proposes that governments in the developing world play limited roles in the financing and provision of health care, and endorses a broader role for the private sector. It also marked a turning point for the World Bank, which began to take a sustained interest in the health sector. The report describes the problems of government-run health systems: Misallocation of resources, inequitable access, and inefficiency.[25] Health care is also presented as too costly for the state to provide. In addition to ideological support, the report also seeks to help the private sector financially; data reveal that implementation of the World Bank proposal would move $38 billion from health to the private markets in South America.[26] Because of its financial clout and political influence, the bank report has shaped how northern donors, aid agencies, and other international agencies conceive of and support health work. Governments willing to implement these health policies receive aid and loans to finance structural changes in the health sector.

In many poor countries, the dismantling of the public health sector has spurred the privatization of the health sector and the growth of private health insurance schemes, as described in Chapter Six. But privatization in these countries is selective, expensive, and confined to sectors that are profitable. A typical result is a proposal to assign a basic package of services to the public sector and reserve tertiary services for the private sector.

In Malaysia, where the public health care system is under threat, there has been an explosion of privately provided health care services in the last two decades or more. In 1996, the Health Ministry contracted support services—cleaning, laundry, disposal of medical waste, maintenance of biomedical equipment, and emergency power supply—at the University Hospital in Kuala Lumpur to commercial companies. In less than four years, hospital costs increased by 250 percent.[27] Skimming has become the order of the day. In one instance, the Health Ministry awarded a contract worth $26 million to a company which subsequently subcontracted it for RM65 million, or $17 million, to a second company. The first company earned RM35 million, or $9 million, in profit for doing nothing. In another example, the Health Ministry tendered a separate contract to the first company mentioned above for RM60 million, nearly $16 million, which again subcontracted it to the same second company for RM40 million, about $10 million. The second company in turn subcontracted it to a third company for RM20 million, or $5 million. These profits were subsidized by taxpayers.[28]

Under this free market model, where free choice and competition are the golden rule, health is not an absolute human right but rather a private good. This approach leads to a growing health gap—the resulting landscape is one of a wealth of options for the affluent minority and scarce public services for the poor majority, abolishing the principles of equity and social justice and the concept of Health for All enshrined at Alma-Ata. In the words of a bank economist,

> Policy lending is where the bank really has power—I mean brute force. When countries really have their backs against the wall, they can be pushed into reforming things at a broad policy level that normally, in the context of projects, they cannot. The health sector can be caught up in this issue of conditionality.[29]

Says a senior African ministry of health official, "They say they want to put us in the driver's seat. But sometimes I feel that I am sitting in the front seat driving a taxi, and they are still telling us where to go."[30]

Conclusion

While corporations, international financial institutions, and international health experts have prevented national governments and WHO from meeting the goals laid out at Alma-Ata in 1978, an international grassroots network of social movements—the People's Health Movement—is working to reinstate a global grassroots commitment to Health for All. The People's Health Movement came together in 2000 for an assembly in Savar, Bangladesh. Coordinating group members represent a range of related aims, such as improving access to safe and effective drugs, monitoring trade agreements, and protecting reproductive rights.

The stated goals of the PHM outlined in their Charter for Health are to: (1) support all attempts to implement the right to health; (2) demand that governments and international organizations reformulate, implement and enforce policies and practices that respect the right to health; (3) build broad-based popular movements to pressure governments to incorporate health and human rights into national constitutions and legislation; and (4) fight the exploitation of people's health needs for purposes of profit. (An excerpt from the charter follows this chapter.)

While advocates have faced major setbacks in meeting the goal of Health for All, the People's Health Movement is gaining momentum. Earlier efforts did not have the advantage of using the Internet as an organizing and communications tool, nor was there the growing awareness of and open protests against a flagrantly unjust world order such as the one we have been seeing recently. Tomorrow is another day.

An earlier version of this article appeared in Third World Resurgence.

THE CHARTER OF THE PEOPLE'S HEALTH MOVEMENT

Excerpted from the People's Health Movement Web site <http://www.phmovement.org/>

The People's Health Assembly

The idea of a People's Health Assembly (PHA) has been discussed for more than a decade. In 1998 a number of organizations launched the PHA process and started to plan a large international Assembly meeting, held in Bangladesh at the end of 2000. A range of pre- and post-Assembly activities were initiated including regional workshops, the collection of people's health-related stories and the drafting of a People's Charter for Health.

The present Charter builds upon the views of citizens and people's organizations from around the world, and was first approved and opened for endorsement at the Assembly meeting in Savar, Bangladesh, in December 2000.

Health is a social, economic and political issue and above all a fundamental human right. Inequality, poverty, exploitation, violence and injustice are at the root of ill-health and the deaths of poor and marginalized people. Health for all means that powerful interests have to be challenged, that globalization has to be opposed, and that political and economic priorities have to be drastically changed.

This Charter builds on perspectives of people whose voices have rarely been heard before, if at all. It encourages people to develop their own solutions and to hold accountable local authorities, national governments, international organizations and corporations.It is a tool for advocacy and a rallying point around which a global health moment can gather and other networks and coalitions can be formed.

Vision

Equity, ecologically-sustainable development and peace are at the heart of our vision of a better world - a world in which a healthy life for all is a reality; a world that respects, appreciates and celebrates all life and diversity; a world that enables the flowering of people's talents and abilities to enrich each other; a world in which people's voices guide the decisions that shape our lives.

There are more than enough resources to achieve this vision.

The Health Crisis

"Illness and death every day anger us. Not because there are people who get sick or because there are people who die. We are angry because many illnesses and deaths have their roots in the economic and social policies that are imposed on us." (A voice from Central America)

In recent decades, economic changes world-wide have profoundly affected people's health and their access to health care and other social services.

Despite unprecedented levels of wealth in the world, poverty and hunger are increasing. The gap between rich and poor nations has widened, as have inequalities within countries, between social classes, between men and women and between young and old.

A large proportion of the world's population still lacks access to food, education, safe drinking water, sanitation, shelter, land and its resources, employment and health care services. Discrimination continues to prevail. It affects both the occurrence of disease and access to health care.

The planet's natural resources are being depleted at an alarming rate. The resulting degradation of the environment threatens everyone's health, especially the health of the poor. There has been an upsurge of new conflicts while weapons of mass destruction still pose a grave threat.

The world's resources are increasingly concentrated in the hands of a few who strive to maximize their private profit. Neoliberal political and economic policies are made by a small group of powerful governments, and by international institutions such as the World Bank, the International Monetary Fund and the World Trade Organization. These policies, together with the unregulated activities of transnational corporations, have had severe effects on the lives and livelihoods, health and well-being of people in both North and South.

Public services are not fulfilling people's needs, not least because they have deteriorated as a result of cuts in governments' social budgets. Health services have become less accessible, more unevenly distributed and more inappropriate.

Privatization threatens to undermine access to health care still further and to compromise the essential principle of equity. The persistence of preventable ill health, the resurgence of diseases such as tuberculosis and malaria, and the emergence and spread of new diseases such as HIV/AIDS are a stark reminder of our world's lack of commitment to principles of equity and justice.

Principles of the Charter

The attainment of the highest possible level of health and well-being is a fundamental human right, regardless of a person's color, ethnic background, religion, gender, age, abilities, sexual orientation or class.

The principles of universal, comprehensive Primary Health Care, envisioned in the 1978 Alma-Ata Declaration, should be the basis for formulating policies related to health. Now more than ever an equitable, participatory and intersectoral approach to health and health care is needed.

Governments have a fundamental responsibility to ensure universal access to quality health care, education and other social services according to people's needs, not according to their ability to pay.

The participation of people and people's organizations is essential to the formulation, implementation and evaluation of all health and social policies and programs.

Health is primarily determined by the political, economic, social and physical environment and should, along with equity and sustainable development, be a top priority in local, national and international policy-making.

A Call for Action

To combat the global health crisis, we need to take action at all levels— individual, community, national, regional and global—and in all sectors. The demands presented below provide a basis for action.

Health as a Human Right

Health is a reflection of a society's commitment to equity and justice. Health and human rights should prevail over economic and political concerns. This Charter calls on people of the world to:

Support all attempts to implement the right to health.

Demand that governments and international organizations reformulate, implement and enforce policies and practices which respect the right to health.

Build broad-based popular movements to pressure governments to incorporate health and human rights into national constitutions and legislation.

Fight the exploitation of people's health needs for purposes of profit.

A People-Centered Health Sector

This Charter calls for the provision of universal and comprehensive primary health care, irrespective of people's ability to pay. Health services must be democratic and accountable with sufficient resources to achieve this. This Charter calls on people of the world to:

Oppose international and national policies that privatize health care and turn it into a commodity.

Demand that governments promote, finance and provide comprehensive Primary Health Care as the most effective way of addressing health problems and organizing public health services so as to ensure free and universal access.

Pressure governments to adopt, implement and enforce national health and drugs policies.

Demand that governments oppose the privatization of public health services and ensure effective regulation of the private medical sector, including charitable and NGO medical services.

Demand a radical transformation of the World Health Organization (WHO) so that it responds to health challenges in a manner which benefits the poor, avoids vertical approaches, ensures intersectoral work, involves people's organizations in the World Health Assembly, and ensures independence from corporate interests.

Promote, support and engage in actions that encourage people's power and control in decision-making in health at all levels, including patient and consumer rights.

Support, recognize and promote traditional and holistic healing systems and practitioners and their integration into Primary Health Care.

Demand changes in the training of health personnel so that they become more problem-oriented and practice-based, understand better the impact of global issues in their communities, and are encouraged to work with and respect the community and its diversities.

Demystify medical and health technologies (including medicines) and demand that they be subordinated to the health needs of the people.

Demand that research in health, including genetic research and the development of medicines and reproductive technologies, is carried out in a participatory, needs-based manner by accountable institutions. It should be people– and public health–oriented, respecting universal ethical principles.

Support people's rights to reproductive and sexual self-determination and oppose all coercive measures in population and family planning policies. This support includes the right to the full range of safe and effective methods of fertility regulation.

People's Participation for a Healthy World

Strong people's organizations and movements are fundamental to more democratic, transparent and accountable decision-making processes. It is essential that people's civil, political, economic, social and cultural rights are ensured. While governments have the primary responsibility for promoting a more equitable approach to health and human rights, a wide range of civil society groups and movements, and the media have an important role to play in ensuring people's power and control in policy development and in the monitoring of its implementation. This Charter calls on people of the world to:

Build and strengthen people's organizations to create a basis for analysis and action.

Promote, support and engage in actions that encourage people's involvement in decision-making in public services at all levels.

Demand that people's organizations be represented in local, national and international fora that are relevant to health.

Support local initiatives towards participatory democracy through the establishment of people-centered solidarity networks across the world.

Chapter 4

SAPPING THE POOR:
THE IMPACT OF STRUCTURAL ADJUSTMENT PROGRAMS

STEVE GLOYD

Since the mid-1980s a standard set of prescriptive economic requirements, known collectively as structural adjustment policies, have been imposed on most poor countries by the International Monetary Fund (IMF) and the World Bank with the purported goal of facilitating economic growth and recovery. Since these countries were said to have "mismanaged" their economies, these policies were imposed as conditions for receiving further assistance from the financial institutions, including new loans, at a time when many poor countries were staggering under heavy debt loads.

But in the last few years, led by activists in the debt cancellation movement, there has been increasing criticism of these policies, as well as scrutiny of the agendas behind the guidelines and exposure of their failure to yield the economic benefits they were designed to produce.

The Development Debate

Structural adjustment programs (SAPs) draw on the Washington Consensus approach to globalization. The Washington Consensus holds that economic growth is the main goal of development and that growth should always be facilitated, even at the expense of social services. The very name of the consensus indicates it is one that reflects the convergent views of the US government and the Washington-based IMF and World Bank, but not necessarily the views of other stakeholders. In fact, the consensus that emerged in the mid-1980s is the result of a long ideological struggle between starkly opposed models of development—development through economic growth at any cost versus more moderate growth incorporating desirable levels of equity.

The first model was popularized in the period after World War II, an era characterized by idealism and hope. The experiences of postwar Japan and Europe, which developed rapidly growing modern market economies after receiving enormous amounts of financial aid from the US, fueled this optimism. The approach was further popularized by the economic and social success of the so-called Asian tigers—Taiwan, South Korea, Singapore, and Hong Kong—between the 1960s and 1990s. All four countries benefitted from US and European financial support.

In contrast, an equity-based development model emerged as early as the 1940s in China, and as late as the 1960s in South Asia and Africa. The Chinese Revolution turned society nearly upside down. The poor gained enormous stature, and the government instituted policies to insure that the income gap would narrow. Barefoot doctors and participatory community activities spread a health consciousness among the entire population. The fall in infant mortality was dramatic; it dropped from approximately 220 per 1,000 live births in 1955 to about 50 per 1,000 by 1980.[1] Furthermore, community-based health programs in parts of Africa, India, and Bangladesh in the 1960s and 1970s also produced huge drops in infant and child mortality.[2] Although the smaller efforts were never implemented at regional or national levels, these successes raised hopes for the potential impact of "scaled-up" efforts.

Two of the most instructive and hopeful examples of social policy and health occurred in the state of Kerala in southern India (30 million people) and Sri Lanka (19 million people). Both governments instituted equity-oriented strategies in the 1940s and 1950s when socialist leaders were elected into office. The strategies were simple, and included: (1) universal and compulsory primary education: Sri Lanka in 1950, Kerala in 1959—these included transportation to schools, free or subsidized lunch at schools to insure minimal levels of nutrition, and support for books; (2) land reform: Kerala starting in 1959 (50 percent got land); (3) housing, water, sanitation: both governments had major projects targeted for the poor between 1950 and 1970; (4) basic curative and preventive health services provided in both countries from 1960 to 1975; and (5) participatory democracy in which genuine elections were held and political power changed hands among political parties.[3]

The changes in infant mortality in both areas were dramatic. Within 20 years, rates had dropped from the range of the poorest countries in the world to levels only shared by much richer countries.[4] Even more instructive was the fact that these gains took place even in the absence of significant economic growth during the period; Kerala was poorer in terms of income than the rest of India and remained so during the period of rapid improvement of social and health status.

The optimism generated by these experiences galvanized the global health community. The evidence suggested that Health for All (the goal of the Alma-Ata WHO-UNICEF conference in 1978) could be achieved if equity-oriented policies, coupled with simple, appropriate health care were implemented at national levels. But, as described in Chapter Three, the commitment to primary health care and the agenda put forth at Alma-Ata was replaced with an approach that narrowed health care to limited disease-oriented programs.

The new, apparently apolitical approach to health fit well within the broader ideological framework which began to emanate from the increasingly conservative governments of the US and Europe (Reagan, Kohl, Thatcher). Their approach accepted (rather than challenged) the reality of "resource scarcity" and returned to "trickle-down" theories of development, which meant that policies encouraging accumulation of wealth by the wealthy superseded policies addressing equity concerns. In the mid-1980s, as this ideology became solidified in the corridors of power in Western governments, nearly all poor countries were dealt a blow with increasingly unsupportable public debt and consequent structural adjustment programs.

Creating the World Bank, the International Monetary Fund—and Debt

The origins of the debt problem were global and affected most poor countries in a similar manner. The colonial relationship underpinning development, described in Chapter One, set up dependent relationships that laid the groundwork for today's current debt situation.

In 1944, during World War II, economists from 44 countries attended a conference on monetary and financial matters at Bretton Woods, New Hampshire and formed the International Bank for Reconstruction and Development (which became known as the World Bank) and the International Monetary Fund.[5] The initial purpose of the World Bank was to finance the reconstruction of postwar Europe, although the Marshall Plan soon assumed that function. The World Bank then focused on loaning money to countries in Asia, Africa, and Latin America, usually for specific projects such as dams. The IMF was set up to make short-term loans to stabilize currencies and balance of payments to prevent another Depression, but since then, however, it has exceeded its mandate and become a global economic adviser and enforcer.

From the beginning, the economists had differences of opinion about the institutions and concern about the potential for global economic imbalances. British economist John Maynard Keynes, who advocated for a balanced global economic system in which there would be strict controls on capital, and surpluses and deficits would not be allowed to accumulate, was particularly concerned about the bias toward global competition and corporate enterprise.[6] This fear has proven to be justified. Today, there are more than 180 member states of the World Bank and IMF, including many poor countries. Third World countries have been party to years of advice, programs, and loans which they are told will lead to economic growth and widespread well-being, but today have immense debts that they cannot repay, and are caught in a cycle of perpetual borrowing.

Another important historical moment in debt history was the 1973 oil embargo that was sparked by demands from the Organization of Petroleum Exporting Countries. OPEC was created in 1960 to coordinate and unify petroleum policies among producing countries in order to secure prices, ensure a regular supply of petroleum to purchasing countries, and to be able to negotiate the output controlled by Western multinationals.[7] In 1973 this consortium dramatically increased the price of oil during the Arab oil embargo; the price per barrel increased from $5 in 1972 to $7 in 1973, and it reached more than $35 per barrel by 1981.[8] Most OPEC countries did not have the capacity to use the windfall of money and thus invested their oil dollars into Western banks. With a relative glut of money, bankers embarked on a period of aggressive, arm-twisting, and sometimes predatory lending. Personal benefits often accrued to the government officials who tendered or approved the loan process, increasing the likelihood of loans being accepted. Interest rates were low, and repayment schedules were made based on those interest rates, as well as the going prices of goods that borrowing countries sold on the world market. Then, in the late 1970s and early 1980s, several policies were implemented by the US and other rich governments which changed the rules, including raising interest rates and placing higher subsidies on their own goods, which decreased the relative value of developing countries' exports.

Another factor that contributed to this burgeoning debt was the unpredictable level of foreign assistance from industrialized countries. Between 1965 and 1998, overseas development assistance (as a percentage of GNP) dropped by more than 50 percent.[9] Much of the aid that had previously gone to governments of poor countries was diverted to international and national NGOs. The public sector took a double hit—not only was the amount of aid as a percent of the GNP reduced, but much of the money that countries did receive went to NGOs instead of governments. Assistance fluctuated tremendously due to the shifting geopolitical interests of rich-country governments, especially that of the US. The rich countries also influenced the grant and lending policies of the World Bank and other multilateral donors. Thus, the lower levels of foreign aid to poor-country governments further reduced overall revenues that could have been used to repay debts.

Local corruption also played a role in the growing debt. US-supported dictators such as Marcos in the Philippines, Mobuto in Zaire, Suharto in Indonesia, and the Duvalier family in Haiti transferred many billions of dollars of these loans (and aid) to personal bank accounts outside of their countries. Protection by the US government undermined any efforts by local civil society to stop their thievery. Many leaders in poor countries also spent substantial amounts of government revenues on arms (from Northern suppliers) in order to prop up unstable governments.

Some debts have an especially odious history. Apartheid, the racist ruling system in South Africa from 1948 to 1990, was declared a "crime against humanity" by the UN in 1973. Nevertheless, the IMF continued to loan money to the regime well after this declaration was made. The regime spent billions of dollars on its military and police forces to suppress the liberation movement. As of 1998, the foreign debt that piled up during apartheid was conservatively put at $26 billion.[10] And the amount is much higher if neighboring countries, also affected by the regime, are taken into account. So more than a decade after liberation, South Africans continue to pay for apartheid. (Activist organizations like Jubilee South not only call for debt cancellation, but for reparations from Northern countries, the IMF, and World Bank to compensate for colonial and imperial rule, military debt, and the slave trade.)

Historically, it is clear that the responsibility for poor-country debt lies more with global economic and political systems than with the countries themselves. A handful of poor-country leaders called for debt cancellation in the 1980s, arguing that the debt was created by external circumstances. These arguments were disparaged by the US government, and their voices were isolated. (Ironically, 80 years previously, the US government argued a very different line. Just after having occupied the colonies of Cuba and the Philippines after its victory in the Spanish-American War, the US government refused to pay their debts to Spain. The US government called these "odious debts" and thus illegitimate.[11]) Nevertheless, the legitimacy of the current round of debts has not been questioned by lending nations, and the responsibility of debt repayment continues to fall solely on the shoulders of the debtor nations.[12]

The Destabilizing Effects of Structural Adjustment Programs (SAPs)

When it became clear that countries could not pay off their mounting debts, the IMF initiated what it called structural adjustment programs (SAPs). The SAPs were austerity measures, in line with the Washington Consensus, designed to liberate public funds for debt repayment and to improve the conditions for local businesses to export goods to gain foreign currency. According to the IMF, SAPs would jump start the economic engines of poor countries so they would be able to generate sufficient resources to raise the standard of living.

Conveniently, the same measures also increased the poor countries' economic and political dependence on the countries who imported their goods. Representatives from the World Bank, the IMF, and other first world interests called poor-country governments bloated, and blamed the inefficiency of business sectors on high levels of public spending and cumbersome bureaucracies. As a result, health and education budgets were severely pruned, as social services were seen as goods to be paid for by the consumer. SAPs were imposed on poor, indebted countries, without exception, and were implemented in a remarkably similar fashion in each country. Rescheduling of the debt was made conditional on accepting other aspects of the SAPs. (Debt rescheduling permitted governments to continue to pay off debt over a longer time period with smaller monthly payments.) In the 1990s additional loans, called structural adjustment loans (SALs), were designed to help generate the cash for the short-term needs of debt repayment.

SAPs also usually mandated a decrease in spending in all sectors of government. SAPs often dictated massive layoffs of public sector workers and caps on total worker numbers in the government or in specific ministries. The ministries of education and health were often the hardest hit, since they usually employed large numbers of people, primarily nurses and teachers. "Efficiency" measures such as bigger classes and bigger schools, militated against rural education.[13] Long-term caps were also placed on the maximum number of workers that could be hired and on total ministry budgets. As a result, many government health professionals either transferred to the private sector or joined the brain drain in search of work in other countries.

In addition to layoffs, other public programs needed to be cut to meet the parameters of the SAPs. Subsidies for basic foodstuffs (oil, bread, sugar), fuel, public transport, water, sanitation, and medicines were cut or eliminated. Other social expenditures such as credit systems and agricultural support were also cut or severely reduced. (Curiously, IMF officials did not focus on the reduction of poor-country military expenditures, which have consistently amounted to a large proportion of total public sector spending.)

Countries under SAPs were also instructed to increase exports by devaluing currency and improving conditions for private sector investment. In most countries local currency was devalued to make locally produced goods cheaper on the international market. SAPs also often required countries to float currencies to reach a value determined by market forces; because there is little to no demand for developing country currencies, and there was no floor set for the devaluation, the currencies were sure to float to a very low value. Prior to SAPs, many countries had laws in place requiring companies to reinvest their profits in that country, and requiring partial (often 51 percent) government ownership of foreign ventures. These restrictions were usually lifted, and the tax structure on foreign business was reduced considerably. Some SAPs also required new laws limiting the power and scope of unions, and most have encouraged the formation of export processing zones (EPZs), geographical areas exempt from labor laws and tariffs.

Finally, poor countries were pressured to privatize their economies using "free market rules." SAPs encourage market-determined prices for all commodities, including those basic commodities (food, housing) that had been subject to price controls. The SAPs also called for elimination of protections for small businesses and liberalization of import controls.

The SAPs have had an enormous public impact in nearly every country where they were imposed. Their effects on national economies and on economic growth have been varied. In Latin America and Asia, some adjusting countries, such as Argentina, have experienced significant economic growth. Some observers have attributed this growth to SAPs while others have alternative explanations. But Argentina has seen the shadow side of IMF conditioning as well; it had been exemplary in abiding by IMF advice, including the privatization of state enterprises, liberalization of foreign trade and investment, and tightened government fiscal and monetary policies, until it came to a crisis point and finally defaulted on $155 billion of its foreign debt at the end of 2001.[14] Other countries have seen local industries negatively affected by the opening of their markets to foreign imports, such as the milk industry in Jamaica, as shown in the documentary film *Life and Debt*.[15] In Africa, even experts from the IMF and World Bank have agreed that the SAPs have not resulted in significant economic growth.[16]

The overall social impact of SAPs has been devastating for the poor. For the urban poor, SAPs have meant increased prices for basic foodstuffs. Many have lost jobs, and unemployment and underemployment rates are high and growing, especially in Africa.[17] In poor countries, many who are lucky enough to remain employed exist on a nonliving wage, largely as a result of increasing prices due to the drop in value of local currency. Cheap credit that had allowed farmers to invest in agricultural inputs and to stabilize cash flow was curtailed in many countries. In urban and rural areas, people now pay for social services that previously had been provided at nominal cost or fee such as public school fees. Families also pay much more for services that had previously been subsidized, such as water, sewage, electricity, and telephone.

In Mozambique, the value of the metical has dropped from 32 to the US dollar in 1982 to 24,500 per dollar in 2000. The Zimbabwe dollar underwent an even more severe devaluation between 1982 and 2002. Salaries have risen, but not nearly enough to compensate. New jobs created by external investment have not significantly increased the real value of wages. They often pay minimum wage, which is now consistently around $20 per month in most African countries, not nearly enough to support an individual, much less a family. At the same time, international NGOs and corporations typically pay their local management level workers on a scale between local and US or European levels. Thus, huge disparities are growing between a new social elite, low wage workers, and the unemployed.

Health services for the poor were particularly hard hit by the SAPs. Money dried up for subsidies on medicines and, subsequently, on basic supplies such as gauze, tape, IV tubes, bed sheets, and hospital food. The costs of medicines and supplies have been transferred to patients, many of whom cannot afford to pay them.[18] And health workers' salaries have not kept pace with the price rises created by the SAPs. In Mozambique, a nurse who might have been earning the equivalent of $150 per month in 1980 was earning $30 to $35 per month in 1995.[19] Morale has suffered because of the huge reduction in the real value of their salaries and because the number of health workers has not increased enough to meet demand. Health workers throughout Africa have responded by working fewer hours (to be able to generate other sources of income), charging patients additional under-the-table fees, and selling medicines from public health facilities for personal profit.[20] In hospitals, there is little money for paint, lightbulbs, windows, doors, toilets, screens, or for any physical rehabilitation of crumbling health facilities. Supervision, logistics, and management support are frequently neglected, so drugs and supplies that might otherwise be available do not reach their destinations. Budgets for vehicle maintenance and fuel either do not exist or, if they do, they are frequently exhausted in the first months of the fiscal year. Per diems offered by international agencies can temporarily improve morale; however, their effects are not only shortlived but tend to link what had previously been routine activities with per diem compensation.[21] In Mozambique, immunization outreach activities simply stop every August or September, when the budget for per diems runs out.[22] Ten years ago, health workers from the same area would rarely have required per diems, and would have more reliably carried out outreach activities when transport was much less available.

In poor countries, the public response to SAPs has been intense and negative. From the mid-1980s through the 1990s, many countries operating under SAPs have had significant social unrest. Demonstrations, riots, and strikes caused by SAP–related food prices, fuel prices, wages, layoffs, and working conditions have occurred worldwide. Governments have frequently resorted to force to suppress the social upheaval caused by the SAPs. In the US, where few in the press know or write about SAPs, this global public outcry gets little visibility. Most residents in poor countries know the terminology of SAPs better than do their well-educated counterparts from countries imposing these policies.

Yet the impact of SAPs on health in poor countries has been somewhat difficult to measure, in part because many of the programs were introduced during periods of economic recession in poor countries. Recessions by themselves cause reductions in well-being and health. In general, it is clear that the rapid decline in death rates in the 1970s and 1980s has leveled off, or even reversed direction, leading to much higher mortality rates than have occurred in recent history. Some, but by no means all, of the leveling off is due to HIV/AIDS. But the major determinants of the health status of the poor, including basic education, family income, and food security and nutrition, lie outside of the health sector.

Most international development agencies initially went along with SAPs but had reservations. In 1987, UNICEF published *Adjustment with a Human Face,* a report which criticized the negative effects of SAPs on children and mothers and proposed a policy designed to protect the well-being of the most vulnerable living under structural adjustment regimens. UNICEF officials argued that public health services could contract as long as certain services, especially immunizations and oral rehydration therapy programs, were supported.[23] The leadership of the World Health Organization (WHO) was relatively silent on the impact of the SAPs, even though the policies seriously undermined accessible, comprehensive health care services. UNICEF and WHO supported the Bamako Initiative in 1987, which fostered community financing and fee-based systems for essential drugs. Most African countries' governments had stopped providing pharmaceuticals and sometimes even salaries, so instituting fees and was considered to be a necessary measure. But the poorest of the poor were hurt the most by the imposition of fees—although people were "willing" to pay the fees, many families living in extreme poverty could not afford to.

In the 1990s, resistance to SAPs began to reach the rich countries. Frequent demonstrations in Europe and North America against IMF and World Bank policies began to shake the conviction of the policy makers and economists who determined adjustment policies. The Jubilee Movement has consistently called for debt forgiveness from a social, moral, and religious base. Nonprofit organizations such as Oxfam (UK) and Global Exchange campaigned continuously for rethinking the debt problem and SAPs. Anti-globalization organizations also have placed debt reform or forgiveness on their priority agenda. The cumulative effect of the advocacy efforts, tied to the fact that the SAPs have had a poor record in improving economic growth, have influenced World Bank and IMF policy, and the rhetoric of reform has gradually emanated from both organizations.

Debt Relief: Too Little Too Late?

In his report to the Millennium Summit in September of 2000, Kofi Annan highlighted the seriousness of Africa's debt crisis, pointing out that many African countries were spending up to 40 percent of government revenue to service foreign debts.[24] African governments are paying scarce resources to the rich elite in rich countries. Furthermore, the cycle of debt is such that without relief or cancellation, countries will remain permanently indebted. Countries are getting deeper and deeper into debt at the same time that they are spending more money to service their debts. For example, in 1986, Nigeria borrowed five billion dollars; by 2000 it had paid back sixteen billion dollars, and today still owes over thirty billion dollars.[25]

The principal response to the call for relief has been the Enhanced Structural Adjustment Facility (ESAF), for Heavily Indebted Poor Countries (HIPC). Launched in 1996, it's often referred to as the HIPC Initiative. Over a series of meetings in Toronto, Naples, and Cologne, a strategy of special terms for selected countries was developed. The IMF and World Bank agreed that if HIPC countries consistently followed the terms of the SAPs over a period of three years, they would be considered for debt reduction in the ensuing three years. Currently, under the reformed version of the program, called the enhanced HIPC Initiative, there are 42 eligible countries, 34 of which are in Africa. Most of the countries receiving debt relief are still paying more on debt service payments than on public health.[26]

After Mozambique qualified, its debt dropped only slightly. After entering the second round, Mozambique received a decrease in its debt service payment from $114 million per year to $55 million. This payment remained, however, substantially greater than the government's contribution of $42 million to the health sector. Nevertheless, the reduction did permit the government of Mozambique to increase its health expenditures to $7.50 per capita per year, up from only $4 three years earlier.[27]

One major criticism of the HIPC Initiative is that the process is controlled by the IMF and World Bank, the very institutions responsible for implementing SAPs. They continue to dictate how public sector money can be spent. As of 2003, most poor countries in the world, and nearly all countries in Africa, continue under the regime of SAPs and are at the mercy of IMF rules. A report from Uganda, released at the end of 2002, suggested that because of SAP limitations, the Ugandan Ministry of Health was going to be required to return the value of a grant received from the Global Fund to Fight AIDS, Tuberculosis, and Malaria because the ministry had an IMF-imposed spending cap for health.[28] Fortunately, Uganda has since decided to disregard the spending cap due to the public health emergency it faces.

In nearly 20 years of SAPs in Africa, there has been little to no overall improvement in economic growth despite some well-advertised short periods of "success." There has also been little improvement in health. Ironically, this poor performance occurred in the 1990s, a period of unprecedented global economic expansion—a time when proponents of globalization claim it is improving the quality of life for people from poor and rich countries alike. In contrast, equity-oriented strategies in Kerala, Sri Lanka, and China have yielded better basic services and living conditions over the past 15 to 25 years. SAPs have been destructive to the social infrastructure, and they have also circumvented opportunities to implement equity-oriented strategies.

Finally, little attention has been devoted to questioning the paradigm that national economic growth will lead to development. It has become conventional wisdom that the impressive gains in health and well-being that occurred in South Korea, Taiwan, Hong Kong, and Singapore were associated with impressive gains in per capita GNP. It is less well-known that each of these countries undertook major equity-oriented initiatives that were not dissimilar to what occurred in Kerala and Sri Lanka: Well-funded universal education; housing, water, and sanitation initiatives; land reform (especially in Taiwan); and public provision of simple health services.[29]

If we want to improve health in the poor countries of the world, experience has consistently demonstrated that the public sector has a critical role to play in helping to create the conditions for social development and improving people's lives. The policy makers and economists of the IMF and World Bank have pushed many countries down paths that have undermined the capacity of governments to respond to the needs of their populations. We need to overturn the policies of structural adjustment, relieve countries of crushing debts, and reestablish government's ability to provide all basic services, including but not limited to health care.

EXPANSION OF THE NEOLIBERAL MODEL

A market-based development model that favors the health of corporations over people is essential to the financial success of imperial governments and the global institutions housed within their borders. Through the process of corporate-centered globalization, the US, other first world governments, the World Bank and IMF, and regional development banks are exporting this model.

In this profit-driven model, public goods such as medical care are viewed as commodities. Not surprisingly, in developing countries that still provide public services, these commodities are seen by these interests as having large, untapped markets. In the last fifteen years, the World Bank and regional development banks have become major players in designing—and enforcing—health sector reform, and the state's role in social services, including health care, has shrunk. Chapter Five reveals the faulty logic and negative consequences of bank-imposed health sector reform and loan packages in Guatemala. Chapter Six shows how managed care corporations have been able to take advantage of this by exploiting the void purposefully created by the international financial institutions like the World Bank and regional banks like the Inter-American Development Bank (IADB). Because of the openings created by the banks, these corporations are circling now greedily circling Chile, Argentina, Brazil and other large countries.

Chapter Seven shows how trade agreements are setting up a legal framework that allow corporations and other first world interests to exploit new markets (such as health care and water) overseas. And in Chapter Eight, we see the deleterious health effects of militarism and imperial expansion.

Chapter 5

THE FAILURES OF NEOLIBERALISM: HEALTH SECTOR REFORM IN GUATEMALA

JUAN CARLOS VERDUGO

In recent years, the World Bank has shifted from lending solely for large infrastructure projects to including service sectors such as health and education in its lending portfolio. With this shift the World Bank can capitalize on the large funds invested in social services, which in most countries are largely paid for by governments. Working in the social sectors can also be seen as an attempt by the World Bank to improve its image, since it has been critiqued for mammoth projects, like dams and pipeline construction, which dislocate people and cause environmental devastation in poor countries.

The World Bank has also become a major promoter of health sector reform, or HSR. Starting in 1987 with an influential paper titled *Financing Health Services in Developing Countries: An Agenda for Reform,* and followed by a 1993 report titled *Investing in Health,* the bank has championed HSR, which limits the role the state plays in providing health care. *Financing Health Services in Developing Countries* criticized the "inefficiency" of publically provided primary health care in the developing world, and pushed the private sector as the solution. While the World Bank recognizes the role of government support in *Financing Health Services,* it calls for a "different approach," comprised of four directives: governments should charge users of public health facilities; provide insurance or other risk coverage; use nongovernment resources effectively, and decentralize government health services.[1] Similarly, *Investing in Health* placed emphasis on market-oriented reforms, like recovering costs by charging fees for services.[2]

Prior to the World Bank's interest in health sector reform in the 1980s and the 1990s, the World Health Organization (WHO) and national ministries of health played the primary role in health system planning. Now countries consult World Bank officials about health sector reform, and in some the World Bank designs these reforms in full.[3] In Latin America, the World Bank and the Inter-American Development Bank (IADB) are the major sources of external health care financing, and the number and amount of the loans keep rising.[4] Lending for population, health, and nutrition sectors increased from an annual average of $103 million between 1981 and 1984, to $1.8 billion in the period between 1995 and 1997.[5]

In answer to socioeconomic problems, "free market" advocates push for privatization, the removal of trade barriers such as tariffs, and the marginalization of the state as a social provider. This framework dominates debates about health care in Latin America, and it is being incorporated into the discourse of political actors, including those who are considered to be progressive. But average citizens have little understanding of its consequences. For many, neoliberalism has become accepted as a necessary evil, sold to the public as the only possible path for developing countries attempting to stay in line with current globalization trends.

In order to legitimize health sector reforms, the banks assert the following as "absolute truths": (1) reforms are nationally designed; (2) the state has the capacity to control both public and private sectors;[6] (3) there is a virtuous combination of efficiency, effectiveness, and equity generated by reform; and (4) states can protect the poor by providing subsidized health care services.

From Civil War to the Peace Accords: An Overview of Guatemalan History

Guatemala is a country blessed with cultural and ethnic diversity and plagued by a history of violence and social exclusion. Resources and opportunities are concentrated in Guatemala City, while the rural population is largely denied the basic services required for human development.[7] More than 60 percent of Guatemala's population is rural, the vast majority of whom are indigenous, and most live in poverty.[8] Guatemala has one of the highest levels of inequality in Latin America.[9] The export model of agriculture, which has fueled Guatemala's economy, has relied on worker submission and forced labor of indigenous populations since colonial times.

Although social improvements began to emerge in the 1940s—the period between 1944 to 1954 is widely referred to as "the Springtime of Democracy"—these reforms were halted in 1954 when a CIA-sponsored coup overthrew the progressive Arbenz government. A series of military dictatorships followed that favored the concentration of wealth in the hands of an elite few and, as a result, poverty and social exclusion for the majority of the population. This, in turn, set off a 34-year civil war. At least 200,000 civilians were killed, and one million internal and external refugees were created.

From 1954 to the mid-1980s, the state health sector was essentially abandoned, resulting in low coverage and poor quality of services. Although the economy grew at a rate of 5 percent during the 1960s and 1970s, the government spent only between 1 and 2 percent of the GDP on health.[10] The small changes that happened in those years were essentially "additive reforms" that did not transform the system. Indeed, the country underwent a "privatization through attrition," given that the state had essentially abandoned the health sector.[11] As a result, the for-profit health sector grew to the point that the relatively small middle- and upper-class population could sustain it. There was also a great proliferation of private nonprofit entities including nongovernmental organizations (NGOs), churches, and community organizations working to meet the basic public health and community needs of the population.

In the late 1980s and early 1990s, state leadership was transferred from the armed forces to a civil government elected in the polls. This transfer of power permitted the government to begin to focus on nonmilitary efforts such as the "modernization" of the state and to make reforms in different social sectors, including health and education. From an economic perspective, the "growth model" pushed by neoliberals inside and outside of the country was exhausted at the end of the 1970s, and the economic crises of the 1980s pushed the country to develop structural adjustment programs under the supervision of the International Monetary Fund (IMF) and the World Bank.

In 1996, the Peace Accords were signed between the guerrilla forces and the government, initiating a new stage for Guatemalan society. The accords composed of distinct agreements, established a new national pact that inspired hope for many Guatemalans. At last, they looked forward to enjoying participation in the political arena, as the country appeared to be moving away from state repression. Economic and social reforms promised greater development and prosperity.

Although the accords included some progressive elements, liberalization and economic transformation occurred in a slow and disjointed way. Restrictive social policies and the privatization of industries, like electricity, communications, and postal services, were quickly implemented because there were no strong social or political movements to defend the interests of poor Guatemalans.

In the 1990s, health sector reform began to take shape as part of the structural adjustment program. The government, under the auspices of the IADB, completed studies of the health sector in the early 1990s. These studies implicitly endorsed state "modernization" as defined, and pushed for at a national level, by the IMF and World Bank. In 1995, the IADB and the government signed an agreement for a loan to fund a health sector reform. In 1996, when a business-friendly party came to power (the PAN, or National Advancement Party), it used the Peace Accords to legitimize health sector reform with a focus on health care at the community level, but with a redefined role for the state in the health sector.

In Latin American countries where it has a presence, the IADB has promoted the division of health sector functions among the public and private institutions. The Ministry of Health (MOH) acts as the director—in charge of shaping policy, regulating, and setting guidelines—while the private sector administers funds and delivers health care services.[12] This way, the IADB inserts free market mechanisms into the health sector such as offering very basic health care services, introducing fees for services, and supporting the increasing participation in health care by private institutions.

In Guatemala, health sector reform has introduced a variety of structural, legal, and administrative changes within the Ministry of Health,[13] but the most significant transformation has been the implementation of the so-called Comprehensive Health Care System, or Sistema Integral de Atención en Salud (SIAS), at the primary care level.[14]

Starting in 1997, the government transferred its administration and delivery of primary health care services to private entities through signed agreements (*convenios*). As of 2002 there were 160 agreements signed with 91 agencies, including national and international NGOs, faith-based organizations, private companies, cooperatives, and municipal governments. Currently the program covers more than three million Guatemalans.

Under SIAS, the population is divided into jurisdictions of approximately 10,000 people for private organizations to serve. Contracts are offered to these organizations, and each is funded according to budget of Q40, or $5, per person. The basic package of services is divided into four programs: maternal care, infant and child care, emergencies and common illnesses, and environment and sanitation. For every 10,000 people there is one ambulatory doctor, one institutional facilitator, four community facilitators, 84 health wardens (*guardianes de salud*), and a minimum of five trained traditional birth attendants, as well as one malaria volunteer per community.[15] Only the doctor and the institutional facilitator (and occasionally the community facilitators) are full-time and receive salaries; the other health workers are volunteers. The health wardens and traditional birth attendants receive Q50 ($6.50) each month to attend a daylong training. In other words, SIAS is a system based on the work of volunteers. More than 90 percent of the health workers receive only a monthly fee to cover travel.

SIAS, designed in the mold of selective primary health care as described in Chapter Three, offers minimal state investment in health and extremely limited services for the poorest Guatemalans. A study of SIAS by the Instancia Nacional de Salud—a coalition of grassroots health organizations that came together in response to health sector reform—identified a number of concerns, including the exclusion of civil society in its design, inadequate staffing and personnel, the limited services available to people seeking medical care, and the difficulty of "quality control" because of the number and kinds of different providers.[16] While there has been no formal evaluation of SIAS by the Ministry of Health or external agencies, other countries (like Honduras and Zimbabwe) have expressed interest in implementing similar programs.[17]

Guatemala uses a framework that formalizes the exclusion of the population from comprehensive care and renounces the state's responsibility to ensure the right to health. Access to care has been determined by free market mechanisms and the logic of private organizations. In sum, primary level care has been handed off by the state, and left to the vagaries of the private sector and the market.

The Peace Accords have not achieved the expected goals in terms of health care, and the most sensitive and critical topics affecting society—such as poverty and equitable access to social services—have been neglected. That said, there have been important advances. The war and open oppression have ended. A political opening for progressive parties (evidenced by their participation in two consecutive elections) has been made, and political engagement by Guatemalans of all backgrounds has increased, across the board. With these changes, there is at least hope that Guatemala will be able to construct, in an environment of tolerance and respect for human rights, the conditions for a firm and lasting peace.

The Invisible Hand of the Inter-American Development Bank

In 1999, the Ministry of Health was awarded the prize for Innovation in Public Health by the Pan-American Health Organization (PAHO), the IADB, and the World Bank. Guatemala was acknowledged for work accomplished during the initial phase of the health sector reform process.

Without downplaying the commitment of the Ministry of Health authorities and workers in the process, it is important to analyze how this award might be understood from the perspective of international institutions, particularly that of the IADB, the main sponsor of the reform. Guatemala is a country that has been characterized by great political instability, a lack of defined political-economic policies, political parties lacking clear agendas, and high turnover of Ministry personnel. However, in reviewing health policies and plans of Guatemalan governments over the last decade, the same underlying neoliberal political strategies prevail.[18] Obviously the IADB has played a crucial role behind the scenes.

Since 1991, the IADB has had tremendous influence over the design of health policy in the country, and it should be considered a permanent actor in this sector. For example, the IADB financed the basic study of the health sector, which served as a basis for reform proposals. The health sector reform process stalled during the first two governments of the 1990s, and it was not until the National Advancement Party (PAN) took office in 1996 that steps were taken to move forward. Following the PAN government, the Guatemalan Republican Front (FRG) came into office in 2000 and did not change the overall direction of health policy.[19]

The IADB applied pressure on Ministry of Health officials at the highest level during the presidency of Ramiro de León Carpio (1993–1995). In interviews, ministry officials commented that the IADB imposed changes on the director general of health services of the Ministry of Health, and, in the words of one of the Ministry of Health advisors, the IADB had practically besieged the ministry headquarters.[20]

But the Guatemalan citizenry was not invited to participate in the design process of the reform; in fact, Guatemalans have been provided with little to no information about these machinations. Most do not know about the agreements signed with the IADB, the government's relationships with international financial institutions; nor do they know how policies are formulated by the Ministry of Health and the IADB. In the case of SIAS, the lack of information provided to health care personnel generated passive and active resistance. For example, during the first few years, the idea persisted that SIAS was a temporary policy. While health workers should be seen as essential to the success of any reform, they received limited information about the changes, worked without a human resources policy, contended with deteriorating labor conditions, and had few opportunities to participate in health policy design. Many health workers feel their concerns have not been considered.

The importance of the government agreement with the IADB is illustrated by its incorporation into the 1996 peace negotiations, and in the new health sector framework defined by the Peace Accords. Indeed, in the original copy of the loan document, all of the legal changes—such as the new health code and the law of coordination of the health sector—were reviewed by the IADB representative before going to the Guatemalan Congress for discussion and approval. This process allowed unfettered interference with the legislative and executive branches of the government.

In a reform process that has taken more than 12 years, the IADB is the only permanent actor that has influenced health policy in a consistent and considerable way.[21] Changing governments have taken on different measures of the institution's guidelines, without having a reform agenda or health policy of their own. And though health workers and the population are permanent participants in the health sector, they have had minimal influence in the process.

A Public and Private Mix: A New Role for the Ministry of Health

The neoliberal reforms imposed on Latin American countries arise out of a misinterpretation of the economic crises of the late 1970s and early 1980s. According to international financial institutions (IFIs), the state played too big a role in providing social services, an argument that stems from a critique of the welfare state in Europe.[22] IFIs have pressured governments throughout Latin America to implement solutions, such as structural adjustment, that aim to reduce government spending on social services. According to this concept of state modernization, the government's role is to establish clear rules and stability for the private sector and the market, while maintaining sufficient coercive measures to control growing social demands.

This "solution" is especially problematic in Guatemala, where the state apparatus is one of the smallest in Latin America. Furthermore, Guatemala has never had a high level of social expenditure, so it seems unlikely that economic crises in the 1980s were due to government interventions. Indeed, instead of making a commitment to an inclusive national agenda and productive social investment in the country, Guatemala has invested heavily in its military and private sector protections. Not surprisingly, education, housing, and health care continue to languish.

In its newly defined role as "director" of the health sector, the Ministry of Health has shown itself to be especially weak at regulating the private organizations that administer and deliver services through SIAS. It was not until five years after SIAS began that the Ministry of Health established a monitoring system to regulate the delivery of administrative, financial, and health care service by private providers.[23] The Ministry of Health has had difficulty directing the health care sector for many reasons. They include:

Weakness in central authority, lack of resources, and limited operational capacity. Historically, Ministry of Health employees have dealt with poor conditions; low wages; limited infrastructure, equipment, funds, and staff; and many related logistical problems. These enduring problems create a work environment that reduces motivation and, though a good portion of health workers make a concerted effort to achieve their work goals, may promote complacency. Consequently, any additional work—such as regulating the private nonprofit and for-profit service providers—is perceived as an imposition by the central levels of the Ministry of Health.

The challenges of regulating health care provided by a multitude of private organizations. Health services are more complex and more difficult to regulate than other services—such as janitorial work or laundry—that can be measured and supervised in a direct and immediate way.[24] In the case of SIAS, the diversity of contracting organizations at the primary care level (church institutions, cooperatives, NGOs, grassroots organizations that are different in nature, interests, and objectives) makes this task more difficult. The organizations have unequal technical and financial capacities, previous experience, and stability. Some have been in their locations for longer periods of time, and are regarded more (or less) highly because of their familiarity to Guatemalans seeking medical care. These differences make it impossible for the Ministry of Health to ensure equity and equality. This heterogeneity is especially striking if we take into consideration the limited amount of money the Ministry of Health dispenses to these organizations. Wealthier organizations can supplement the limited funds from the government and improve service delivery; poorer organizations cannot. As a result, there is tremendous variability in how health care is provided.

The challenges of transferring regulatory control to departmental and municipal levels. Health sector reform was initiated through a parallel structure already established by the Ministry of Health with strong encouragement from the IADB. This was done to facilitate the implementation of SIAS. Because very little input from health workers at local levels was solicited, today they are resistant to taking on the responsibilities of regulating SIAS.

The difficulty in regulating a "flawed" market. The health market is considered "imperfect," and for that reason, state directorship rather than privatization is even more justified. Yet a weak state and Ministry of Health makes regulating the "imperfections" of the health market in Guatemala very challenging, considering that more mature states carry out these tasks with many limitations.

For instance, state regulation should standardize treatments and control prices in the health sector. But these processes would be much easier for the Guatemalan government to monitor if they were under the state's direct control. In the US, government regulation has been effective for Medicaid and Medicare, the two insurance systems under direct state control.[25] In fact, Medicaid and Medicare are much more efficient than private insurance companies.[26]

"Extreme Efficiency" Doesn't Work

Providing health care at the lowest possible cost with the greatest possible benefit is a fundamental objective for the World Bank and the IADB. However, in Guatemala the "extreme efficiency" of SIAS has caused a great deal of ineffectiveness and inequity.

This extreme efficiency is exemplified by the $5 dollar per person per year annual government expenditure on health. This minuscule expenditure allows for only basic services, provided in the context of a limited infrastructure, an overreliance on volunteers, and a fixed "package" that is not adaptable to local needs. These services are very similar to those presented by the World Bank in its 1993 report *Investing in Health*. The only publically funded components are immunizations; the monitoring of infant growth; prenatal care; pap smears; treatment of common illnesses, with a restricted stock of medications; and training for traditional birth attendants and health wardens.

In practice, this translates to mostly curative actions—such as being able to consult with a doctor once a month or access to some vaccinations for children—that address few acute illnesses. Guatemalan villages are visited by a doctor once a month, but most deaths are caused by such acute illnesses as diarrhea and respiratory infections. And effective measures like health prevention (e.g. community education on how to prevent illness, or improve nutrition) and promotion (e.g. community projects to improve access to basics like water) are given very little emphasis in SIAS. For example, SIAS mandates the improvement of environmental and sanitary conditions—such as water treatment, which would reduce diarrheal and other illnesses—but because there is no funding, these interventions are not carried out. So the population, especially children, continues to suffer and die from entirely preventable diseases.

Infrastructure that is essential for providing quality care is not financed by the Ministry of Health. For example, the Ministry does not fund the construction and maintenance of community convergence centers, where doctors carry out their monthly consultations. As a result, many doctors do not have permanent centers where they can meet with patients. Instead, they improvise, using rooms in people's homes or churches, which makes it difficult to carry out important procedures such as pap smears and other procedures that require privacy.[27] One doctor working in the system says, "Sometimes I have to see my patients on a rock under a tree. All of our community centers are temporary. It can be difficult to examine a pregnant woman under a tree."

An ambulatory care doctor and an institutional facilitator are the only health personnel contracted full time (and without benefits) for approximately 10,000 people. More than 90 percent of health workers receive a monthly fee to cover travel costs but are expected to work as volunteers. As one health warden stated in an open discussion, "We do not have time to do all the work that is asked of us. Sometimes we leave people who are sick in our area. We do not have the economic means to maintain ourselves."[28] Additionally, the training of volunteers is inadequate; they undergo no formal orientations before beginning their work, and receive monthly trainings from the doctor, often after s/he has finished a long day of clinical care.

At the primary care level, SIAS is centralized, does not allow for adaptations to the diverse and local contexts in Guatemala, and has rigid spending allotments. Not surprisingly, this results in inequities. Ideally, the model should be carried out differently in each region, depending on how dispersed the population is, the likelihood of natural disasters, environmental and climatic variations, limited communication networks and roads, and other conditions which can increase health risks.

The Poor Subsidize the Market

Policy makers have adopted the term "subsidization," which has generally meant that the state is responsible for creating and supporting a safety net for the most vulnerable in the society. In the neoliberal context, subsidization by the state mandates the creation and maintenance of conditions which allow the market and the private sector to flourish. The Guatemalan government, strongly influenced by international financial institutions, has generated conditions in which the poor subsidize the market. The federal budget is largely financed by consumer taxes under a regressive tax code that lets the rich off the hook because they don't pay according to their income and wealth. There are regular and periodic increases in the value-added tax (VAT), a sales tax that everyone pays, and which disproportionately affects low-income and poor Guatemalans. But there have been no recent attempts to increase direct taxes, such as the income tax.

Furthermore, the government has spent billions to prop up the financial sector, but has not increased spending on education, health, or housing. The majority poor contribute significantly to the state budget through taxes, but they do not receive social services in return. And, as we have seen, the health budget is also "subsidized" by the labor of the poor. In addition to using volunteers to keep spending low, the SIAS health care model formally exploits the self-care strategies of families and self-sufficiency of communities. The poor must work to receive services, something that the middle and upper classes never have to do. Other policies have taken advantage of the networks and collective strategies of the poor in order to limit state-financed services.

The Guatemalan government has created conditions beneficial to the market and detrimental to poor people. Through the use of antiorganizing laws and security forces to put down popular organizations and trade unions, the government suppresses the discontent caused by structural adjustment.

Working to Create Alternatives

Guatemala offers a clear example of how reforms imposed by multilateral and transnational agencies affect health care. This analysis is critical to understanding the real consequences of bank-led health sector reform, which have been widely implemented in the developing world. Health sector reforms are social experiments with limited potential for solving the grave health problems faced by poor countries like Guatemala.

In Guatemala, one of the most important outcomes of the health sector reform process has been the creation of the Instancia Nacional de Salud (National Health Advocacy Platform.) Since 1997, this progressive, grassroots, community-based coalition has lobbied the government for better public health services. The Instancia did not have input into SIAS's design, but the coalition has monitored the reforms. Spurred on by these imposed changes, Instancia developed a proposal for primary health care as an alternative to the neoliberal model, and it is implementing the proposal in San Juan Ostuncalco, Quetzaltenango and the Boca Costa of Solola.[29] (See more on Instancia Nacional de Salud in Chapter Thirteen.)

Promoting a balance of curative care, prevention, and promotion in individual, family, and community programs is fundamental to the alternative model sponsored by the Instancia Nacional de Salud. The community health workers implementing the proposal are full-time salaried workers who have undergone an intensive six month training. This approach stresses multicultural and gender equity, while breaking from historical patterns of exclusion and discrimination against women, Mayans, and the poor in Guatemala by highlighting concepts of inclusion. Finally, a commitment to health care as a human right is central to this effort.

Even though the Instancia Nacional de Salud is in the initial phases of implementing the alternative proposal, the coalition is in regular dialogue about it with the Guatemalan Ministry of Health. The goal is not only to provide primary health care to these communities in the pilot program, but to influence the way the government provides health care at the primary level to all Guatemalans.

Translation by Meredith Fort.

Chapter 6

HMO'S ABROAD:
MANAGED CARE IN LATIN AMERICA

CELIA IRIART, HOWARD WAITZKIN, AND EMERSON MERHY

The basic challenge is that what is called globalization is really another name
for the dominant role of the United States.

—Henry Kissinger[1]

At the beginning of the 1990s, international financial institutions (IFIs) and
other lending agencies, such as the World Bank and the Inter-American
Development Bank (IADB), termed the 1980s a "lost decade" in Latin
America. During that period, the economies of most Latin American countries
did not grow, and some governments could not pay their foreign debts. Led by
the World Bank, these lending agencies implemented structural adjustment
programs (SAPs) designed to incorporate Third World countries into a new
economic order, driven by what some call the "Washington Consensus." As
instruments of first world interests, SAPs and other plans mandated that
developing countries reduce spending on social services, control monetary
expansion, and, most importantly, begin to reform their state structures.[2]

This chapter describes how this change was an early step in a process that
has mandated profound and ultimately negative transformations in Latin
America. SAPs required that markets be opened to foreign investors who then
took over in areas—like health care—that had been previously managed by the
state. (For more on SAPs, see Chapter Four.) We focus on the multinational
financial corporations now doing business as insurers and health care providers
in Latin America, presenting evidence from Argentina, Brazil, Chile, and
Ecuador. We outline the impact of these changes on the access to and quality
of health care, and spotlight activists and organizations that are actively
opposing this process.

We also give some background on health sector reform. In developing countries, including those in Latin America, these reforms have usually been initiated at the behest of IFIs after a country has experienced some, or all, of the symptoms of socioeconomic crisis: intermittent recession, increasing internal and external indebtedness, growth of fiscal deficits, high inflation, and structural unemployment. Not surprisingly, as crises like these deepen in developing countries, the power of lending agencies has grown. Yet instead of reflecting on the roles that their policies may have played in creating the predicament, IFIs like the World Bank and the IADB have usually identified the cause for these kinds of socioeconomic upheavals on the state's inefficiency in managing productive enterprises and services and on "overspending" on social services, like health or education.

Their requirements for reform are driven by four basic, yet implicit, assumptions: 1) services, natural resources, and public goods previously controlled by the state should be privatized; 2) large capital investments are needed; 3) the demand for labor will decrease; and 4) the first world should emerge from the economic crisis with as little trauma as possible.[3]

Managed Care or Damaged Care?

Most Latin American governments responded to the financial crisis of the 1980s and 1990s by accepting of policies initiated by the World Bank, the IADB, and International Monetary Fund (IMF). Getting urgently needed international funds was contingent on the adaptation of SAPs and other reforms.[4]

Reforms in the health care sector started with the premise that costs were increasing because of "mismanagement," and that mismanagement—not a lack of resources or other pressures—was the main cause of this sector's crisis. In the widely debated 1993 World Development Report, *Investing in Health*, the World Bank argued that inefficiencies of public-sector programs hindered the service delivery, as well as the reduction of poverty.[5] This report proposed that incentives be established for private insurance, privatizing public services, promoting of market competition, and an emphasis on limited primary health care and prevention interventions.

Specifically, the World Bank has supported managed care initiatives that convert public health institutions and social security funds to private management and/or ownership. These initiatives require new loans, and thus, come with a burdensome string attached—increased foreign debt for the participating countries. Furthermore, these new policies respond to economic "demand" for services, rather than "supply" of services based on need.

Theoretically, this approach allows fixed costs to be reduced and more efficient management of resources, since excess services are controlled and financing is directed toward providers of presumably higher quality care, though competition. Yet according to this logic, providers are forced to both lower their costs and offer higher quality services in order to obtain financing.[6] This logic also undermines the belief that health care is a human right. Indeed, through SAPs and reports such as *Investing in Health*, the World Bank has promulgated an ideology that health is a private matter, and health care a private good.

Equally troubling, the political process accompanying these reforms in Latin American countries has usually been "hidden," restricted to the executive branch of government to reduce political conflict and resistance. In general, policy implementation bypasses the legislative branch in favor of presidential decrees. At each stage, the only actors involved are those who participate in each sector—whether public, private, or medical social security.

This approach hinders the development of a more holistic and societal perspective on reform—policy changes intended for the private sector, for example, cannot be considered by public sector or social security sector actors, as within their purview. Indeed, this comparatively "silent policymaking" has been acknowledged as an explicit goal by such informants as a World Bank official based in Argentina, and a high official of the Ministry of Health and Social Action of that country.[7]

The Role of the Big Banks and Finance Capital

In the health care sector, structural adjustment implies acceptance by Latin American governments of projects and programs initiated by lending agencies, especially the World Bank. Governments gain access to loans, but also they must also agree to carry out major cutbacks in public services. Administered with these international loans, health sector reform typically bring new legal norms (such as laws, decrees, ordinances, or ministry of health regulations) that facilitate reduced state participation in the financing, administration, and delivery of services, while enhancing the role of the private sector.

For example, in Argentina, Decree 578/93 obligated public hospitals to obtain contracts with the social security and private sectors, as well as to collect user fees from people without social security or private coverage. Other decrees deregulated social security institutions and decreased the number of health care services that the participants received through salary contributions and increasing out of pocket costs in order to decrease state expenditures.[8] In Brazil, the government changed a law that had allowed foreign capital to own only up to 49 percent of any Brazilian health-related (service or insurance) concern; foreign businesses may now own up to 100 percent of these companies. Not surprisingly, in many official pronouncements of the countries we studied, health care has shifted from being a universal right the state is responsible for to a marketplace "good" that individuals may purchase. This is a fundamental change—health is no longer a public good, but a private privilege.[9]

Multinational corporations have invested finance capital in Latin American health systems through 1) the purchase of established companies in Latin America dedicated to the sale of indemnity insurance or of prepaid health plans; 2) association with other companies under the framework of a "joint venture"; and/or 3) agreements to manage social security and public sector institutions. For multinational corporations, Latin America is a favorable environment for profit making. The majority of countries accepted SAPs then had to deregulate their economies, and as a result, foreign companies were able to manage public and social security funds with little or no investment.

The new norms also permit private national and multinational businesses to operate mediating agreements between social security institutions and providers. Also, these companies have entered into the service industry, and manage billing processes. This administrative work brings in a high rate of reimbursement, in same cases 20 percent or more of the managed funds.

Furthermore, as wealth has become more concentrated in the upper middle class and well-off classes, some people have opted out of the public system and for additional private insurance. Finally, it is become possible for corporations to operate across national boundaries since "free trade" treaties in some regions permit it, especially in the countries of the Common Market of the South MERCOSUR (Argentina, Brazil, Uruguay, and Paraguay). And with the impending Free Trade Area of the Americas (FTAA), this could be the case for all of Latin America.[10]

The list of investors in Latin America includes some of the largest insurance companies in the US.[11] Others are subsidiaries of European insurance corporations, or mutual funds that capture capital invested by universities, foundations, and corporations in First World countries. In our research, the main multinational companies operating in the countries under study were: Aetna, CIGNA, the EXXEL Group, the American International Group (AIG), International Medical Group (IMG), Prudential, and

International Managed Care Advisors (IMCA). By 1999, Aetna International had already put together health plans with 3.3 million members in seven Latin American countries. The CIGNA International health care unit enrolled 1.5 million members in five countries. American International Group attracted more than 300,000 health insurance customers in the region. Heavy investment by multinationals is well established in Argentina and Chile, has begun in Brazil, and is in the very early stages in Ecuador. During the late 1990s, Aetna International invested more than $510 million in Latin American health care ventures. Since 1997 CIGNA has invested $475 million overseas, mostly in Brazil. Both Aetna and CIGNA have reported more than $800 million in Latin American health care revenues annually.[12] These corporations tend to buy shares in several companies within each country and then to merge them, sometimes with the participation of local investors.

While access to health care for the poor is shrinking, the investments are paying off for the corporations. Between 1996 and 1999, revenues of multinational health care corporations grew much faster in Latin America than in the US, where managed care transformed into a slow-growth field with a relatively small rates of profit and with declining stock market values. During this same period, American International Group's revenues in Latin America have increased 20 percent annually on average.

Interviews and a review of publications by US corporations show that these multinationals are working to expand their business operations into the medical social security and public sectors in Latin America, since the scope of the private market is somewhat limited. (This trend has also been seen in the United States, where corporations have approached the "ceiling" in the private insurance market. As a result, they have pushed for public changes that allow them to access the huge public sector funds that support the Medicare and Medicaid programs.)

In contrast to the US, social security systems that guarantee health care and retirement benefits for many employed workers in large private or public enterprises are publicly funded in most Latin American countries. Employers and workers contribute to these social security funds; workers without coverage and the unemployed rely on public sector institutions, including public hospitals and clinics.

Throughout Latin America, social security systems have become very large funds, managed by the government or by publicly regulated agencies. North American executives see these funds as new and major sources of revenue. For instance, a managed care executive whom the EXXEL Group recruited from Indianapolis has noted: "It's a very lucrative market . . . . The real opportunity here for an investor-owned company is to develop tools in the *prepagas* [private prepaid] market in anticipation of the *obras sociales* [social security] market."[13]

The privatization of government health programs and social security systems has already permitted major capital expansion for corporations. And perceptions of the public system as inefficient, expensive, and corrupt seriously discredits public and social security institutions and makes this privatization more palatable. This has already happened in Colombia and Argentina, where the arguments for privatization resembled those favoring managed care within the US Medicare and Medicaid programs.[14]

Public Costs, Private Profits

What are the consequences of allowing the profit motive to define health policy? As in the United States, critics of managed care in Latin America have shown how this change has restricted access for vulnerable groups and diverted funds towards administrative costs and investor return away from clinical services.[15]

Copayments required under managed care plans have introduced new barriers to access and increased strain on public hospitals and clinics. In Chile, approximately 24 percent of patients covered by the ISAPRE *(Instituciones de Salud Previsional)* managed care organizations receive services in public clinics and hospitals because they cannot afford required copayments.[16] Indigent patients undergo lengthy means testing; at some hospitals in Argentina, the rejection rate for such applications averages between 30 and 40 percent.

Despite the additional barriers for patients, public hospitals in Argentina that have not converted to managed care principles face an influx of patients covered by privatized social security funds. For instance, in 1997, public hospitals in the city of Buenos Aires reported approximately 1.25 million outpatient visits by patients covered by the privately administered social security fund for retired persons. Before turning to public hospitals, these elderly patients often had not been able to access health care at the privately administered hospitals due to copayments, or they had been refused treatments by private practitioners because the health care providers had not been paid by the social security fund, among other bureaucratic failures.

As for-profit managed care organizations have taken over the administration of public institutions, increased administrative costs have diverted funds from clinical services. To attract patients with private insurance and social security plans, Buenos Aires' public hospitals have begun to hire management firms that receive a fixed percentage of billings. Meanwhile, copayments are being demanded for vaccines and other preventive measures that create barriers for people to receive services. In Argentina for example, the percentage of *private* vaccination facilities grew 94 percent between 1980 and 1995.[17]

Privatization and cutbacks in public sector budgets also have implied a decrease in preventive programs. As a result, illnesses that had declined or disappeared—such as cholera, leptospirosis, dengue fever, and typhus—have reemerged as epidemics in Latin America. National health indicators in Argentina have shown that pulmonary tuberculosis in children under 5 years of age increased 153 percent between 1991 and 1996 and childhood diarrhea increased 41 percent during the same period (the population of children under 5 increased by only 12.5 percent in this period).[18] In Buenos Aires, the richest and most populous province in the country, polio immunization coverage decreased 23.3 percent between 1992 and 1998, and DPT (diphtheria, pertussis, tetanus) vaccination coverage decreased 24.4 percent. This deterioration occurred despite a strong growth rate during those years in the Argentinean economy, averaging 5.5 percent annually.[19]

Finally, Latin American managed care organizations have also attracted healthier patients, while sicker patients gravitate to the public sector. In Chile, the ISAPREs have aimed to capture and enroll younger workers without chronic medical conditions. As a result, only 3.2 percent of patients covered by the ISAPREs are more than 60 years old, in comparison to 8.9 percent of the general population and 12 percent of patients seen at public hospitals and clinics.[20]

Reflections on the Future

Latin American countries should anticipate that reforms which open the door to managed care companies will likely result in the same inequities caused by managed care companies in the US and in some European countries. After taking huge profits and contributing to the destruction of public health care systems, managed care organizations and health insurance companies leave when profit margins fall. In the US, companies have operated Medicare and Medicaid managed care programs for a number of years, and then left these markets—leaving people without coverage and health providers bankrupt.

For example, managed care organizations (MCOs) have exited from Medicare and Medicaid programs in multiple geographical areas in the US. Data gathered by the Centers for Medicare and Medicaid Services (CMMS) on withdrawals from the Medicare program showed that by December 2000, Aetna withdrew from Medicare managed care markets in 11 states, including New York, California, Pennsylvania, Connecticut, Florida, Georgia, Illinois, Kentucky, Louisiana, Ohio, and Washington. CIGNA withdrew from Medicare markets in 13 states, including Arizona, California, Colorado, Delaware, Florida, Georgia, Maryland, New Jersey, New York, Ohio, Pennsylvania, Texas, and Virginia. Aetna's pullout affected an estimated 355,000 members in 11 states, including New York and California, while CIGNA's pullout affected about 104,000 members in 13 states, including Georgia, California, and Delaware. According to a recent estimate, MCO pullouts have affected more than 2.2 million beneficiaries between 1998 and 2002.[21]

Lending agencies and managed care organizations cannot point to many reform successes. However, failures are systematically presented as problems of the state: corruption, lack of technical capacity, etc. And official missions of lending agencies continue to evaluate, several times a year, the progress of agreed upon reforms in the countries that receive the loans in order to authorize new loans, or examine the terms of the old ones. Interestingly enough, these official missions never seem to alert either the lender or the recipients, in advance of a crisis, of the failures that they later say had been obvious all along.

The explosion of the Argentinean crisis in late 2001 provided dramatic evidence of the effects of ten years of structural adjustment policies and strict application of the lending agencies' recipes. In 2002, Argentina had an official unemployment rate of 26 percent, and public hospitals are crowded with middle and working class patients who lost their jobs and, therefore, their health insurance. Hospitals and clinics, though public and free once again, are underutilized because of the lack of basic medicines and even elementary diagnostic procedures.

Working conditions in health care are similarly grim. In public hospitals, health care workers toil under precarious conditions. During the most acute periods of the crisis, salaries are arbitrarily cut and payment was not guaranteed. In addition, salaries were not paid in the national currency, but in parallel bonds issued by provincial and national governments. In 2004, there are regular shortages of most basic medications and supplies, including those for disease prevention and screening.

What did these remarkable failures cost? Argentina increased its external debt from US$320 per capita in 1975 to US$3,800 in 2000. This external debt represented 73 percent of the national GDP—all goods and services produced in the country—in 2000.

The People Respond

In keeping with this disturbing picture, similar to that of many other countries, a number of social and political movements in Latin America are gaining influence and demonstrating that policies that benefit only multinational financial capital are regressive and detrimental to the entire population. New movements comprised of unemployed and landless workers, worker self-management groups (factories organized and controlled by their workers), peasant organizations, poor populations in urban neighborhoods, Indians and Blacks, class-based women's and other marginalized groups, are forming and creating a network of resistance.

Their protests span a huge range of demands. In Brazil, the Landless Workers Movement (MST) is demanding land and housing. In Paraguay, the Democratic Convergence Front, a broad coalition of peasant organizations, leftist parties and trade unions came together to demonstrate and block roads to force the president to retract the privatization of the state electrical network. In El Salvador, a coalition of health care workers, peasant groups and students have worked together to stop the privatization of health care.

Other demands include jobs, worker control of factories, demilitarization, access to water and other natural resources, and education, to name a few. Local, country-specific struggles are coming together to fight against the Free Trade Area of the Americas (FTAA) and Plan Americas (an extension of Plan Colombia to all of the Americas). But their demands, which have fallen on the deaf ears of the executive, legislative, and judicial branches of governments, are only a part of their activities.

These movements are also developing new social and economic structures outside of the existing framework of the capitalist system. The leaders are unemployed workers, landless workers, peasants whose organizations emphasize systems of democratic governance. Groups in various Latin American countries are developing strong connections, enabling them to exchange ideas about approaches to improving their living conditions.

Intellectuals and university affiliates in the North and South are invited to share their ideas and help in the organization of activities such as "popular universities" and technical projects (in agriculture and other productive areas). Intellectuals are also being asked to develop international connections between Northern and Southern solidarity movements, provided they are open to the ideas of the movements and do not confine their attention only to the traditional leftist parties.

The response of ordinary people to the globalization process and its effects on their lives has opened up an international movement that permits us to close this chapter paraphrasing the Porto Alegre World Social Forum slogan: "Another world is not only possible, but desirable." More and more, committed people are becoming engaged in its creation.

Chapter 7

TRADE AND HEALTH CARE:
CORPORATIZING VITAL HUMAN SERVICES

ELLEN SHAFFER AND JOSEPH BRENNER

In 1854, renowned English physician John Snow, often referred to as the father of public health, ushered in a new era in medicine by tracing a cholera epidemic in London to a contaminated water pump.[1] Snow's findings contributed to the development of government policies and other organized efforts to prevent, monitor and control disease, and to maintain and prolong life in entire populations.[2]

As budgets and authority wane for the world's health ministries and the World Health Organization (WHO),[3] protections for public health—guarantees for safe housing, food, water, and economic security—are giving way to new organizing principles. With little public attention, internationally binding trade agreements, which assure that commerce in services (like health care) is not "unnecessarily" burdened by regulations (including those that safeguard public health), are being put into place.

Equally alarming, these trade agreements supersede democratic decision making by local, regional, and national governments and shift the power to tribunals. Secret tribunals, like those of the World Trade Organization (WTO) or the North American Free Trade Agreement (NAFTA), determine which local regulations or legislation may stand and impose fines and trade sanctions on governments for going against their wishes. Instead of regulating tariffs on commodities like steel, the trade agreements currently being negotiated, such as the General Agreement in Trades and Services (GATS) and the Free Trade Area of the Americas (FTAA), will facilitate the privatization of vital services such as health care and water and deregulate standards for food, the environment, and working conditions. (A timeline of trade agreements, past and present, follows this chapter.)

Meanwhile, national and international bodies, including the WHO and national governments, are just starting to cooperate effectively on critical threats to global health. Some of these threats were enumerated by a National Academy of Sciences study in 1997. They include epidemics of water-related diseases such as cholera and malaria (which are preventable by providing universal, affordable access to safe water and sanitation); the spread of tuberculosis and AIDS; emerging drug-resistant diseases; biohazards; income inequality and financial instability; depletion of natural resources; and global warming.[4] Obviously, protecting population health, public health systems, and access to vital human services is still a necessity, even as international trade and economic policies are being determined.

While the present direction of trade negotiations is disturbing, the agreements are not complete. In this chapter, we review trade agreements and negotiation and dispute processes, with particular focus on the General Agreement on Trade in Services (GATS); and the Free Trade Area of the Americas (FTAA). The GATS is of special concern because of its potential to limit access to health care and other essential services and the FTAA is of interest because of its potential size. With 34 countries participating, the FTAA would be the largest trade bloc ever, and would affect public health regulations and access to goods and services for more than 800 million people. We suggest that an informed health care community call for an assessment of the impact on health by these agreements, and for a moratorium on further negotiations on trade in health care and other essential services until such an assessment is complete.

Global Trade: Who Makes the Rules?

International trade has been conducted for millennia. But in the past twenty-five years, cross-border financial transactions and exchanges between multinationals have occurred at an accelerated pace, and these corporations have been able to consolidate their power and influence. Today, they are increasingly successful in pressuring governments to adopt trade policies which benefit their bottom lines.

These "free trade" policies, largely guided by a set of principles sometimes referred to as the "Washington Consensus," restrict the ability of governments to regulate industry and provide public safeguards in a number of ways. They reduce public funding and establish user fees and copayments for social services that were previously subsidized, while allocating money for corporate welfare. They also lead to privatization of services, decentralizing administrative and financial procedures and weakening controls at the national level.

Until recently the liberalization of trade meant eliminating financial measures, such as tariffs, alleged by neoliberals and conservatives to discourage competitive trade from foreign producers and slow down development. Part of the Bretton Woods system, the General Agreement on Tariffs and Trade (GATT) was created in 1947 to reduce tariffs and import quotas and impose requirements for foreign and domestic goods to be "treated equally." Bretton Woods also led to the creation of the International Monetary Fund (IMF) and the World Bank, described in Chapter Four.

GATT was a second attempt at a trade regime after the failure of the broader International Trade Organization (ITO), which was negotiated in the Havana charter in 1948. The ITO, which would have been part of the UN system, was to have a broad regulatory mandate, including trade, employment rules, and business practices. But because of pressure from the business community and US government concerns about the ITO impinging on its sovereignty, the US Senate, which in effect scuttled the entire framework, refused to ratify it. Instead the GATT was created with a more narrow focus on eliminating tariffs on manufactured goods.[5]

In the early 1980s, US President Ronald Reagan and British Prime Minister Margaret Thatcher began planning to expand the GATT focus to also cover services, agriculture, investments and intellectual property rights. This expansion translated into the 1986–1994 round of GATT negotiations, known as the Uruguay Round, which was pushed largely by US-based global corporations and government officials.[6] After this round, the GATT was succeeded by the World Trade Organization (WTO), which came into effect on January 1, 1995, with 76 member countries;[7] since then membership has almost doubled and now includes 146 countries. Based in Geneva with a staff of 550 nonelected bureaucrats, the WTO oversees international trade agreements. A number of the agreements directly affect health, including the General Agreement on Trade in Services (GATS), the Agreement on Agriculture, the Agreement on Trade Related Aspects on Intellectual Property Rights (TRIPS), the Agreement on the Application on Sanitary and Phyto-Sanitary Standards (SPS), and the Agreement on Technical Barriers to Trade (TBT).

These agreements have implications not only for global health, but also for food and environmental safety and labor standards. For example, the TRIPS agreement has been used to uphold patent protections for pharmaceutical companies, limiting people's access to essential drugs, and to protect profits of agrochemical companies while limiting farmers' control of seed exchange and access to agricultural inputs. (TRIPS is described in more detail in Chapters Nine and Twelve.)

World Trade Organization: Against Public Health

While international conventions and declarations designed to protect the environment or health such as the Framework Convention on Climate Change and the Alma-Ata Declaration on Primary Health Care depend on action by each country, the WTO's centralized enforcement system is highly effective. WTO disputes are adjudicated by three person tribunals that deliberate without public scrutiny, and the WTO can impose substantial financial penalties on nations that do not comply with its rules and can authorize trade retaliation between countries.

In its relatively short life, the WTO has not hesitated to overturn national government decisions that protect public health in the interest of trade. For example, the European Union's ban on the sale of beef from cattle treated with artificial hormones was overturned by a WTO panel in 1999 after complaints from the US.[8] To justify its ban, the EU relied on the precautionary principle, an important basis for public health policy, which asserts that potentially dangerous substances should be proven safe before they are marketed. The WTO ruled that the ban was illegal under the SPS in part because it did not rely on a risk assessment approved by the WTO and authorized the US to retaliate with sanctions against European goods.[9]

For some countries, especially developing countries with limited budgets, the possibility of being tried in a WTO tribunal is sufficient to induce them to back down on laws that protect public health and well being. In 1988, Guatemala adopted the WHO-UNICEF Infant Formula Marketing Code into laws prohibiting infant formula companies from using advertising labels that made their products appear to be healthier than breast milk. For four years US-based Gerber Products launched a campaign to eliminate the law and refused to comply. In 1995, Gerber gained US support to challenge the law in a WTO tribunal, and the threat of trade sanctions were enough to have the government exempt imported baby food products from Guatemala's infant health laws.[10]

Shrinking the Public Sector

One major aim of free trade agreements is to downsize the public sector. Neoliberals and conservatives argue that privatization and deregulation increase prosperity, but analysts are increasingly suggesting that they are contributing to the rise in poverty, economic inequality, and instability throughout the world, and therefore lead to increased preventable illness and death.[11] These trends reverberate throughout health care systems around the world, placing more demands on safety net providers and other poorly funded services, spurring the global migration of health care workers, and creating uneven quality safeguards.

There is growing consensus among economists that while markets are important for a successful economy, there is also an important role for the state.[12] For example, Nobel Prize–winning economist Joseph Stiglitz recently cited Brazil's strong regulatory policies as a reason for that country's successful handling of its electricity crisis, "while the US let market forces (and companies like Enron) handle the matter."[13] All analysts, including the World Trade Organization's, agree that privatization of services can only proceed effectively to the extent that there is accountability.[14]

Whether assuring common rules and a level playing field for commerce, providing vital human and social services such as health care, education, and water, or protecting the commons through national parks and clean air standards, public sector accountability is a necessary prerequisite. Safe work places, living spaces, prescription drugs, and consumer products, as well as near-universal vaccination and many other major health accomplishments, are products of government action, legislation, and regulation, not of unregulated market forces. Trade agreements not only impose these rules, they increasingly curtail the rights and abilities of governments to determine whether they wish to abide by them. For example, the WTO can override government prohibitions against purchases of goods made by child labor.

Tariffs and subsidies are important development tools that industrialized countries have used historically and continue to use. But poor countries with fragile economies are accused of "protectionism" when they try to implement them. In many developing countries, tariffs are an important source of government funds, accounting for 10 to 20 percent of revenue, and in some cases even more. In most industrialized countries, tariffs are less important, representing on average only 1 to 2 percent of total government revenue. When a developing country eliminates or reduces tariffs, it has to replace them with other taxes, which are potentially much more difficult to impose. As the WTO urges developing countries to eliminate subsidies, industrialized countries continue to subsidize their farmers. Farmers and the poor in developing countries depend on support from their government in order to survive. The US and European countries use a double standard to the disadvantage of the developing world.

Turning Vital Services into Commodities

The WTO's General Agreement on Trade in Services (GATS) could have a devastating effect on public health and health care in member countries. The GATS explicitly proposes opening up services to private competition and reducing regulations on health care, environmental services such as drinking water and sanitation, research, and education.

The services market is a new frontier in global commerce considered to be highly profitable by multinational service corporations and their host governments. Commercial services accounted for around one-fifth of world exports of goods and services, reaching $7 trillion in 1998.[15] Nearly 90 percent of all mergers and acquisitions in developing countries were in the services sector in 1999, mostly resulting from the privatization of state enterprises.[16] Furthermore, services now account for 60 to 70 percent of gross domestic product (GDP) and employment in industrialized countries, including traditionally private commercial enterprises such as banking and insurance; and traditionally public sector services, including telecommunications, health care, environmental services (such as water and sanitation), education, and corrections.

Water provides a perverse opportunity for commercial expansion. In the developing world over a billion people lack access to safe drinking water and 2.4 billion lack adequate sanitation. In the developed world an aging water infrastructure and the demands of development on water supplies promise scarcity, and an opportunity for private water companies. It is estimated that the private provision of clean and safe water could generate $800 billion to $1 trillion a year, and private corporations have increasingly sought a role. Absent adequate government oversight and accountability, private water companies have often raised charges to unaffordable levels, even as service, quality, and access worsened. In Chapter Ten, Patrick Bond describes how the privatization of water in South Africa led to a cholera outbreak and intense hardship for the poor.

Initiated in 1995, the GATS is still under negotiations by WTO member countries, but the framework is already in place. GATS establishes "disciplines," or limits, on broadly defined "government measures," that pose "barriers to trade" in the area of services. Measures include those taken by "central, regional or local governments and authorities, and nongovernmental bodies in the exercise of powers delegated by" those government bodies.[17] These disciplines restrict what governments can do to regulate services, in the interest of facilitating trade by foreign service providers. It is at once complex and sweeping, and crucial details are not publicly available.

Even so, because of some political sensitivity to the importance of necessary services for life, welfare and equity, the GATS negotiations have developed differently than other WTO agreements. GATS is structured to allow countries to establish limits, at least initially, on the services and regulations they are willing to subject to some of the more far-reaching GATS guidelines. These are "Market Access" rules, which prevent countries from regulating or limiting the amount of services, how they are provided, or the percent of foreign ownership; and "National Treatment" rules, which state that a country cannot provide more favorable conditions to domestic companies than to foreign companies. For example, governments would not be able to restrict transactions with companies in countries with repressive labor practices or poor environmental practices. Similarly under GATS, a country could not choose to promote progressive practices within social service industries (such as education).

But some GATS guidelines apply automatically to all services. These are the "top down" disciplines, which no WTO member countries would be exempt from. Under these universal rules, government measures must not present unnecessary barriers to trade.[18] As described above, the decision on whether a public health protection is "necessary" rests with the WTO, not with the government in question. And while governments may exempt or enact measures to protect health, they cannot "unjustifiably discriminate" or use such measures as "disguised restrictions on trade in services." Again, WTO trade tribunals decide what is necessary and justifiable. Finally, governments must commit to avoiding the "trade-distortive effects" of subsidies.[19]

Under GATS, once a country has committed to open up (or "list") any service, it becomes very difficult to backtrack; governments must wait for three years to initiate the withdrawal of a commitment once it has been made. Furthermore, withdrawal requires compensation, often in the form of further liberalization or financial penalties, and also requires the consent of other WTO countries. For example, if a WTO member country agrees to open up health care under GATS, and then later decides to change national policy to offer universal or expanded health care services to its population, a WTO tribunal can rule that the country is not GATS compliant and impose a penalty that it deems appropriate.

GATS negotiations are far from complete. Currently countries are determining which services they are willing to "offer" and which services they would like other countries to offer. In addition, much of the final wording, even of important "top down" disciplines that apply to all services and all countries, is still under consideration. In recent years, labor unions and organizations such as Public Services International and Public Citizen's Global Trade Watch have been organizing to inform the public about the potential negative effects of GATS on essential services. This round of negotiations is scheduled to be completed in January, 2005, but disagreements between rich and poor countries may delay that deadline.

GATS Negotiations Put Health Care at Risk

Health care is a very large "market" that corporations are eager to tap into and GATS could be the means by which corporations do so. World expenditure on health care is more than $3.5 trillion.[20] In the 1990s, international financial institutions such as the World Bank and International Monetary Fund encouraged developing countries to privatize curative health care and many public health activities, leaving only the poorest population to be served by the public sector. Affiliates of US health insurance companies established a significant presence in Latin America starting in the mid-1990s. (See Chapter Six for details.) The resulting privatization of formerly public health systems has diverted funds and other resources from critical health needs to administration.[21] Copayments and other mechanisms have driven up the cost of care, increasing family spending on health care, and presenting barriers to access. Increasing demand is straining public hospitals and clinics.

The United States, an even clearer example of problems resulting from health care privatization, spends nearly half of the entire world's health care budget (equal to about 15 percent of its GNP).[22] Yet the US has over 40 million persons uninsured by either private or public means, and ranks 22nd—just between Slovenia and Portugal—in life expectancy.[23] In contrast, Canada has a heavily subsidized system of publicly financed, provincially based universal coverage and spends less than 10 percent of its GNP on health services.[24] Canada ranks tenth in life expectancy, tying with France, and after Japan and Sweden, among others.[25]

There is already substantial trade in health care services among nations and that commercial activity primarily benefits wealthy individuals and corporations, at the expense of social objectives such as expanded primary care systems. Some developing countries have created "niche markets" that provide high-quality specialized health services at lower cost than in developed countries, attracting foreign users.[26] These include Cuba, Jordan, India, and Tunisia, and China for traditional therapies. There is little evidence, however, that revenues generated by niche markets are channeled to improve the domestic infrastructure and systems for providing medical care and public health services. In fact, greater economic activity in commercial health care services does not necessarily result in any net economic benefit to national economies or to the population. Niche marketing of specialty services exacerbates two-tier systems and drains public health resources.

If a country chooses not to commit health care services through the GATS agreement, the liberalization of other services can affect health care, for example, administrative services (data processing, cleaning and maintenance, research, etc.), financial services (insurance and loans), and construction and environmental services (including waste disposal).[27] It is likely that the privatization of these services would result in increased costs for citizens and governments. In addition to increased costs, an ever downsizing public sector (especially in the developing world) will find it increasingly difficult to regulate contracts with foreign companies.

Bilateral and Regional Trade Agreements

As the WTO rounds continue, industrialized countries are also pursuing nation-to-nation bilateral agreements, such as the recent agreement between the US and Chile; and regional agreements, such as the North American Free Trade Agreement (NAFTA) between Canada, the US and Mexico to augment the WTO. These bilateral and regional agreements give industrialized nations, and the corporations that influence them, the power to impose rules that are even less favorable for developing countries than those established through the WTO. The Free Trade Area of the Americas, which is currently being negotiated, would create the largest regional trade bloc to date, establishing rules for every country in the Western Hemisphere, with the exception of Cuba.

FTAA is intended to facilitate trade and reduce regulation in agriculture, government procurement, investment, services, and intellectual property rights. It also proposes rules for market access, subsidies, settlement of trade disputes, and competition policy. Unlike GATS, all services would be subject to privatization and deregulation under FTAA purportedly to reduce barriers to trade in services presented by public sector provision of services and by regulation. Unlike GATS, no FTAA provisions are in force yet—the agreement is scheduled to kick in 2005. Latin American governments like Brazil and Ecuador have expressed serious reservations about signing on, buttressed by massive popular demonstrations against the agreement.

As with GATS, the FTAA exempts services supplied in the exercise of governmental authority, but states that these must be supplied "neither on a commercial basis, nor in competition with one or more service providers." *No vital human service in the US would be exempted under these definitions, including health care and water.* As presently drafted, the FTAA would facilitate further privatization and deregulation of vital human services.

Another worrisome aspect of the FTAA is the power it would give to corporations over national and local governments. A foreign investment provision of NAFTA gives private companies the right to challenge laws and regulations ("measures") adopted by democratically elected governments and officials. The text proposed for the FTAA includes a similar provision. Under NAFTA, any "measure" may be overridden by the tribunal if it decides that it is not "necessary," or "unduly burdensome to trade." Governments may also be liable for the company's loss of unearned future profits.

There are many examples of what NAFTA's foreign investment provision means for public health and welfare. Sun Belt Water of Santa Barbara, California, sued the government of Canada for $14 billion because British Columbia banned the export of bulk water. The claim was based on future profits the company would have realized had it not been precluded from entering the water-export business in that province. California and other parts of the US face similar proposals by private companies seeking to export water both to and from the state. Public scrutiny and regulatory protection of the population could be effectively chilled by the threat of lawsuits and penalties, to the detriment of the public's health. If NAFTA investment provisions are adopted by the FTAA, the US and state governments would be similarly prohibited from imposing performance requirements on foreign investments.

In another case, the Metalclad Corporation took the Mexican state of San Luis Potosí to a NAFTA court in 1997 for not being permitted to install a toxic waste site in the state, claiming that the state violated NAFTA provisions when the governor declared the site an ecological zone. The secret tribunal decided in favor of Metalclad and required the Mexican government to pay $16.7 million.[28]

Our Stake in Public Health

Opposition to these unfair trade terms is growing. In August 2002 the California legislature approved Senate Joint Resolution 40, calling upon Congress, the president, and the United States trade representative that investment provisions such as NAFTA's threaten democracy and should not be included in future agreements such as the GATS and the FTAA.[29]

Trade representatives and economic ministers from the 146 WTO nations negotiate the details of agreements such as GATS and TRIPS. These officials have the responsibility to respond to the concerns of their citizens who are working to promote access to health care, water, and other basic needs. In the United States, because of the Trade Promotion Authority bill passed in the summer of 2002, Congress is not allowed to amend or modify international agreements presented for a vote. However, there are many opportunities in the interim for Congressmembers to communicate with the US trade representative, and for Congressional committees to shape the language that is presented for a final yes or no vote.

WTO and bilateral trade meetings in Seattle, Doha, Quito, and Cancún have been influenced by informed activists who have been present at the meetings to manifest civil society's views on trade. There is a growing concern in many countries about the impact of global trade agreements on health and human welfare. National and international public health and health care communities have an opportunity to advocate for laws that protect public health and prioritize health over trade.

The authors wish to acknowledge Alicia Yamin, Howard Waitzkin, and Celia Iriart for contributions to the chapter.

TRADE AGREEMENT TIMELINE

Complied by Megan Morrissey

- 1944 – North American Treaty Organization (NATO) established to defend its 16 member nations and ensure peace and economic stability in Europe.

- 1944 – Bretton Woods Agreements create the World Bank and International Monetary Fund (IMF) to boost "postwar economies" and urge international economic cooperation.

- 1947 – General Agreement on Tariffs and Trade (GATT) signed in Geneva, setting rules for reducing impediments to international trade among member states.

- 1957 – European Economic Community Treaty (EEC), one of the four constituent treaties creating the European Union, signed in Rome.

- 1960 – The Organization of the Petroleum Exporting Countries (OPEC) formed to coordinate and unify petroleum prices in first five member nations Iran, Iraq, Kuwait, Saudi Arabia, and Venezuela.

- 1960 – Central American Common Market (CACM) signed, unifying the national economies of Guatemala, Honduras, Nicaragua, and El Salvador.

- 1960 – Latin American Free Trade Agreement (LAFTA) signed, otherwise known as the first Montevideo Treaty, in which 11 countries agree to eliminate tariffs.

- 1961 – Organization for Economic Cooperation and Development (OECD) founded to promote economic growth and free trade among northern industrialized states.

- 1965 – Dickenson Bay Agreement establishes the Caribbean Free Trade Association (CARIFTA) among member nations Antigua, Barbados, and British Guyana.

- 1968 – CARIFTA agreement adds eight new members from the English-speaking Caribbean.

- 1969 – Andean Pact formed between trading partners Bolivia, Peru, Ecuador, Chile, Colombia, and Venezuela.

- 1973 – Caribbean Community and Common Market (CARICOM) signed, replacing CARIFTA and uniting 12 member states under a single economic regime.

- 1973 – Trilateral Commission founded by David Rockefeller to create a forum for corporate executives to address government officials and media representatives.

- 1976 – The Group of Seven (G7) is initiated when Canada joins France, West Germany, Italy, Japan, the US and the UK as a powerful bloc on the world economic scene, with a mandate to influence organizations such as the World Bank and IMF.

- 1980 – Latin American Integration Association (LAIA/ALADI), the second Montevideo Treaty, signed by 11 nations, replacing LAFTA and promoting the creation of a Latin-American common market.

- 1988 – Canada-United States Free Trade Agreement signed, lowering tariffs in key industries and increasing trade between the two nations.

- 1989 – Asia-Pacific Economic Co-operation (APEC) established to liberalize trade and boost economic cooperation among North America and East Asian nations.

- 1991 – Andean Trade Preference Act (ATPA) signed, providing Bolivia, Colombia, Ecuador and Peru duty-free access to the US market for a range of products. In turn, US provides aid for strengthening democracy and fighting narco-terrorism.

- 1991 – Treaty of Asunición launches the Southern Common Market (MERCOSUR) agreement among Argentina, Brazil, Paraguay, Uruguay, and Bolivia.

- 1992 – Treaty on European Union signed following negotiations on monetary and political union, leading to the creation of the Euro.

- 1994 – North American Free Trade Agreement (NAFTA) comes into effect, removing barriers to trade and investment between Canada, Mexico, and the US.

- 1994 – General Agreement on Tariffs and Trade (GATT) re-written to regulate trade in goods while reflecting changes in contemporary geopolitics since GATT 1947.

- 1995 – World Trade Organization (WTO) established to exert control over trade practices and laws on a global scale. Initial membership of 76 grows to 147 in nine years, with 30 observer nations.

- 1995 – WTO General Agreement on Trade in Services (GATS) signed by all WTO members, extending the multilateral trading system to services (such as transportation, health, insurance, education, etc.).

- 1995 – Negotiations on Mutual Agreement on Investments (MAI), which would place rules on governments and corporations restricting the promotion of trade, begin.

- 1997 – Russia joins the G7, creating the Group of Eight (G8), which has broadened efforts to influence non-member countries and international organizations.

- 1998 – Free Trade Area of the Americas (FTAA) formal negotiations begin in Miami, laying plans for free trade among all Western Hemisphere nations except Cuba.

- 1998 – MAI negotiations are twice stalled by popular protest, preventing OECD countries from signing the agreement.

- 2000 – African Growth and Opportunity Act (AGOA) passed to accompany the US Trade and Development Act, making ties with African and Caribbean markets and promoting a US-Sub-Saharan Africa Trade and Economic Cooperation Forum.

- 2001 – WTO holds its Fourth Ministerial Conference in Doha, Qatar, kicking off the Doha Round of Negotiations. The Doha Declaration on TRIPS and Public Health was a major step forward in the struggle for access to medicines.

- 2003 – Middle East Free Trade Area (MEFTA) announced, creating ties between the US and the economies of Jordan, Israel, Morocco, and Bahrain.

- 2003 – Andean Sub-regional Integration Agreement instated to create economic and social cooperation between Bolivia, Peru, Ecuador, Colombia, and Venezuela.

- 2003 – WTO's Ministerial Conference held in Cancún, Mexico. Due to resistance from developing countries and strong protests, no agreement is reached.

- 2004 – US-Central American Free Trade Agreement (CAFTA) signed, linking the economies of Nicaragua, Honduras, Guatemala, Costa Rica, and El Salvador to the US after a year of accelerated negotiations.

- 2004 – Chile-United States bilateral free trade agreement begins, immediately eliminating tariffs on 85 percent of goods.

- 2004 – Caribbean Basin Initiative (CBI) forms Title II of the US Trade and Development Act of 2000. The move to facilitate trade between the US and the Caribbean is the culmination of 20 years of legislation and three separate Acts.

- 2005 – Final deadline for the establishment of the FTAA, an intended successor to NAFTA and the largest trading bloc in history.

Chapter 8

MILITARISM AND THE SOCIAL PRODUCTION OF DISEASE

SEIJI YAMADA

If globalization is rapidly coming to define the current world order, it is important to recognize the mechanisms by which globalizing forces are able to exert and maintain their power. Militarism plays a role in that process, as well as in the social production of disease. This discussion will necessarily be historical, examining the past in order to understand the role of US militarism in the formation of the American empire. To illustrate the effects of militarism on people's health, this chapter draws on examples from around the world and focuses on the example of the Marshall Islands, which were used as testing grounds for nuclear weapons in the past and are being used for the weaponization of space in the present.

Economic and Military Domination

"Globalization" can be read as a process that implies specific forms of international integration, those which privilege private capital. The neoliberal program for poor nations consists of privatizing national industries, making cutbacks in the public sector, focusing on production for the export market, and floating national currencies. The result is the free flow of capital to the areas with the lowest production costs: Those with cheap labor and a lack of environmental regulations. In these states, lax human rights environments, characterized by the suppression of labor organizing by state security forces, keep labor costs low. The ability to pollute with impunity allows corporations to externalize the environmental and health costs of doing business. Institutions such as the World Bank and the International Monetary Fund (IMF) enforce the neoliberal program for developing nations through structural adjustment programs (SAPs) that poor countries must institute in order to receive loans. (Chapter Four describes the effects of these policies more fully.)

As long as the integration of the world economy toward a market model proceeds apace, the imperial center need not resort to force. When the elites encounter resistance to economic domination, however, violence is employed. To the extent that Third World armies or proxy forces can be utilized to carry out the violence, the domestic political costs of mobilizing the armed forces of the US are minimized.

It is no longer impolite in the mainstream media to refer to the American empire.[1] The US is the world's most dominant nation-state politically, economically, and militarily. Politically, in some respects, it remains one nation among many, such as in the UN General Assembly. In the economic realm, it competes with Europe and Asia. In the military realm, however, it reigns supreme. Indeed, military might translates into political capital, as it did when the military victors of World War II gained permanent seats with veto power on the UN Security Council. The tendency is thus for the US to "lead with its strength," choosing to resolve conflicts by military threat or actual attack.

In some cases, the interest of US corporations are readily identifiable, as in the interventions in Guatemala in 1954 (agrobusiness), in Chile in 1973 (copper mining), and today in the Middle East (petroleum). The stated reason for the unprovoked assault on Iraq in 2003, the danger it posed to the US, was ludicrous even prior to the invasion, contributing to the widespread perception that control of petroleum reserves is what was at stake for the US.[2,3] Of course, no "weapons of mass destruction" were found afterward.

The oil resources of the Middle East have long been recognized as "a vital prize for any power interested in world influence or domination."[4] As revealed in British intelligence documents declassified at the end of 2003, in 1973 after the imposition of the Organization of the Petroleum Exporting Countries (OPEC) oil embargo, US defense secretary James Schlesinger drew up plans for an American seizure of Middle East oil fields.[5]

Even when the military is not engaged in conflict, the US military serves as a means for the government to subsidize the high technology industry. Further, as military spending does not encourage democratic forms, economic and social control by elites is ensured.[6] The armaments industry, worth $200 billion worldwide, is dominated by US companies. Five of the six largest arms contractors in the world are American: Lockheed Martin, Boeing, Raytheon, Northrop Grumman, and General Dynamics.[7] In addition, other corporate sectors benefit from military spending. For example, Kellogg Brown and Root, an engineering division of Halliburton, built bases in

Afghanistan and the detention camp at Guantanamo Bay prior to receiving the contract to rebuild Iraq's infrastructure.[8]

The economic imperative for the behavior of the US state, however, is not always so apparent. Vietnam, for example, was of relatively insignificant economic importance. The main threat that it posed was the threat of a good example, demonstrating that it is possible for a people to choose their own path, without the tutelage of their masters. The societies of Vietnam, Cambodia, and Laos had to be destroyed to prevent such an occurrence. Thus, political domination in and of itself is a desideratum, to be ensured by military domination. The American people, meanwhile, are misled into thinking that the interests of the corporations and the strategic interests of the US are their interests. The Vietnam War helped to lift this veil of ideological mystification, however. As the human and material costs of war mounted, broad segments of the US population began to question its morality.

The elites in the US utilize whatever device is convenient, in the words of Noam Chomsky, "to frighten the public into supporting policies undertaken to serve the interests of the state and domestic power centers; when one pretext loses its efficacy (like 'Communism'), others take its place at once, with scarcely a murmur from the educated classes."[9] Thus, the cold war served as an ideological cover for US interventions in its own sphere of influence.

With the fall of the Berlin Wall, the Communist threat was no longer a credible reason for massive military spending. The War on Drugs was used for a time as the justification for military aid to Colombia.[10] The Clinton administration's Plan Colombia of 2000 provided $1.3 billion of largely military aid to Colombia over two years, ostensibly to control drug production and trafficking. Subsequent to September 11, the need to refer to the War on Drugs wore off, so that in 2002, the US began to allow its aid to be used in combating "illegal armed groups," which ostensibly refers to the paramilitaries and the guerrillas. In reality, this has meant military operations in which government and paramilitary forces actively collaborate.[11] According to the Colombian Commission of Jurists, of extrajudicial killings in the period April–September 2000, the paramilitaries were responsible for 80 percent, the guerrillas for 16 percent, and the state for 4.5 percent.[12]

The collapse of the Soviet Union did not slow the development of ever more sophisticated weapons systems. Ballistic missile defense is opposed by scientists who view the technical difficulties as insurmountable and who see little utility in such a system.[13,14] In June 2002 the US withdrew from the Anti-Ballistic Missile (ABM) Treaty, and in 2004, the system will begin to be deployed in Alaska and California. While space is already used for military purposes such as reconnaissance, ballistic missile defense represents the weaponization of space.[15] The goal is the absolute military superiority of the US, allowing it to act with impunity around the globe. "[M]issile defense is about preserving America's ability to wield power abroad. It's not about defense. It's about offense."[16]

Deployment and continued testing of the missile defense systems costs nine billion dollars per year. The entire project may eventually cost a trillion dollars.[17] As noted above, this represents a transfer of wealth by the state to the dominant armaments corporations. Boeing's space and communications division in Seal Beach, California, is the lead contractor; a consortium of Lockheed Martin and Bechtel operates facilities in the Marshall Islands; Raytheon constructs the extra-atmospheric kill vehicles; and Lockheed-Martin constructs the booster's upper-stage assembly.

Since the middle of the 20th century, the human race has had the capability to annihilate itself. In the summer of 2002, India and Pakistan stepped close to the nuclear brink. In the aftermath of September 11 and the US bombing campaign in Afghanistan, Chomsky began a lecture in India with musings on whether humankind was nearing the end of its allotted life span as a species.[18] After his talk, Chomsky was queried by the audience: If the US saw fit to combat terror by striking at its presumed source in Afghanistan, why should India not root out the source of its terrorism in Pakistan? (Ironically, many of the *jihadis* active in the India-Pakistan conflict received support from the US during the campaign against the Soviet occupation of Afghanistan.[19]) As is evident from the enumeration of military deaths in both Gulf Wars, the US preference is for enemies that do not fight back. In the case of South Asia, it is evident that if India and Pakistan were to project military power in the manner of the US, Armageddon might ensue. But the US government itself has plans for the use of a variety of nuclear weapons against an array of countries.[20] It turns out that the unthinkable has been rather systematically thought out.

September 11 provided the opportunity to redeclare a War on Terror (the Reagan administration had declared a War on Terror when it took office), a great boon to the military. At $399.1 billion for the 2004 fiscal year, the US military budget is larger than the combined military budgets of the next 20 countries.[21] Even the deployment of the ballistic missile defense system, of no conceivable utility against hijackers armed with knives, has met little opposition in the period since.

Global "emergencies" to which the US responds provide ample opportunity for expansion of the empire. Having occupied Japan after the Pacific War, US troops remain in Japan today. Thirty-seven thousand US troops remain in Korea. The cold war purportedly over, US troops remain in Europe. Since the 1990s, the number of US bases around the world has been rapidly accelerating.[22]

Following its 1991 bombing of Iraq, the United States wound up with military bases in Saudi Arabia, Kuwait, Bahrain, Qatar, Oman, and the United Arab Emirates. Following its bombing of Yugoslavia, the US wound up with military bases in Kosovo, Albania, Macedonia, Hungary, Bosnia and Croatia. Following its bombing of Afghanistan, the US established military bases in Afghanistan, Pakistan, Kazakhstan, Uzbekistan, Tajikistan, Kyrgyzstan, and Georgia.[23]

The Social Production of Disease

The most obvious way in which militarism leads to the social production of disease is through outright war, which leads to death of combatants and civilians. Wide and increasing disparities in death rates between combatant nations result from modernization of the technologies of war. While the two Gulf Wars did not cause the numbers of casualties of the major conflicts of the 20th century, they represent important moments in the recent development of the American empire. In the first Gulf War of 1991 it is estimated that 79 US soldiers died,[24] in contrast to the 100,000 Iraqi combatants that were killed, give or take 50,000, according to the Defense Intelligence Agency.[25] Tactics such as bulldozing live Iraqi soldiers (mostly Shiite and Kurdish peasants drafted into the army) in their desert trenches made accurate estimates of casualties impossible.[26] In the second Gulf War of 2003, during the period of formal hostilities, 159 American and British personnel were killed[27] and between 4,000 and 7,000 Iraqi soldiers were killed.

There are also civilian deaths caused by social upheaval, as well as the disruption of production and distribution of necessities such as food and water, and deaths caused by infectious disease occurring under conditions of deprivation. The first Gulf War provides examples of each type of impact. It's been estimated that approximately 205,500 Iraqis died as a result of the first Gulf War and the chaos afterward.[28] Of these, 35,000 deaths were caused by postwar violence and 111,000 caused by indirect effects such as the destruction of the infrastructure.[29] And the shooting war was followed by economic sanctions, originally placed on Iraq in August 1990, after Iraq invaded Kuwait, and in place until the second US-led invasion, in April 2003.

The total number of excess deaths in children under five over the life of the sanctions are estimated to range from 350,000 to 540,000.[30] While some deaths were caused by the Gulf War, most of these deaths resulted from shortages of essential goods and lack of purchasing power. Economic sanctions, while not a form of military intervention, certainly qualify as a form of warfare.

Additionally, when lands are used for military purposes, people are deprived of resources necessary for health and are made economically dependent on military installations. The US military took over Mâkua Valley on the northwestern coast of Oahu in 1942 and converted it into live-fire training grounds. Mâkua Valley, which contains numerous historical and cultural sites, has been forcibly cleared of its native Hawaiian residents seven times, most recently in 1996.[31] After military exercises started 270 fires over a period of 12 years, live-fire training was halted in 1998. US senator Daniel Inouye suggested that without the ability to train at Mâkua Valley, the military might leave Oahu, which would have resulted in economic loss to the area.[32] Within a month of September 11, 2001, community opposition to such training was lifted, an illustration of the manner in which public fears further military interests. In July 2003, an intentional burn of Mâkua by the army burned 2,100 acres instead of the intended 900 acres.

The presence of military forces also disrupts local economies and social systems and fosters dependence on the global market economy, creating receptive conditions for abuses of human rights, black markets, substance abuse, and commercial sex work, with the attendant spread of disease. During the Korean conflict, Japan served as a rest-and-relaxation post for US soldiers. Entertainment districts with prostitution surround the US military bases in Okinawa and Korea. Before US bases in the Philippines were closed, some of the most extensive sex trade districts were in Angeles City, adjoining Clark Air Force Base; and in Olongapo, adjoining Subic Naval Base.[33] The sex trade in Thailand was greatly expanded by the presence of the US soldiers on leave from military service in Vietnam. Subsequently, Asia's earliest AIDS epidemic occurred in Thailand.[34]

Finally, war and militarism cause ecological destruction. For example, a variety of toxic substances contaminated the sites of the former bases in the Philippines.[35] Depleted uranium from armor-penetrating weapons contaminated areas of the Balkans and Iraq. Depleted uranium is U-238 (made by depleting natural uranium of fissile U-235), so its radioactivity is less than that of natural uranium. The health consequences of exposure to depleted uranium are controversial.[37] However, the chemical toxicity of uranium as a heavy metal and the radiological toxicity of depleted uranium are not.[38]

The Marshall Islands: A "Strategic Trust"

In terms of human health and ecological damage wrought by military activity in peacetime, the use of the Marshall Islands for nuclear weapons testing must be considered a signature event. From 1946 to 1957, the US tested 67 nuclear weapons in the Marshall Islands. The world's first thermonuclear device utilizing hydrogen fusion, a project code-named Mike, was detonated on Enewetak in 1952. The 15-megaton Bravo blast of 1954 was America's largest. It rendered Bikini uninhabitable, and exposed the people of Rongelap and Utrik to nuclear fallout. Many suffered from acute radiation sickness. A dose-effect relationship between the radiation exposure and the incidence of thyroid cancer has been demonstrated in the Marshall Islands. Displaced by weapons testing, the people of Enewetak[39] and Bikini[40] atolls were forced into nomadic lives.

Currently most of Kwajalein, the largest atoll in the world, is taken up by the Ronald Reagan Ballistic Missile Defense Test Site (RTS), a military base for testing. The RTS is equipped to track intercontinental ballistic missiles (ICBMs) launched from California and to launch the interceptor missiles being tested for the ballistic missile defense (BMD) system.

Depending on the level of activity on the base, two to four thousand non-Marshallese live on Kwajalein Island, the largest island in the Kwajalein atoll. Most of the residents are employees of private US contractors. Kwajalein Island has wide-open spaces. Long-term residents live in comfortable bungalows, with temporary workers housed in air-conditioned quarters. The streets are shaded with trees. Its residents use bicycles, as private cars are not allowed. The stores are well-stocked, and the grocery store carries fresh fruits and vegetables. The grounds are kept up by Marshallese men, and the linens on the beds of the temporary quarters are changed and washed by Marshallese women. A small number of Marshallese with professional jobs are allowed to live on Kwajalein, but the vast majority of Marshallese workers on Kwajalein arrive on the ferry from nearby Ebeye Island in the morning and must return there within three hours of completing their shifts. At the Kwajalein dock, Marshallese workers place their hands on a machine that reads their handprints.

Ebeye Island is three miles and a 20-minute ferry ride from Kwajalein Island. Its 0.36 square kilometers (66 acres) are home to 9,000 to 10,000 people. Some were residents of the central corridor of islands within

Kwajalein atoll, displaced by the missile testing facilities. Displacement consequent to weapons testing and jobs at the RTS have brought people to Ebeye from all over the Marshall Islands.

On Ebeye, many of the crowded houses (with an average of nine people per household) are made of corrugated tin and plywood. There is little greenery on the island; most of its surface is either built upon, paved, or covered with coral stones. There is no space for the crop plants that used to make up the traditional diet of the Marshallese: taro, breadfruit, arrowroot, pandanus. During the rains, the sewage backs up. The reef around Ebeye is too polluted for the people to gather resources. The electricity goes out, occasionally for extended periods, making refrigeration unreliable. Thus, the people subsist on imported white rice and canned meats with little access to fresh vegetables or fruits. The result is malnutrition in children, and high rates of obesity and diabetes in adults.[41] The crude prevalence of diabetes in adults 30 years of age or older is 20 percent.[42] At the hospital, which is often lacking basic medical supplies and until 2001 did not have running water, children are seen for malnutrition and vitamin A deficiency. Also, until 2001, boys and young men met the ferry with containers to carry water from Kwajalein to Ebeye, a major source of potable water. Such difficult water conditions led to a cholera epidemic on Ebeye in December 2000.[43] Since then, a desalination plant, which had functioned only intermittently up until that time, has become fully operational.

The people meanwhile participate in the cosmopolitan culture, though on Ebeye the only television available is US armed forces cable TV. Communities have become fragmented, and the people lead more sedentary lifestyles. Extended families have disintegrated and cultural norms regarding the care of children have been forsaken. The Marshallese people are not only exploited for their labor—for many of the American men working on Kwajalein, "going to Ebeye" means seeking out sexual liaisons with Marshallese women.

One of the ironies of globalized capitalism is that many Marshallese have migrated to the US where they make beds and keep grounds in Hawaii's tourist industry, pick crops in Oklahoma, and pack chicken in Arkansas. Arkansas now has the largest settlement of Marshallese in the US. Indeed, the Marshallese people find themselves sharing the postcolonial legacy of peoples worldwide, as they migrate from the periphery to the center to join the international working class in low-wage economic sectors.[44]

The use of Kwajalein atoll for the purposes of missile testing ostensibly continues as an agreement between sovereign nations. That the Republic of the Marshall Islands is one of the very few nations that consistently votes together with the US and Israel on United Nations General Assembly resolutions on Israel (another is the Federated States of Micronesia) demonstrates just how politically independent the Marshall Islands are.

Important cultural values inevitably fall victim to military domination. In the Marshall Islands, traditional land use dictated that chiefs provide for their peoples. Currently however, Marshallese landowners, who are the traditional chiefs of Kwajalein atoll, readily accept money paid as rent for the RTS as their private earnings. Taking a page from US power politics, the landowners even hired a former US senator to lobby the US government for better lease terms.[45]

The racism inherent in the apartheid-like Kwajalein-Ebeye setup is palpable, though for the most part, the American residents of Kwajalein do not recognize it as such. Indeed, racism was inherent in the decisions to conduct nuclear and ballistic missile testing in the Marshall Islands. After all, who would willingly volunteer their home to be a target for missiles shot from another continent?

Conclusion

While the Marshallese experience is distinctive, other populations and communities have experienced how militarization adversely affects health. These commonalities might be the basis for a global resistance movement. Thus, the people of Vieques in Puerto Rico, Diego Garcia in Mauritius, Okinawa, or Hawaii—all islands with significant military presence—have much to learn from each other. The victory of the people of Vieques in shutting down the practice bombing by US military in their backyard is cause for celebration and solidarity. In addition, the Marshallese experience with radiation-induced diseases confers an affinity with the Navajo (who worked in uranium mines), the people of Ukraine (where the Chernobyl nuclear accident occurred in 1986), Iraq (who have been exposed to depleted uranium munitions), and Hiroshima and Nagasaki. The Marshallese people have forged ties with the international anti–nuclear weapons movement in the past. Yet protests by the Marshallese people against the US occupation of Kwajalein Island have been muted in recent years; at present, Greenpeace activists are those most visibly demonstrating and working against ballistic missile defense.[46]

We must oppose ballistic missile defense because it won't work, because it is destabilizing, and because it is a cover for the weaponization of space and the further extension of offensive military capabilities. The ballistic missile defense program, as promoted by the arms industry, is an instrument of oppression of the Marshallese people and others around the world. Global health activists must oppose nuclear weapons and the weaponization of space. We need to restart the antinuclear movement, beginning with a campaign to take nuclear weapons off of hair trigger alert and to ban the use of tactical nuclear weapons.

If we support a better world, we must all oppose the increasing diversion of society's resources to the military and the corporate sector that profits from the manufacture of arms and the waging of war. US citizens must oppose their government's military adventurism. The editor of the medical journal *Lancet*, Richard Horton, suggests the military approach to terrorism is destined to fail. Rather, we should utilize public health as a tool against terrorism.[47] Prior to the invasion of Iraq, Jeffrey Sachs said the one hundred billion dollars that the war would cost could be used to prevent 30 million premature deaths from disease.[48] Directing society's resources toward equitable improvement of the human condition, rather than its destruction, is the way toward peace, justice, and—ultimately—health for the peoples of the world.

HOW ECONOMIC GLOBALIZATION POLICIES AFFECT HEALTH

In Section Three, we expose some of the direct health effects of corporate-centered globalization. Chapter Nine describes how trade agreements and agroindustry corporations are decimating small-scale farmers' livelihoods and the global food supply on which our survival rests. In Chapter Ten, we investigate a South African cholera epidemic linked to World Bank-inspired privatization and commodification of water.

In Chapter Eleven, the economic factors leading to a global resurgence of malaria are documented and critiqued. Chapter Twelve examines the worst global health problem in 700 years: the AIDS pandemic. Not since the Bubonic Plague have so many people been killed by one disease. Treatment for AIDS does exist, but the vast majority of people living with the disease are unable to afford treatment because the pharmaceutical industry has priced it beyond their means.

These stories demonstrate that the poor are currently far from being potential beneficiaries of economic globalization. In fact, they are increasingly denied their rights to health and other basic needs.

Chapter 9

STOLEN HARVEST:
THE HIJACKING OF THE GLOBAL FOOD SUPPLY

VANDANA SHIVA

India has a major farm crisis. This is not the first such crisis in the country that was provoked by external forces, however. More than 3.5 million people starved to death in the Bengal famine of 1943. At the time, India was being used as a supply base for the British military. Food grains were appropriated forcible from the peasants, while export of food grains continued. The starving Bengal peasants gave up over two-thirds of the food they produced which, coupled with speculation, hoarding, and profiteering by traders, led to skyrocketing prices. The poor of Bengal paid for the empire's war through hunger and starvation.

A half century after the Bengal famine, a new and clever system has been put in place, which is once again making the theft of the harvest a right and the keeping of the harvest a crime. Hidden behind complex "free trade" treaties are innovative ways to steal nature's harvest, the harvest of the seed, and the harvest of nutrition.

In April 2003, agricultural debts and farmer suicides began to climb among potato growers in Uttar Pradesh (UP). While the farmers were spending 255 rupees per quintal on production, potatoes were being sold for Rs.40 per quintal, leaving farmers at a loss of Rs.215 for every quintal produced.[1]

That independent farmers are struggling to survive against immeasurably difficult odds is borne out by the number of suicides by farmers throughout the country. By 2000, more than 20,000 farmers had taken their own lives, victims to the high costs of production, spurious seed, crop loss, falling farm prices, and rising debt.

The crisis for potato growers, like the crisis for producers of tomatoes, cotton and oil seeds, and other crops, is directly related to World Trade Organization (WTO) and World Bank–driven trade liberalization policies, of which the new Indian agricultural policies are direct outcomes. The policies of globalization and trade liberalization have created the farm crisis at three levels:[2] (1) a shift from "food first" to "trade first" and "farmer first" to "corporation first" policies; (2) a shift from diversity and multifunctionality of agriculture to monocultures and standardization, chemical and capital intensification of production, and price deregulation of the input sector, with virtual monopolies especially of seeds, leading to rising costs of production; and (3) deregulation of produce markets and withdrawal of the state from effective price regulation, leading to a collapse in prices of farm commodities.

From Farmer First to Corporation First

The new agriculture policies are based on withdrawing support from farmers and creating new subsidies for the agroprocessing industry and agribusiness. In a debate on the potato crisis, the UP agriculture minister referred to subsidies given for cold storage and transport. These subsidies do not go to farmers and producers. They go to traders and corporations.

The entry of Pepsico corporation in Punjab was the first example of this trade first policy. When the market rate of tomatoes was Rs.2.00 per kilo, Pepsico was paying farmers only Rs.0.80 to Rs.0.50 per kilo, but collecting 10 times that amount as a transport subsidy from the government. Cold storage owners in UP have received millions of rupees in subsidies, but this is not a subsidy to farmers. A farmer pays the cold storage owner for storage, and cold storage owners are hiking charges to exploit the crisis. This represents a massive drain of financial resources from indebted farmers to traders, from producers to business and industry.

The annual budgets since liberalization have been adding to the subsidies for the corporate sector—tax holidays for building silos and cold storages, incentives for exporting, subsidized transportation to the ports of the trader's choice. The recently announced five-year export policy of the government has allocated one billion rupees to subsidize corporations to transport grain to the ports. In addition, public money is used to take land away from farmers to build transportation facilities for agribusiness to help them transport the grain even faster.

Under this pressure to cultivate cash crops, many states in India have allowed private corporations to acquire thousands of acres of land. The state of Maharashtra has exempted horticulture projects from its land-ceiling legislation. Madhya Pradesh is offering land to private industry on long-term leases, which, according to industry, should last for at least 40 years. In Andhra Pradesh and Tamil Nadu, private corporations are today allowed to acquire over 300 acres of land for raising shrimp for exports. A large percentage of agricultural production on these lands will go toward supplying the burgeoning food-processing industry, in which mainly transnational corporations benefit.

Monocultures and Stealing of Seeds

The impact of the new agriculture policy has been to promote a shift from food grains to vegetables and perishable commodities. While grains can be stored and consumed locally, potatoes and tomatoes must be sold immediately. A vegetable-centered policy thus decreases familial and local food security and increases farmers' vulnerability to the market. While this promotes monocultures of perishable commodities, the word used for these monocultures is "diversification," in typical globalization doublespeak.

The state minister for agriculture and the UP agriculture minister both cited the variability of size and the standardization of the agroprocessing industry as a reason for not procuring potatoes from Indian farmers. Size does not matter for the Indian kitchen. Our *aaloo ki sabzi* and *aaloo paratha* do not need the russet burbank that McDonald's needs for its french fries. Seed monopolies and genetic uniformity go hand in hand. For more than 10,000 years, farmers have worked with nature to evolve thousands of crop varieties to suit diverse climates and cultures. Indian farmers have evolved thousands of varieties of rice. This tremendous diversity has been the basis of our food supply, but today it is under threat from genetic erosion and genetic piracy. Monocultures and monopolies are destroying the rich harvest of seed given to us over millennia by nature and cultures.

From the 250,000 to 300,000 species of plants alive today, at least 10,000 to 50,000 are edible. About 7,000 species have been farmed and used for food. Just 30 species provide 90 percent of the world calorie intake, and only four species—rice, maize, wheat, and soybean—provide most of the calories and proteins consumed by the world's population through global trade.

As Hope Shand of Rural Advancement Foundation International (RAFI) has stated,

> There is no doubt about the global economic importance of these major crops, but the tendency to focus on a small number of species masks the importance of plant species diversity to the world food supply. A very different picture would emerge if we were to look into women's cooking pots and if we could survey local markets and give attention to household use of nondomesticated species.[3]

Local markets and local cultures have allowed crop diversity to thrive in our fields, enabling farmers to continue evolving diverse breeds and conserving seeds and plant varieties. Ensuring the continued use of these seeds and plants is the best way to conserve them.

As global markets replace local markets, monocultures have replaced diversity. Traditionally, 10,000 wheat varieties were grown in China. These had been reduced to only 1,000 by the 1970s. Only 20 percent of Mexico's maize diversity survives today. At one time, more than 7,000 varieties of apples were grown in the United States. More than 6,000 are now extinct. In the Philippines, where small peasants used to cultivate thousands of traditional rice varieties, just two green revolution varieties occupied 98 percent of the entire rice-growing area by the mid-1980s.

Industrial agriculture promotes the use of monocultures because of its need for centralized control over the production and distribution of food. In this way, monocultures and corporate monopolies reinforce each other. Today, three processes are intensifying monopoly control over seed, the first link in the food chain: genetic engineering in combination with economic concentration, patents, and intellectual property rights.

Economic Concentration

Dominating the seed, pesticide, food, pharmaceutical, and veterinary products industries are Monsanto; Novartis, which was formed via a merger of Sandoz and Ciba-Geigy; and Aventis, which was formed with the merger of Astra/Zeneca and DuPont. DuPont has fully acquired Pioneer Hi-bred, the world's largest seed company, which, according to the *Wall Street Journal,* "effectively divides most of the US seed industry between DuPont and Monsanto."[4]

In March 1998, the USDA and the Delta and Pine Land Company announced the joint development and patent on a new agricultural biotechnology benignly called "Control of Plant Gene Expression." The new patent permits its owners and licensees to create sterile seeds by selectively programming the plant's DNA to kill its own embryos. The patent, which has been applied for in at least 78 countries, applies to plants and seeds of all species. The United States Department of Agriculture (USDA), a government agency, receives a five percent of the profits from the sales of these seeds, which it considers a built-in "gene police."[5]

The result? If farmers save the seeds of these plants at harvest for future crops, the next generation of plants will not grow. Pea pods, tomatoes, peppers, heads of wheat, and ears of corn will essentially become seed morgues. Thus the system will force farmers to buy new seeds from seed companies every year. RAFI and other groups have dubbed the method "terminator technology," claiming that it threatens farmers' independence and the food security of over one billion poor farmers in Third World countries.

According to USDA scientist Melvin Oliver, "The need was there to come up with a system that allowed you to self-police your technology, other than trying to put on laws and legal barriers to farmers saving seed, and to try and stop foreign interests from stealing the technology."[6]

Molecular biologists are examining the risk of the terminator function escaping the genome of the crops into which it has been intentionally incorporated, and moving into surrounding, open-pollinated crops or wild, related plants in nearby fields. Given nature's incredible adaptability and the fact that the technology has never been tested on a large scale, the possibility that the terminator may spread to surrounding food crops or to the natural environment is a serious one. The gradual spread of sterility in seeding plants would result in a global catastrophe that could eventually wipe out higher life forms, including humans, from the planet.

According to RAFI, "if the terminator technology is widely utilized, it will give the multinational seed and agrochemical industry an unprecedented and extremely dangerous capacity to control the world's food supply."[7] By RAFI's estimate, by 2010 the terminator and related-seeds market could constitute 80 percent or more of the entire global commercial-seed market, valued at twenty billion dollars per year.

Third World governments and farmers have rejected these "gene control" technologies. The Indian government has stated that it will not allow the terminator technology to enter India. The Consultative Group on International Agricultural Research, the world's most important agricultural research system, has stated firmly that it will not use the technology in its breeding work. In response to Monsanto's planned advertising campaign "Let the Harvest Begin," African governments wrote the declaration "Let the Harvest Continue!"

> We do not believe that such companies or gene technologies will help our farmers to produce the food that is needed in the twenty-first century. On the contrary, we think they will destroy the diversity, the local knowledge, and the sustainable agricultural system that our farmers have developed for millennia, and that they will thus undermine our capacity to feed ourselves.[8]

"Never before," writes Geri Guidetti of the terminator technology,

> has man created such an insidiously dangerous, far-reaching, and potentially "perfect" plan to control the livelihoods, food supply, and even survival of all

humans on the planet. In one broad, brazen stroke of his hand, man will have irretrievably broken the plant-to-seed-to-plant-to-seed cycle, the cycle that supports most life on the planet. No seed, no food, unless you buy more seed. The Terminator Technology is brilliant science and arguably "good business," but it has crossed the line, the tenuous line between genius and insanity. It is a dangerous, bad idea that should be banned.[9]

When Indian farmers sow seed, they pray, "May this seed be exhaustless." Monsanto and the USDA, on the other hand, seem to be saying, "Let this seed be terminated so that our profits and monopoly will be exhaustless."

As a result of international outrage, Monsanto announced in October 1999 that it would abandon its plans to commercialize terminator technology. However, Monsanto will continue to develop other hazardous technologies, including those to control seed.[10]

Patents and Intellectual Property Rights

Seed and crops have been celebrated as sources of life's renewal and as the embodiment of fertility. In Asia, rice has been an important source of both nourishment and cultural identity. On the Indian subcontinent, Basmati rice has been grown for centuries and is referred to in ancient texts, folklore, and poetry. This naturally perfumed variety of rice has always been treasured and eagerly coveted by foreigners. Today, there are 27 distinct, documented varieties of Basmati grown in India.

In recent years, Basmati rice has been one of India's fastest growing export items. Every year, India grows 650,000 tons of Basmati, covering 10 to 15 percent of the total land area under rice cultivation in India. Annually, between 400,000 and 500,000 tons of Basmati are exported. The main importers of Indian Basmati are the Middle East (65 percent), Europe (20 percent), and the United States (10 to 15 percent). At $850 a ton, Indian Basmati is the most expensive rice being imported by the European Union. Pakistani Basmati costs $700 a ton, and Thai fragrant rice costs $500 a ton.[11]

But new intellectual property rights regimes, which are being universalized through the Trade Related Intellectual Property Rights (TRIPS) agreement of the WTO, allow corporations to usurp the knowledge of the seed and monopolize it by claiming it as their private property. Over time, this results in corporate monopolies over the seed itself.

A recent patent threatens to pirate farmers' innovation, and monopolizes this trade. On September 2, 1997, the Texas-based company RiceTec was granted patent number 5663484 on Basmati rice lines and grains. RiceTec got patent rights on Basmati rice and grains while already trading the rice in its brand names such as Kasmati, Texmati, and Jasmati. The patent will allow

RiceTec to sell internationally what it claims to be a new variety of Basmati, developed under the name of Basmati.

Patents are supposed to be granted for industrial inventions that are novel in ways that are not obvious. Yet the aroma of Basmati rice, which the patent claims as new, is not novel. RiceTec's Basmati cannot be both novel and similar to traditional Basmati at the same time. In granting the patent, the US Patent Office has protected not invention but biopiracy.

If this false claim to invention is maintained, it could actually be used to penalize Basmati farmers for infringing on the RiceTec patent. The livelihoods of 250,000 farmers growing Basmati in India and Pakistan would be jeopardized. Market monopolies would exclude the original innovators from their rightful access to local, national, and global markets.

In 1998, the WTO ruled that India's failure to amend its patent law was illegal. This ruling forced India to recognize US-style patent regimes and was in essence a decision against Indian democracy. India is being held guilty under the WTO "constitution," because the Indian people, the Indian Parliament, and the Indian government have acted democratically in accordance with the rights and duties bestowed on them by their national constitution.

The piracy of Basmati is just one example of how corporations are claiming "intellectual property rights" to the biodiversity and indigenous innovations of the Third World, robbing the poor of the last resources that allow them to survive outside the global marketplace.

The most effective means for challenging such patents is through the recognition and legal protection of farmers' rights. Indigenous innovation is also recognized and protected by the Convention on Biological Diversity (CBD), an international treaty signed by the world's governments at the 1992 Earth Summit in Rio, which aims to protect biodiversity, recognize countries' sovereignty over their biological wealth, and promote sustainability and equity in the use of biological resources.

The value of conserving biodiversity in general and agricultural biodiversity in particular is now undisputed. Both the CBD and the Leipzig Global Plan of Action commit governments to conserving agricultural biodiversity and recognizing farmers' rights. Governments that have agreed to the CBD are obliged to respect, preserve, maintain, and promote the wider application of knowledge, innovations, and practices of indigenous and local communities, when relevant to the conservation and sustainable use of biological diversity.

Intellectual property rights and patents, however, reorganize relationships between the human species and other species, and within the human community. Instead of the culture of the seed's reciprocity, mutuality, permanence, and exhaustless fertility, corporations are redefining the culture of the seed to be about piracy, predation, the termination of fertility, and the engineering of sterility.

The perverse intellectual property rights system that treats plants and seeds as corporate inventions is transforming farmers' highest duties—to save seed and exchange seed with neighbors—into crimes. Further, seed legislation forces farmers to use only "registered" varieties. Since farmers' varieties are not registered, and individual small farmers cannot afford the costs of registration, they are slowly pushed into dependence on the seed industry.

These practices are not limited to farmers in India. Josef Albrecht is an organic farmer in the village of Oberding in Bavaria. Not satisfied with commercially available seed, he developed his own ecological varieties of wheat. Ten other organic farmers from neighboring villages also used his wheat seeds. In 1996, the Upper Bavarian government fined Albrecht because he traded in uncertified seed. He has challenged the penalty, and the Seed Act that levied it, on the grounds that the act restricts the free exercise of his occupation as an organic farmer. During the Leipzig Conference on Plant Genetic Resources, Albrecht initiated a noncooperation movement against seed legislation, in the same Leipzig church where the democracy movement against the Communist government of East Germany was organized in 1986.[12]

In Scotland, many farmers grow and sell seed potato. Until the early 1990s, they freely sold seed potato to other seed potato growers, to merchants, and to farmers. In the 1990s, these sales became illegal. Seed potato growers had to grow varieties under contract with the seed industry, which specified the price at which the contracting company would take back the crop, and barred growers from selling the crop to anyone. The companies started to reduce the acreage and reduce the prices. In 1994, seed potato bought from Scottish farmers was sold for more than double the price to English farmers, while the two sets of farmers were prevented from dealing directly with each other. The seed potato growers signed a petition complaining that the stranglehold of a few companies amounted to a cartel. The farmers also started to sell noncertified seed directly to English farmers. The seed industry claimed it was losing four million British pounds in seed sales through this direct trade between farmers. In February 1995, the British Society for Plant Breeders sued a farmer from Aberdeenshire, who was forced to pay thirty thousand pounds in compensation to cover royalties lost to the seed industry by direct farmer-to-farmer exchange.

In the United States, direct farmer-to-farmer exchange is also illegal, as established by a case filed by Asgrow Seed Company, now owned by Monsanto, against Dennis and Becky Winterboers. The Winterboers are farmers who own a 500-acre farm in Iowa. Since 1987, the Winterboers have derived a sizable portion of their income from selling their crops to other farmers to use as seed. In 1994, Asgrow (which has plant-variety protection for its soybean seeds) sued the Winterboers on the grounds that this direct trade violated the company's property rights. The court ruled against the Winterboers, and the Plant Variety Act, which the Winterboers had hoped would protect sales between farmers, was amended. The 1995 amendment established an absolute monopoly for the seed industry, making farmer-to-farmer exchanges and sales illegal.

Monsanto further negates farmers' rights with its Roundup Ready Gene Agreement, the signing of which is necessary in order to purchase the company's Roundup Ready soybeans. The agreement prevents the grower from saving the seeds or from selling or supplying the seeds or material derived from them to any other person or entity. The agreement requires a payment of five dollars per pound of seeds in addition to the regular price of the seeds as a "technology fee." If any clause of the agreement is violated, the grower has to pay 100 times the value of the damages. Finally, the agreement gives Monsanto the right to visit the farmer's fields, with or without the farmer's presence or permission, for three years after the agreement is signed.

But the agreement has no liability clause. It has no reference to the performance of Roundup Ready soybeans, and Monsanto is not responsible if the seeds fail to perform as promised, or if Roundup causes ecological damage. This is especially relevant given the failure of Monsanto's genetically engineered cotton, called Bollgard, to resist damage from bollworms as advertised.

In 1998, Monsanto hired Pinkerton detectives to harass more than 1,800 farmers and seed dealers across the United States, with 475 potentially criminal "seed piracy" cases already under investigation. A group of seed-saving farmers in Kentucky, Iowa, and Illinois were forced to pay fines to Monsanto of up to $35,000 each. According to Monsanto's Scott Baucum, "We say they can pay [either of] two royalties—$6.50 at the store or $600 in court."[13]

The most dramatic case of criminalization of farmers is that of Percy Schmeiser of Saskatchewan, Canada. In a landmark case, Monsanto is suing Schmeiser for saving seeds, despite the fact that he did not buy Monsanto seeds. Rather, his fields were invaded by Monsanto's Roundup Ready canola. Pollen from Roundup Ready crops is blowing all over the Canadian prairie and is invading farms such as Schmeiser's. But instead of paying Schmeiser for biological pollution, Monsanto is suing him for "theft" of its property.

Monsanto also sponsors a toll-free "tip line" to help farmers blow the whistle on their neighbors. According to RAFI's Shand, "Our rural communities are being turned into corporate police states, and farmers are being turned into criminals."[14]

Price Regulation

Since the World Bank is advising all countries to shift from "food-first" to "export-first" policies, these countries all compete with each other, and the prices of these luxury commodities collapse. Trade liberalization and economic reform also include devaluation of currencies. Thus exports earn less, and imports cost more. Since the Third World is being told to stop growing food for consumption and instead to buy food in international markets by exporting cash crops, the process of globalization leads to a situation in which agricultural societies of the South become increasingly dependent on food imports but do not have the foreign exchange to pay for imported food. Indonesia and Russia provide examples of countries that have moved rapidly from food-sufficiency to hunger because of the creation of dependency on imports and the devaluation of their currencies.

Moreover, while the government of India continues the gimmick of announcing procurement prices and procurement centers, government intervention in price regulation and procurement has completely disappeared under globalization. The government announced Rs.195 per quintal as the procurement price of potatoes, and the opening of eight centers for procurement. However, no government procurement has been done to support farmers and ensure a fair price. Prices have therefore fallen to Rs.40 to Rs.100 per quintal, a bonanza for the agroprocessing industry which makes even more profits from chips, but a disaster for the grower who is being pushed to suicide in despair. With potatoes at Rs0.40 per kilo, the agroprocessing industry is paying less than Rs.0.08 to farmers for chips they sell at Rs.10.00 for 200 gms. For 1.31 million metric tons of potatoes this amounts to a transfer of 20 billion rupees from impoverished peasants of UP to global multinational corporations such as Pepsico and McDonald's. The plight of potato farmers in Punjab is similar.

The dysfunctionality of agriculture under globalization is beneficial to agribusiness, which is harvesting the artificially accumulated stocks and artificially manipulated collapse of domestic markets to make super profits. This stolen harvest, however, is being paid for with the very lives of farmers.

An earlier version of this essay appeared in Stolen Harvest: The Hijacking of the Global Food Supply (South End Press, 2000).

Chapter 10

THE POLITICAL ROOTS
OF SOUTH AFRICA'S CHOLERA EPIDEMIC

PATRICK BOND

Neoliberal views on the management of health and environmental issues emerged in South Africa just as they were achieving virtual hegemony internationally. In this chapter, we consider debates about water pricing and their implications for public health, especially with regard to cholera and diarrhea. The South African case illustrates the furious struggle underway across the world between rights-based and market-based allocations of natural resources, and their disastrous implications for health—tens of thousands of unnecessary deaths due to waterborne diseases.

Dashed Expectations

Ironically, advocates of rights-based development had a strong headstart in the form of a broad popular mandate given to South Africa's first democratic government. The African National Congress (ANC) campaign platform in the first democratic election was the 1994 Reconstruction and Development Program (RDP). It was followed by the 1996 Constitution, which guarantees that "everyone has the right to an environment that is not harmful to their health or well-being. . . .Everyone has the right to have access to healthcare services, including reproductive health care; sufficient food and water; and social security."

The difference between rhetoric and reality quickly appeared. Shortly after liberation was achieved in mid-1994, the minimum price of water was set by neoliberal bureaucrats at "marginal cost"—that is, the operating and maintenance expenses associated with covering the next unit of water's production cost. In contrast, expectations had been raised in the RDP that the new government would provide water as an essential staple *free of cost* for at least a "lifeline" amount to all residents. This would have required a nationwide water-pricing policy with higher unit amounts for higher-volume water consumers, especially large firms, mines, and (white) farmers. It was by no means an impossible task, but the first post-apartheid water minister, Kader Asmal, refused to grasp the nettle. His rejoinder to the demand that he respect the RDP promise of a 50 liter per day lifeline supply of water was telling.

> The positions I put forward are not positions of a sellout, but of positions that uphold the policy of the South African government and the ANC. . . .The RDP makes no reference to free water to the citizens of South Africa. The provision of such free water has financial implications for local government that I as a national minister must be extremely careful enforcing on local government.[1]

It took a leap of logic to redefine the word "lifeline" to mean, not free, but instead the equivalent of the full marginal cost, namely the break-even cost of supplying an additional unit of water to the customer. Under the influence of his own bureaucrats and the World Bank, Asmal's slippery semantic solution was applied with increasing ruthlessness during the late 1990s. The main criticism of a free lifeline and rising block tariff offered by World Bank water official John Roome was that municipal privatization contracts "would be much harder to establish" if poor consumers had the expectation of getting something for nothing. If consumers didn't pay, Roome continued, Asmal needed a "credible threat of cutting service." Roome's advice was later termed, in the World Bank's 1999 *Country Assistance Strategy* for South Africa, "instrumental."[2]

Neoliberal hostility to subsidies was a general phenomenon among a key strata of post-apartheid policy makers. In 1996, Dr. Chippy Olver, then deputy director-general of the Department of Constitutional Development and subsequently director-general of the Department of Environmental Affairs and Tourism (and main manager of the World Summit on Sustainable Development) told the *Mail & Guardian* newspaper that low-income people should *not* receive lower-priced electricity than large firms. (In fact, poor people pay, on average, four times more.) He remarked offhandedly, "If we increase the price of electricity to users like Alusaf [an aluminum smelter], their products will become uncompetitive and that will affect our balance of payments."[3] The same logic, in the case of water, proved deadly in KwaZulu-Natal, the country's eastern province straddling the Indian Ocean, and home to more HIV-positive and low-income South Africans than any other province.

The Cholera Epicenter

Cholera came first to Ngwelezane, an African municipality ("black township" in local parlance) located not far from the massive Richards Bay port and industrial complex north of Durban, which houses the profitable Alusaf facility. Over a period of two years beginning in mid-2000, more than 150,000 people across South Africa, nearly all low-income black Africans, contracted cholera. More than 300 died, many as far off as Johannesburg, Limpopo Province, and a thousand kilometers away in the Eastern Cape.[4] The outbreak hit hardest and longest in rural KwaZulu-Natal villages where water supplies were infected with the cholera bug during the 2000 winter season. The *Sunday Times* investigated the epicenter two months later.

> This week, a startling picture emerged of the sequence of events that led up to the outbreak around Ngwelezane. Authorities discovered that some areas were still receiving free water in terms of a 17-year initiative of the former KwaZulu government to deal with the 1983/4 drought. "It was eventually noticed, and it was decided to switch off the supply," said the chief executive of the Uthungulu Regional Council, B.B. Biyela. "The people were given sufficient warning and the supply was cut off at the beginning of August."

> The first cases indicating cholera were noticed in [the local villages of] Matshana and Nqutshini in the second week of August. The first case confirmed was on August 19. At this point, health officials asked the Mhlathuze Water Board to reconnect the free water supplied by the former homeland government to the Nqutshini area.[5]

The connection fee of 51 rand (then US $7) imposed by Biyela was unaffordable for thousands of people. The disconnections saved a few thousands dollars but cost the provincial KwaZulu-Natal health authorities and the sick people millions.

The officials' failure to fully anticipate the social and environmental benefits of state services was typical of the post-apartheid commodification process. As a result, water and sanitation services broke down periodically, despite the increasing prices charged by the municipalities and water boards in their effort to raise funds. According to Lance Veotte, water coordinator for the South African Municipal Workers Union (SAMWU):

> The working class residents of the Ngwelezane Township pay much more for water than the white middle and upper class area, even though both are part of the same Empangeni municipality. Businesses in Empangeni pay $16 service charge and 30c per thousand liters. Rural communities who were affected by the cholera have to pay a flat [monthly consumption] rate of $2, which means that the rural poor are paying the highest price for water in the newly formed Mhlatuze municipality. Black people continue to subsidise whites.

> Samwu members who work in health services went to the area for three months in an attempt to curb the epidemic. They reported that not even the clinics had water—clinics and schools must also pay or face disconnection. This is an extract

from the report of the members: "People are forced to use muddy water also used by cattle and goats. 93 percent of the rural schools here only get water from boreholes but 70 percent of these boreholes are out of service. Many schools run out of water regularly and have to resort to using dams, pools and rivers: Unsafe Water! Only three percent of the area has flush toilets! The remaining community members have pit latrines which were found to be not properly ventilated which attracts the breeding of flies and other insects. In any case, 90 percent of the toilets are not properly built.[6]

Problems had been flagged by the Department of Health more than a year earlier:

> It is common knowledge that lack of water and sanitation is a common cause of cholera, diarrhoeal or other illnesses that afflict so many in our country and that there is a relationship between various communicable diseases, including TB, and conditions of squalor. Yet we often have not structured our institutions and service delivery systems in ways that can easily respond to these realities.[7]

The Department of Health wasn't sufficiently in touch with catchment-area water officials until it was too late because, as services undergo commercialization, their management has been increasingly fragmented. And the state has typically skimped on functions required for integration, such as local-level environmental health officers, who are particularly scarce in cholera-prone KwaZulu-Natal and Eastern Cape.[8] Water, electricity, health, and other agencies adopt corporatized organizational forms, and, in the process, fail to pursue logical, constructive linkages and spillovers.

This happens across the spheres of government as well, because water boards like Umgeni Water have been notoriously quick to commercialize and pass on unprofitable customers in rural water schemes to nearby municipalities. Because those towns or even cities are also in the process of water privatization, their officials claim they cannot afford to continue subsidizing low-income people. Once the state has surrendered its responsibility to provide water, a company that has a privatization or outsourcing contract often has no qualms about cutting off the service to those who cannot afford to pay the full cost-recovery market price plus a profit markup.

Another incident from KwaZulu-Natal demonstrates institutional and incentive problems that have emerged in rural water projects. According to *Sunday Times* reporter Mawande Jubasi, cutoffs were still occurring in cholera zones fully 18 months after the epidemic began:

> David Shezi stole water for his eight children after he could no longer take the humiliation of seeing them begging for water from neighbors. But while he sat in a cell at a police station on KwaZulu-Natal's South Coast, the man who went to the police about the theft continued to sell water to desperate people.

Samson Nqayi, chairman of the Dangaye Water Authority, a subsidiary of Umgeni Water, said he complained to police about Shezi and five co-accused to make an example of them. Nqayi, who owns a water truck, sells 25 liters of water for 1 rand to those who have no piped water. He also charges them 500 rand to install pipes to their mud huts. . .

Shezi is poor, earning only 500 rand a month by selling fruit and vegetables to motorists near his home in Umgababa. Five years ago he saved 500 rand to get water connected to his hut. But then school fees, transport and food costs drove him into debt.

When his water was cut off three months ago he became dejected. He used a pipe to bypass his water meter. Then he was arrested with five other men in his village. "I did not want to do it but I had no option," he said. "I should be getting free water. I tried to do it the right way and I failed. Now I am sure I will go to jail because my wife and children were thirsty."

Shezi is among one million poor people in KwaZulu-Natal who are forced into drastic measures to get water. On Friday, 300 members of an informal settlement near Queensburgh, Durban, were collecting water from the cholera-infested Umhlatuzana River. Their supply had been cut by the [Durban] municipality.

These people are the losers in a water war between the national Department of Water Affairs and Forestry, Umgeni Water and the municipalities of Durban, Pietermaritzburg, Ugu and Umgungundlovu. The municipalities and Umgeni Water say they do not have the money to provide free water. They asked Water Affairs and Forestry for R400 million [$57 million] and got only R120 million [$17 million].[9]

What is most important here is that privatizers—whether water seller Samson Nqayi, multinational corporation Suez, or even corporatizing KwaZulu-Natal municipalities and water boards which are moving to full cost-recovery systems—are simply taking no responsibility for the social and personal costs of cholera, diarrhea, dysentery, TB, or other AIDS-opportunistic infections incurred by health clinics and their patients. A company making profits from water sales feels no guilt when poor men, women, and children suffer.

The ability to avoid the social implications of public goods associated with water and electricity allows huge multinational corporations to make enormous profits by expanding infrastructure systems just prior to the point where low-income people would be served. Usually this is a geographic decision that corresponds with residential segregation by race or class or both, so that areas served by privatized services are noticeably "cherry-picked": Wealthy consumers get the services, but poor people are denied access. Even before the logic of privatization sets in, the necessary preliminary work by the neoliberal state—commercializing, delinking water from other state functions, raising tariffs, cutting off people who cannot pay their bills—all have the same effect, as Biyela and other officials proved in Ngwelezane. The theme of this chapter, therefore, is how the commodification of water causes droughts for poor people and floods for rich people and companies.

As a result, the key determinant is not whether water is privately or publicly managed, but whether it is in the process of being commodified. At that point, men like Biyela are just as lethal in the public sector as they would be as chief executive officers of a privatized water company.

Ironically, just as the cholera epidemic began, the lead government water official, Mike Muller, wrote in *Business Day* newspaper to endorse the Mozambique government's private-sector water regulation: "We could learn from their recent experience, which saw them dismiss the managers of newly privatized water services in Maputo for allegedly contributing to a cholera outbreak by failing to maintain services during the recent floods."[10] Tellingly, Muller did not dismiss Biyela, Nqayi, the many others implicated, or resign himself, once it became clear that his department's failure to maintain water services was contributing to the continuing spread of cholera in South Africa.

Nor did Muller mention that the decision to privatize Maputo's water was forced upon national authorities as part of the World Bank's strategy known as the Highly Indebted Poor Countries (HIPC) conditional debt relief initiative. That strategy reached its nadir in a letter from World Bank president James Wolfensohn to Mozambican president Joaqim Chissano in March 1998, celebrating "sharp" increases in water tariffs and calling for even higher prices prior to privatization of the five largest cities' water systems.[11]

Muller even went so far as to deny the obvious water disconnection–cholera link in a Canadian Broadcasting Corporation (CBC) interview in February 2003, shortly after an outbreak of bad international publicity about South Africa's water bureaucracy. CBC's reporter enquired, "So, no responsibility in government policy for the cholera situation?" Muller replied, "I come to the statement: the pandemic of cholera comes down the east African coast every 10 to 20 years and this was one more. South Africa at the moment cannot provide, free full services to everybody." Muller continued, "The policy for cost recovery is an absolutely sensible way of running a water system and the way most water systems run in the world."[12]

However, as cholera continued to spread and social protest rose to new heights, Asmal's replacement as water minister, Ronnie Kasrils, admitted that "lifeline" should really mean "free." But a rapid neoliberal reaction by the departments of Trade and Industry and of provincial and local government—using the argument noted above, that municipalities "should beware not to overtax large and nondomestic consumers"—prevented the government from paying for the cross-subsidy by charging corporations more. A variety of other sabotage techniques also emerged in bureaucracies ranging from the national department to catchment-area water boards to municipalities, with the result that the people needing the free lifeline water supply the most were least likely to receive it.[13]

Typical was the adoption of skewed water tariffs following the December 2000 municipal elections, in which the ANC government had promised that the free lifeline would finally be adopted as formal policy. Invariably, however, those tariffs provided a very small free lifeline block—6,000 liters per household per month—followed by a very steep, rising and convex curve, such that the next consumption block became unaffordable, leading to even higher rates of water disconnections in many settings. Optimally, a different strategy would provide a much larger free lifeline tariff, preferably on a per-person, not per-household, basis, to avoid bias against large families. Then the tariff would rise in a concave manner, to severely penalize luxury consumption.

Johannesburg's tariff was set by the council with the help of the French firm running the concession, Suez. Hence the tariff began in July 2001 with an extreme price increase for the second block of consumption. Two years later, the price of that second block was raised 32 percent, with a 10 percent overall increase, putting an enormous burden on those poor households who used a bit more than 6,000 liters each month. The rich got off with relatively small increases, which did nothing to encourage water conservation.

Clean Water and Cholera Prevention: Common Goods

One of the most rigorous socioeconomic epidemiologies of a cholera outbreak, more than a century earlier in northern Germany, shows a similar process to that of South Africa's in 2000. The ruling class of the city of Hamburg was particularly shortsighted. Evidence was abundant: in the city's terribly inadequate sanitation system, its unfiltered water, its stale air in the working-class ghettos, its lack of good food for lower-income people, the pathetic character of the public health facilities, and the manner in which the Elbe River was reduced to a sewer by firms along its banks and runoff from domestic latrines. Underlying the structural shortcomings was a laissez-faire ideology championed by the leaders of Hamburg's government. According to Cambridge historian Richard Evans, the significance of the cholera epidemic, which killed 10,000 people in 1892, lay mainly "in the realm of politics" because it demonstrated, with a graphic and shocking immediacy, the inadequacy of classical liberal political and administrative practice in the face of urban growth and social change. In the crucible of cholera, the fusion of class interests held together since the 1860s by the liberal ideology of free trade, the primacy of merchant enterprise, and the reconciliation of divergent interests by qualified parliamentary government, came unstuck.[14]

The same kinds of problems Evans observed characterize "normal times" in South Africa under circumstances of class apartheid, even if they are disguised by those in power who would rather blame the victim. One allegation in support of neoliberalism in water and energy pricing was that people suffering a "culture of nonpayment" spent too much of their disposable resources on the state lottery, casinos, or cellphones. An official of the Mhlathuze Water Board, who cut off low-income people's supply at the scene of the cholera epidemic epicenter, told the press in October 2000, "People will gladly pay R7 (a little under a dollar) for a two-liter Coke, but complain bitterly when they must pay the same price for more than 1,000 liters of water."[15] In reality, studies that include highly detailed household-income analysis have shown that in virtually all of the cases of nonpayment, affordability has been the universal problem.[16]

The affordability epidemic was thrown into stark relief in late 2002 by Statistics South Africa, the official government statistical agency. Its October Household Survey confirmed that in real terms, average African household income had declined 19 percent from 1995 to 2000, while white household income was up 15 percent. The average black household earned one-sixth as much as the average white household in 2000, down from one-fourth in 1995. Across racial divides, the poorest half of all South Africans earn just 9.7 percent of the national income, down from 11.4 percent in 1995. The richest 20 percent earn 65 percent of all income. The official measure of unemployment rose from 15 percent in 1995 to 30 percent in 2000. Adding to that figure frustrated job seekers brings the unemployment rate to 43 percent.

As a result, municipalities have deemed a large percentage of the population as undesirable customers of essential services. A national household survey conducted by a government agency and the Municipal Services Project found that 10 million people (of South Africa's population of 45 million) had had their water cut off, and ten million also had been victims of electricity disconnections. Though disputed by the water minister, the same figures emerge from a separate database that draws upon municipalities' own reports of disconnections since the mid-1990s. [17]

One challenge is to move from individual-scale analysis to the broader terrain of disease mitigation as a public good.[18] Simply put, where the net benefits to society outweigh the costs associated with consumption of a good or service, the result is a "merit good." When the merit good benefits apply universally, so that no one can be excluded from their positive effects, the result is a "public good." Providing affordable clean water is a logical example, as even residents of wealthy Sandton (South Africa's wealthiest suburb) learned in February 2001. The local newspaper scared elite readers with the information that due to inadequate water provision for low-income people, including waterborne sanitation, their water table was now dangerously infected with E. coli—a case of ecological blowback associated with class apartheid.

Yet confronted with the common good argument, lead water official Muller replied, "Why do we not calculate the ecological, public health, and gender benefits of water supply to reinforce our budget requests? Such exercises have often been done and will doubtless keep economists busy for years but their calculations are open to endless challenge."[19] Challenge or not, the monetary figures are impressive. Diarrheal disease is responsible for almost 25 percent of the deaths among black and colored children between one and four years of age in South Africa.[20] According to Ibinibini Mara of the Anti-Diarrhoeal Core Advocacy Group, recent research has estimated that 43,000 people, mostly poor black children, aged from infancy to five years, die from diarrheal diseases in South Africa each year, making it one of the leading causes of death. There are about 24 million cases of diarrhea each year, of which 3 million require medical treatment. The costs of diarrheal disease treatments are estimated to be 3.4 billion rand ($437 million) in direct medical costs, aside from the indirect costs and pain, suffering, and social dislocation caused. A cost-benefit analysis on the impact of diarrheal diseases in South Africa by the Group for Environmental Monitoring in 2001 estimated the economic production losses at around twenty-six billion rand (more than $3 billion) a year.[21]

The importance of water and sanitation interventions is clarified by University of the Western Cape public health scientists David Sanders and Pam Groenewald:

> Diarrhoeal disease is the most important water related disease worldwide both in terms of morbidity and mortality.... A recent burden of disease study in developing countries, using the DALY (disability adjusted life year) to measure burden of disease, ranks diarrhoeal disease as one of the largest causes of disease burden. It is estimated to account for 8.1 percent of total DALY loss in these areas. Infants and children carry the main burden of inadequate water and sanitation-related disease with more than 80 percent of the DALY loss due to diarrhoea being the result of infections in children under age 5.

> Studies have reported 0 to 81 percent (median 21 percent) lower child mortality rates amongst children with improved water and sanitation facilities than those without such facilities. Other studies have reported 40 to 80 percent reduction in

diarrhoea mortality in infants and children with the provision of piped water in the house. Several studies analyze the impact of improved water and sanitation on morbidity rates due to diarrhoeal disease. The expected decrease in morbidity rates associated with access to adequate levels of water and sanitation is regarded to be between 22 and 46 percent. One study shows that a decrease of between 35 to 50 percent can be expected, if improved water and sanitation are combined with excreta disposal and hygiene education. Another shows that up to 70 percent of diarrhoeal disease cases can be attributed to inadequate disposal of child faeces and garbage and poor caretaker hygiene.[22]

However, because of attitudes such as those expressed by Pretoria water officials, the obvious causal linkages are, unfortunately, in dispute—even in Geneva, where one would least expect it. Thus the World Health Organization's (WHO) 2001 Sachs Commission background report favorably cited the 1993 *World Bank World Development Report on Health*, to the effect that earlier state investments in water systems were wasted:

> Not only is improved water and sanitation not particularly cost effective as a health measure, it is also high in total costs....Between 1981 and 1990, more than US $134 billion was invested in efforts to expand water supply and sanitation services, approximately 34 of the sum coming from donors. Although some regions were able to make progress in improving access, few attained any of the goals set. [23]

Inexplicably, the WHO report failed to recognize that at the same time, the Bretton Woods Institutions were forcing dramatic cuts in operating subsidies on debtor countries, a practice that continues today. When impoverished water consumers could no longer maintain the systems—for example, refilling diesel tanks to run boreholes, or replacing broken piping—naturally the capital investment was lost. Yet from this experience, which should have encouraged advocacy on behalf of higher state operating subsidies, the Sachs team drew the opposite lesson, namely that "improved water and sanitation [are] not particularly cost effective as a health measure." Moreover, the researchers endorsed regulated water privatization as "an important tool to ensure the delivery of expanded [privatized] services to the poor." One tautological rationale—again, without conceding that Washington financial bureaucrats ordered cuts in social and infrastructural spending—was that "in many places it is the poor themselves, rather than their governments, who are acting to improve their lives by investing in water and sanitation."[24]

A central problem in trying to win more funding (both for capital investment and crucial recurring expenses) to improve water and sanitation so as to mitigate against cholera, diarrhea, and other waterborne diseases should now be obvious: persistent neoliberalism. It is worth reminding ourselves that it is not only in relatively wealthy South Africa that the World Bank insisted on full cost-recovery. In even more impoverished parts of Africa, the World Banks advised its staff in its *Sourcebook on Community Driven Development in the Africa Region—Community Action Programs,*

> . . . work is still needed with political leaders in some national governments to move away from the concept of free water for all. . . [and to] promote increased capital cost recovery from users. An upfront cash contribution based on their willingness to pay is required from users to demonstrate demand, develop community capacity to administer funds and tariffs, and to insure 100 percent recovery of operation and maintenance costs.[25]

Water as a Human Right

In contradistinction to the urban and rural water commodification strategies, which have had such a devastating impact in South Africa and across the continent, community, labor, and health activists argue that water is a human right and should be decommodified, and demand access and management systems that make this right real, not just rhetorical. In turn, rejecting Paris or London water privatizers and the World Bank suggests that the strategy also entails a deglobalization component, at least when it comes to resisting the depredations of transnational corporations and international financial agencies.

This is, however, never merely a matter of technical information or persuasive policy options. It will take serious political struggle, such as the Cochabamba, Bolivia, water war in April 2000 that rolled back the World Bank's privatization agenda and led to the departure of Bechtel's water subsidiary, at a cost (the company alleges) of $25 million.

There are grounds for optimism that because of such protest, making profits from water sales will become excessively difficult. By 2003, Suez was recording serious problems not just in Johannesburg, but in the US (Atlanta), Argentina, the Philippines, and Puerto Rico. As British journalist Nick Mathiason reported at the outset of the March 2003 Kyoto World Water Forum meeting, "Many of the biggest private sector water companies" were in retreat:

> Suez, the biggest water company in the world, is reducing its exposure in developing countries by a third. It had plans to reduce costs by 340 million this year and a further 68 million next year and now intends to cut deeper. Not surprisingly, in a harsh macro-economic climate, the company now favours "currency risk-exempt financing," having had its fingers burnt in Argentina and the Philippines....

> Likewise, Saur—the third biggest water firm—has in the last two years withdrawn from a contract in Mozambique while Vivendi, the second biggest player in the world, has expressed concern about the financial viability of servicing the poor in developing countries, preferring locations where customers or governments can guarantee payment.[26]

According to David Hall of the Public Service International Research Unit in London, Suez suffered protests and criticism in Casablanca and Jakarta. In December 2002, it pulled out of Manila due to massive losses and in January 2003, was pushed out of Atlanta, the largest water commercialization experiment in the US. The company's chief executive, Gerard Mestrallet, committed to "reduce investments" in the Third World. In the event of further failure, as witnessed in Manila and Argentina, of nations paying agreed profits in hard currency, Suez would "prepare to depart." [27]

World Bank records of private sector investments in the utilities of developing nations show a collapse in 2001 to half the $120 billion level of 1997. "We have agreed to take the commercial risk, but it is the political risks that kill you," admits Mike Curtin of Bechtel Group which suffered large losses in the April 2000 anti-privatization revolts in Bolivia. "My fear is that the private sector is being driven out of the water sector."[28]

For the sake of health, driving profit from water is crucial. For the sake of establishing democracy and socioeconomic justice, it is only the first step; making states genuinely accountable to the human rights of citizens remains the fundamental challenge, and moving in that direction through the agendas of deglobalization and decommodification of water provides some excellent lessons.

Chapter 11

THE REGLOBALIZATION OF MALARIA

TIMOTHY HOLTZ AND S. PATRICK KACHUR

Malaria is considered the world's oldest human disease; the plasmodium parasite may have emerged as long as 1.5 billion years ago, and it is estimated to have killed 27 billion people throughout history.[1] It continues to kill today. According to the World Health Organization (WHO), every year there are approximately 300 million malaria infections, resulting in at least one to one and a half million deaths annually.[2] Ninety percent of these deaths occur in sub-Saharan Africa, and most are in children under five years old.[3] The impact of malaria is probably underestimated by these rough figures, as the true number of malaria deaths is difficult to determine, especially in sub-Saharan Africa. Despite this uncertainty, according to best estimates today, the burden is roughly the same magnitude as 50 years ago. In 1950, there were an estimated 200 million malaria infections and 1.2 million deaths worldwide; but by 1970 that number had been cut to 500,000 annual deaths.[4] Since then, however, numbers have steadily risen.

Tragically, the reversal is due mainly to a resurgence of malaria in sub-Saharan Africa, although the problem continues to a lesser degree in Asia and parts of Latin America. In 1950, the estimated number of annual deaths in Africa barely topped 300,000 and hovered there for 20 years.[5] Given the growth in population, the death rate due to malaria was clearly falling. By 1990, however, almost 800,000 deaths per year were ascribed to malaria in Africa, and by 1999 that number had hit one million.[6] There has also been a striking increase in the number of malaria epidemics on the continent, with epidemics in 35 areas between 1997 and 2002. For example, between October 2000 and March 2001, a severe malaria epidemic in Burundi caused three million cases and 13,000 deaths among a population of 6.5 million. Every 30 seconds, one child dies from malaria in sub-Saharan Africa.[7]

These numbers beg the obvious questions: Is there a global commitment to fight this pervasive yet easily cured infectious disease among the world's poorest people? Is it possible that the globalization of poverty is causing a retrenchment and resurgence, or re-globalization, of malaria in the poorest countries? How can we fight this ancient disease in solidarity with those who are at greatest risk of contracting malaria?

Human malaria is a disease caused by one of four species of protozoan parasites, specifically *Plasmodium falciparum*, *Plasmodium vivax*, *Plasmodium ovale*, and *Plasmodium malariae*. It is typically transmitted by the bite of an infective female *Anopheles* mosquito. *Anopheles* mosquitoes are affected by climate and geography, with transmission rates highest during the rainy season. Symptoms among nonimmune persons include spiking fever, chills, shakes, body and muscle aches, headache, diarrhea, vomiting, and a cough. Infection with *P. falciparum* is the most dangerous. It can cause cerebral malaria, coma, and death within hours. *Plasmodium falciparum* is particularly dangerous in children under five years old, because they do not have an adequate immune response to prevent serious infection. In areas where transmission is endemic, repeated bouts of malaria are especially common in children. Repeated exposure leads to chronic anemia, malnutrition, retarded cognitive development, and increased vulnerability to other diseases. Simple microscopic examination of a stained blood smear is the most widely practiced method for definitive diagnosis of malaria and can be practiced almost anywhere given trained staff and materials (frequently absent in poor clinics). Malaria is entirely treatable if appropriate therapy is given promptly. In Central America and the Middle East, chloroquine is the drug of choice; elsewhere other drugs are needed to treat chloroquine-resistant parasites.

Malaria is one of only a few diseases whose prevalence steadily increased during the 1980s and 1990s, despite the available treatments. This resurgence reverses the trend seen since the discovery of modern chemotherapy in the 1950s, and the small gains of the campaign against malaria by the WHO (1955–1972). Of the 150 countries with populations over one million, 44 (29 percent) have endemic malaria; 35 of these countries are in sub-Saharan Africa.[8] In sum, over 40 percent of the world's peoples live in an area where there is a risk of contracting malaria.[9] The worst affected areas outside sub-Saharan Africa are India, Sri Lanka, Burma, the Solomon Islands, and countries in Latin America such as Guyana, Suriname, Peru, and Brazil.[10]

Although interventions to combat malaria exist, they have rarely been implemented adequately in the poorest countries where the malaria burden is greatest. In addition, the twin threats of drug-resistant parasites and insecticide-resistant mosquitoes have outpaced efforts to implement effective malaria-control activities in many endemic countries. Public health infrastructures to deliver and monitor malaria treatment and preventive interventions are notoriously poor. But while prevention and treatment interventions have failed to reach the communities most at risk, other global forces, including pressures to accept "free market" economic systems and structural adjustment programs, have penetrated the peripheries of most malaria-endemic regions. Many of these processes have had a substantial impact on malaria transmission, morbidity, and mortality.

A Hidden Problem of Immense Proportion

Most people in developed nations do not know much about malaria unless they travel to warmer climates where malaria is still persistent. Our current generation generally regards malaria as a "tropical problem," forgetting that malaria was a major problem in the Upper Mississippi Valley in the United States until the early part of the 20th century and has historically been found as far north as Canada in the West, and Siberia in the East. According to a demographer during the mid-1800s, thousands died in seasonal epidemics of malaria throughout the Ohio River Valley.[11] Over a million combatants suffered from malaria during the US Civil War. Malaria was also endemic throughout Europe for centuries, where it was known as ague in Britain and *mal-aria* (bad air) in Italy.[12]

In the process of industrialization, most economically developed countries have accomplished an epidemiologic transition, in which chronic and noninfectious diseases become a more important cause of morbidity and mortality than illnesses of infectious origin. And most industrialized countries have eradicated malaria. For people living in poverty in less economically developed nations, however, this epidemiologic transition has not occurred. For the people in the poorest 20 percent of countries, infectious diseases still account for 60 percent of all deaths, whereas in the richest 20 percent of countries they cause less than 10 percent of all deaths.[13] Malaria is one of the principal causes of this high infectious-disease mortality, along with tuberculosis, HIV/AIDS, diarrheal diseases, and pneumonia.[14]

Many authors have discussed the biologic reasons for the resurgence of malaria, conveniently ignoring the social aspects of the disease. Too often, malaria experts dismiss the role of socioeconomic forces and human behavior in the creation and reinforcement of this pandemic. Instead, the resurgence of malaria is generally blamed on the "bugs" themselves.

To be fair, drug-resistant parasites and insecticide-resistant mosquitoes have, over the centuries, confounded our best efforts to control malaria. Most of the current focus is on the molecular basis for these control problems in the recently mapped genomes of the parasite. Yet these very basic genetic changes have been selected by a complex and highly evolved set of behavioral, cultural, political, economic, and environmental forces that have, in turn, become increasingly globalized. Global market forces have shaped the availability of commodities for malaria control, outstripping public systems' ability to provide needed subsidies or maintain quality in content or delivery. Economically motivated environmental manipulation, such as dams and irrigation systems, has created new or improved opportunities for human populations to come into contact with infective mosquitoes. At the same time, donor-led development priorities and approaches have increasingly shifted the burden for paying for public health commodities onto the consumers, without acknowledging that the persons most at risk can ill afford them. It is hardly surprising that the poor, who suffer the greatest burden of malaria, will do whatever they can to conserve resources. But the result is suboptimal use of insecticides or pharmaceutical medicines, with minimal impact on reducing the disease and substantial increases in drug-resistant parasites and insecticide-resistant vectors.

The rapid spread of resistance to commonly used antimalarial drugs is necessitating the use of more expensive and potentially toxic drugs, and, in some cases, longer treatment courses. The Centers for Disease Control and Prevention (CDC) associates the emergence of antimicrobial drug resistance with globalization of the food supply, increased urbanization and overcrowding, population movements due to man-made and natural disasters, deforestation and reforestation projects, the increased use of pesticides and antibiotics, increased human contact with tropical rain forests, and global travel. Community surveys of drug-use practices throughout the malaria-endemic world have consistently demonstrated that when people purchase their own antimalarial drugs they frequently do so at doses or for durations that are insufficient.[15] Whether because of limited resources, convenience, lack of knowledge, or local perceptions about the disease and its treatment, these practices appear to select for resistant parasites. When chloroquine was highly efficacious its affordability and relatively good safety record encouraged people to use it widely for suspected cases of malaria, even without laboratory diagnosis. In Africa, chloroquine products have become commodified far beyond the formal health sector and are typically available at multiple retail outlets where little or no medically trained staff is available.

Today, resistance to chloroquine is found in every country in the world where there is significant malaria transmission.

Insecticide resistance on the part of the mosquitoes is also an important barrier to malaria control. What is often overlooked, however, is that the development of that resistance is also largely the product of human social and economic activity, such as agricultural practices and migration.[16] Parasites, insects, and humans coevolve at varying rates, according to how rapid the social environment changes.[17] They do not evolve separately. Research by Frank Livingstone, an anthropological epidemiologist, demonstrated how during the Iron Age in Africa, people transformed their ecology through slash-and-burn agriculture, increasing breeding habitats for *Anopheles gambiae* mosquitoes, who fed on humans as their primary source of food, consequently spreading malaria.[18] In other words, human social evolution, in the form of a new economic system, changed the disease ecology and increased the pace of genetic resistance.

The Forgotten Promise of Malaria Eradication

Why did malaria disappear from Europe and the United States, and was the disappeaarnce due to a concerted eradication effort or socioeconomic changes? In the US, draining swamps and spraying with insecticides was begun in earnest during the 1930s. Some of these changes resulted in a lower density of anopheline mosquito populations, while others reduced the probability of transmission. Though malaria continued to be a problem in the country's rural south well into the 1930s, especially in the African American population, it was ultimately social development—improvements in housing, civil engineering, and access to medical treatment—that led to the eradication of malaria from the US.[19]

Progress was made in some poor countries, too. In India and Sri Lanka, large gains were made against malaria in the 1940s, leading to malaria eradication programs being set up in both countries in the 1950s. Intense vector-control measures, focused on house-to-house spraying and indoor spraying of insecticides, such as DDT, were the backbone of the program. From the start, planners of the international malaria eradication program recognized that mosquitoes would eventually develop resistance to commonly used insecticides and sought to deploy these tools as widely and effectively as possible before that happened. Insecticide spraying resulted in enormous successes, as measured by the number of annual cases found. Sri Lanka had an epidemic in 1934–35 that caused 47,000 deaths, yet less than 30 years later the number of deaths had dropped to only 17.[20] By the time the spraying teams were disbanded in the mid-1960s, however, the parasite had begun to reemerge, this time due to *Anopheles'* resistance to DDT. Sri Lanka has not been able to control its malaria problem ever since.

The one factor responsible for the near-total elimination of malaria in places like the US, if little discussed in the literature, is the reduction of poverty. Poverty reduction brings with it improved housing, screened windows, mosquito nets, and access to better treatment for febrile illnesses— all of which continue to elude those who remain most at risk of malaria infection today. This aspect of malaria and its association with "tropical diseases" obscures the social causation of disease without enlisting a more critical analysis.[21] We are led to believe by neoliberal economists that "the location and severity of malaria are mostly determined by climate and ecology, not by poverty."[22] This quote from the report *The Economic Burden of Malaria*, produced by the Center for International Development at Harvard University in 2000, reflects the dominant ideology among the world's decision makers that malaria and other diseases of the tropics are a major cause of impoverishment. Though this is true, so is the reverse: Poverty is a fundamental cause of the excess burden of disease in developing countries.

Sub-Saharan Africa, where the malaria problem is greatest, was never targeted by the WHO for eradication, because it was believed that the obstacles in that part of the world were too overwhelming to be overcome, and that temporary or partial results would only exacerbate the problem.[23] During the African independence years of 1950–70, progress was made on malaria control. Living conditions improved, and access to modern antimalarial pharmaceuticals (namely chloroquine) became more widespread. But by 1980, the slow gains being made against malaria in Africa started to reverse. Drug resistance to chloroquine was first noticed in East Africa in 1972, and it quickly spread to the rest of sub-Saharan Africa. Resistance to sulfadoxine-pyrimethamine (SP, or Fansidar) has also developed in East Africa and is being detected throughout the continent.

Global markets have made only a few malaria treatments available and affordable to most who suffer from the disease. Due to cost, slashed health care budgets, political inertia, and the relatively few affordable alternative treatments, chloroquine is still the chief antimalarial used in most countries in Africa even though resistance levels have reached as high as 80 percent. Newer, more effective drugs are not produced in sufficient quantity or at an affordable cost. Hence, most who suffer malaria rely on partial doses of poorly effective medicines, which tends to intensify antimalarial drug resistance.

As of 2004, national malaria programs are under increasing pressure to purchase more expensive drugs; although they are more effective, their cost makes them inaccessible and fewer patients can be treated. Seldom entering into the discussion is the question of why the more effective drugs continue to be unaffordable. Recent experience with antiretroviral drugs for AIDS treatment has shown that with enough public pressure, the cost of even complex drugs can be markedly reduced by removing production from the control of large profit-making enterprises.

Given this crisis, a major push for the development of new and affordable antimalarial drugs is essential. Nonetheless, not a single major pharmaceutical company has an in-house antimalarial drug development program.[24] For the global pharmaceutical industry, producing antimalarials is not seen as a profitable enterprise. Aside from the drugs that European or North American travelers consume for malaria prevention when they travel to endemic parts of the world, the demand for malaria treatment drugs comes entirely from the poorest countries of the world. At best, consumers or governments in these countries can only afford to pay pennies a dose for treating an infection as widespread as malaria. Some of the malaria treatments that have been developed in recent decades are intrinsically expensive to produce. Others could be more affordable if they came into wide production, but global manufacturers and their stockholders are averse to developing a new production line until a paying customer can be found. Without public expenditure on the development of new antimalarial drugs, the "free market" approach leaves vulnerable populations free to die from malaria.

The economic impact of malaria in Africa is substantial. Economists John Gallup and Jeffrey Sachs have estimated that malaria causes a reduction of between 7 percent and 13 percent of annual gross domestic product (GDP) per capita in sub-Saharan Africa, and an absolute reduction in per capita annual growth rate of 1.3 percent. The average purchasing power parity GDP per capita in 1995 for the malarious countries was $1,526 (and much lower in the poorest of these countries), versus an average of $8,268 in countries without intensive malaria.[25] Malaria causes productivity losses in formal and informal work sectors because of the symptoms suffered by employees, including fever, weakness, and chronic anemia.

Links between Globalization and Malaria Resurgence

Global political and economic forces have been at the heart of the resurgence in malaria transmission experienced in recent decades in poorer countries and communities. The mechanisms by which this has occurred are numerous. International policies increasingly favor the application of free-market principles to the distribution of many of the medicines, insecticides, and other supplies that are needed to treat or prevent the disease. Donor-driven restructuring initiatives have left public institutions in endemic countries with little central authority and without the capacity at the periphery. Consumers are forced to rely increasingly on the private sector to deliver what was once considered a public good. Human migration and land use patterns have been shaped by political developments or economic necessity and have, in many instances, brought people and malaria-transmitting mosquitoes into more intense contact, consistently worsening the situation. In the following section we describe in detail several of the important links between global forces and the resurgence of malaria.

Irrigation and water management projects. Agricultural production is the primary interaction between humans and their environment for most of the world's peoples. Agricultural practices, especially those that clear large swaths of land for large-scale farming and irrigation, have been implicated in the historic spread of malaria. Large irrigation projects, including dams funded by the World Bank, increase opportunities for anopheline mosquito breeding. For example, the Gezira water management scheme in Sudan, where the introduction of new irrigation channels only worsened the malaria problem in the late 1970s.[26] In Swaziland in the 1980s, medical historian Randall Packard found that agricultural practices such as irrigation reintroduced malaria where it had been previously controlled, and did so in the absence of pesticide-resistant *Anopheles* mosquitoes. The creation of large-scale agricultural projects introduced ideal breeding sites for malaria vectors; the importation of nonimmune foreign workers known to be potential carriers introduced the parasite; and ineffective control measures to address illness all led to the reestablishment of malaria.[27] Packard predicted that the continued deprioritization of malaria control and the dependence of the Swaziland economy on sugar exports would only worsen the problem. Indeed Swaziland continues to have a malaria problem to this day: 77 percent of the country's population lives in malaria-risk areas.

Pesticide overuse. Pesticide use is an important component of export crop production, which is itself a key element of the neoliberal economic approach to promoting "growth" for poor countries. With increased export crop production, pesticide use increases, and extremely heavy use has been reported in many areas, such as Central America and the Indian subcontinent. There are convincing data to show that the overuse of agricultural pesticides has not controlled mosquito populations, but rather, has actually contributed to creating ecological niches where anopheline mosquitoes have developed resistance to insecticides such as DDT. Insecticide use is also part of public health efforts to control mosquito populations—it is used to spray the inside of houses to kill resting mosquitoes at night. However, the amount used for this purpose is a minute fraction of the amount used in agriculture.[28]

Reduced health budgets and socioeconomic restructuring. Timely and appropriate treatment of persons ill with malaria is a keystone of malaria control. In most malaria-endemic countries, however, health budgets are woefully inadequate to deal with the illness, let alone the constellation of other health conditions these countries face. In many countries, the budget available for malaria treatment and control has shrunk as new priorities, such as HIV/AIDS, loom larger and larger. Recent trends toward decentralization and socioeconomic restructuring have not been associated with impressive improvements in overall health or life expectancy.[29] Public spending to achieve equity or maximize access for the most vulnerable groups has been difficult to accomplish. One review of health care spending across several African countries examined the impact of public subsidies to improve access to vulnerable groups, and the authors concluded that such an approach more often favors the better off rather than the poorest.[30] (See Chapter Four for a further description of the effects of structural adjustment programs on health systems.)

Commodification of health. With an increasingly globalized market extending to some of the most remote parts of malaria-endemic countries, health and health services have come to be treated much like other commodities. This process, the commodification of health, is closely tied to the "free market" ideology of globalization.[31] This has been especially true for medicines for treating malaria in emerging monetized economies across Africa, Latin America, and Asia. On the one hand, this trend might have created additional avenues for medicines to reach underserved populations, but for the most part public officials have missed the opportunity to exploit this possibility for the public good.

Currently, most antimalarial drug use occurs at the household level without the involvement of trained health workers, and much of it is inappropriate. When consumers are encouraged to purchase medicines for malaria treatment or insecticide for treating a net, these commodities have to be viewed as relative priorities when decisions are made about allocating a household's limited financial resources. Frequently consumers economize by purchasing the cheapest (not necessarily the most effective) alternative in the lowest possible quantity and postpone purchases as long as possible. Almost everywhere, these commodified public health products are marketed far beyond the reach of public sector programs to assure quality or provide consumers the facts they need to make purchases. As a result, malaria drugs in particular have become widely used but in quantities that fail to completely work and ultimately encourage the emergence of resistant parasites.

Poverty. The existence and or continuation of brutal poverty for 2 billion people, the failure of structural adjustment to improve the lives of millions, and the further immiseration of the world's poor is undoubtedly linked to the large numbers of unnecessary deaths from malaria. Despite what mainstream economists say, malaria is deeply entrenched in issues of poverty and social justice. We know that the report card on "globalization" and development is mixed at best, and decidedly negative considering how Africa has fared in the global economy in the last 15 years. Though not recognized, the problems that the poor have with housing quality, sanitation, and malnutrition can each have profound effects on susceptibility to malaria infection and disease. A major cause of the continued high levels of malaria morbidity and mortality is the perpetuation of social stratification, both within and between countries.[32]

Civil war and armed unrest. In 2002 there were an estimated 15 million refugees and internally displaced persons (IDPs) worldwide due to civil unrest, war, food shortages, and political persecution. Refugees and IDPs in tropical climates are at particular risk of developing malaria and other communicable diseases. Armed conflict and civil unrest destroys public health infrastructure, disease control programs, access to medication, and living conditions of the poor. Displacement of persons to malarious ecologies with which their immune systems are unfamiliar puts them at particular risk of malaria. In addition, malaria control programs are as susceptible as any other program to unrest, and the collapse of malaria control throughout sub-Saharan Africa is testament to this uncertainty. Civil wars and civil unrest were common throughout the 1990s in Africa, and have continued into the 21st century. The war in eastern Congo has resulted in over 2.5 million deaths from disease, much of that from malaria and other communicable diseases.[33] The civil unrest in Sierra Leone and Liberia has also caused a collapse in malaria control programs—often it is difficult for patients to obtain even chloroquine for the treatment of fever.

A remarkable story of malaria control during civil warfare occurred in Nicaragua during the 1980s. The Sandinista government undertook a concerted effort to control malaria after gaining power, which included making antimalarials easily accessible even the most remote parts of the country, and undertaking several mass chloroquine treatment campaigns.[34]

Though this method has not been shown to be effective in all settings, Nicaragua managed to keep malaria incidence at a low level in the 1980s despite being under attack by the US-financed contra army. After the resolution of the war and the election of a neoliberal government friendly to US interests, health care was defunded and malaria has made a comeback.[35] As of 2004, Nicaragua's malaria problem is still not under control.

Combating Malaria: What Works

Community-based strategies to prevent and treat malaria infection and reduce the intensity of exposure, especially in young children, are desperately needed in malaria-endemic communities. Insecticide-treated nets (ITNs) have been shown in randomized trials to reduce child mortality by 15 to 25 percent. They are the most efficacious and feasible intervention against malaria.[36] They benefit the individuals sleeping under them and have a community-wide effect because they act like baited traps for mosquitoes. Unfortunately, the percentage of children sleeping under treated bed nets at any one time in sub-Saharan Africa ranges from 15 percent to 40 percent, and usage is consistently lower among poor rural residents.[37] The need to retreat ITNs with insecticide every year is also a challenge to their effectiveness. In addition, the cost of an ITN ($5 to $7) often exceeds the weekly income of an average African, putting them out of reach for many families.

ITNs cost-effectiveness is comparable to that of other highly effective child survival interventions, such as measles vaccination.[38] Shortly after the initial evidence of high efficacy appeared, advocates called for a broad-based international commitment to make ITNs widely available free of charge.[39] Yet gradually, the favored approach to promoting ITNs in rural Africa by global health organizations (WHO and the World Bank) has shifted toward marketing directly to consumers through commercial channels.[40] These market-based approaches may take years to become effective and may initially exaggerate inequities between urban and rural residents. A recent study in Mozambique, for example, found that urban families with better housing and educated mothers were seven times more likely than the poorer rural residents to own a bed net.[41] International advocates have made recent calls for more generous assistance from donors to heavily subsidize ITNs or provide them free of charge, considering this intervention on par with vaccines.[42] The estimated cost of providing ITNs for all of rural tropical Africa would be $295 million annually, a drop in the bucket compared to annual military expenditures by industrialized nations. More grassroots health advocacy will be needed to promote this shift in thinking.

Few poor nations have succeeded in eradicating malaria. The successful models took hold in the 1960s in "insular" countries such as Taiwan, Cuba, Jamaica, and Mauritius. Cuba undertook an aggressive campaign before eradication was declared in 1967, raising awareness about the disease, promoting community action to rid villages and towns of mosquito breeding sites, and providing prompt treatment with chloroquine. Unfortunately, these lessons are not all applicable for non-island settings, such as rural Africa and the forest areas of Southeast Asia, especially now that more expensive and complex malaria treatments are required and the mosquito vectors are less amenable to environmental source reduction.

In recent years some positive developments have occurred. The WHO and other international partners resolved in 2000 to implement the International Decade to Roll Back Malaria (RBM), through widespread use of ITNs, early effective treatment, strategies to reduce the impact of malaria in pregnancy, and detection and control of malaria epidemics, promising to rapidly eliminate 50 percent of malaria-related mortality by 2010.[43] The establishment of the Global Fund to Fight AIDS, Tuberculosis, and Malaria has pledged $259 million to fight malaria over the period 2003 to 2005.[44] Sadly, however, actual funding and commitment to achieve these goals has been lacking for decades. It would take serious investment of resources, both financial and political, to achieve anything close to the promised gains for 2005. The Global Fund is now far short of the funding initially sought, as pledges have been lower than expected and donors have not kept their pledges.[45] As the decade passes, it is very doubtful that the global targets will be achieved.

Conclusion

Most malaria deaths around the world could be avoided if people had the economic resources to access necessary medical care and measures to reduce the risk of infection. Today, as in the last century, most malaria deaths are preventable. Malaria remains such an important public health condition, despite its long history, because of its ability to adapt to changing circumstances and the effect of human economic and social behavior on its transmission. The economic and social forces of globalization, unfortunately, have only perpetuated the transmission of this disease.

Just as parasites have evolved drug-resistant genes and mosquitoes have developed resistance to insecticides, larger trends in the global system have allowed this illness to go unchecked. Large water projects, the overuse of pesticides encouraged by export promotion policies, and the commodification of health interventions have all contributed to the re-globalization of malaria. Ultimately, the failure of neoliberalism to lift millions out of poverty forms the underlying cause of our inability to deal with this disease in the poor countries of the world.

As unprecedented resources for malaria control are being solicited through new international initiatives, opportunities for new approaches to reducing malaria may be unfolding. Although imperfect, effective technologies for malaria control are known. There is hope that significant resources will be applied for the first time in decades. However, unless global systems are adapted to make wise use of these resources, the problem will continue unabated. The development, testing, and dissemination of new drugs and other approaches to controlling malaria must be removed from the hands of profit-making corporations and supported by public funds. Essential tools such as treated bed nets and effective drugs must be made available as public goods to all who need them, not as commodities to be purchased only by those who can afford them. Broad multisectoral efforts to address pesticide overuse and dam and irrigation projects are important and will require long-term planning and governmental support. Grassroots organizing, political pressure, and global solidarity are critical now to stop the resurgence of this re-globalized disease.

Chapter 12

THE BATTLE AGAINST GLOBAL AIDS

PAUL DAVIS AND MEREDITH FORT

There are 900,000 people in my country. 25 percent of them have HIV.
Swaziland is being erased by greed and trade policy.

– Phetsile Dlamini, Health Minister of Swaziland[1]

Accoording to the United Nations, there are 40 million people living with
HIV, the vast majority in the developing world.[2] Eight thousand people
die every day of AIDS-related complications, and currently there are 15
million children that have lost one—or both—of their parents to the disease.[3]

The pandemic has hit Africa especially hard. According to a report by the
Central Intelligence Agency's National Intelligence Council, the number of
AIDS infections in sub-Saharan Africa may double in five years.[4] In Botswana
and Zimbabwe, infection rates are exceeding 45 percent among residents of
metropolitan areas. And in Zimbabwe, UNICEF reports life expectancy will
fall to 27 years old by the end of the decade.[5] (In July 2001, the Harare City
Council began requesting residents to bury their dead deep enough to leave
space for the next.)[6]

The crisis is quickly growing elsewhere. Millions have been infected in
Africa, China, and India, but the fastest growing rates of infection are now in
the countries of the former Soviet Union, including Russia and the Ukraine.[7]
Even more numbing than these statistics is the assessment by the World
Health Organization (WHO) that it will be 30 to 40 years before AIDS even
begins to plateau.[8] The United Nations Program on AIDS has stated that the
40 million infected with HIV so far represent an epidemic "in its infancy,"
with 70 to 100 million expected by 2010.[9]

The death toll inflicts the heaviest burden on working-age people—the
women and men who head families, schools, businesses. Governments, too,
are affected; entire nations are being depopulated of their most productive

citizens, leaving a country of orphans and elderly people. Increasingly bereft of economic opportunities and without the resources needed to fight AIDS, people throughout the developing world are creatively doing whatever they can to survive the nightmare. Reports Stephen Lewis, a UN envoy to Africa,

> I visited a little Catholic community center in Windhoek, Namibia, in February. It was a place where people living with AIDS could network, find a support group, have a meal, try to earn some money through an income generating project. What was the project in that instance? The Sister running the center took me out back to show me. A group of men were making miniature papier maché coffins for infants, and as they affixed the silver handles, they said to me with a mixture of pride and anguish: "We can't keep up with the demand."[10]

Economic Contributors to the Pandemic

The staggering number of HIV/AIDS-related deaths in developing countries dramatically illustrates how corporate-centered globalization impacts the health of poor people all over the world. As outlined in Chapter Two, the sustained process of labor and resource extraction by first world countries underlies the global economic forces that contributes to increased poverty and disparity in the Third World. Furthermore, as explained in Chapter Five, AIDS began its rapid spread in sub-Saharan Africa at the same time that provision of social services in many resource-poor countries was being undercut by austerity measures imposed by international financial institutions (IFIs) such as the International Monetary Fund (IMF) and the World Bank.

By the late 1980s and early 1990s, IFIs had required many public system clinics in Africa to begin charging "user fees" for services following the 1987 Bamako Initiative, which introduced the principle that the world's poorest countries (all of them in Africa) should implement fees and cost recovery for public health services. As a result, health services utilization rates declined and the poorest were most affected.[11] For example, in Zimbabwe in 1991 attendance at one government clinic fell from 1,200 in March to 450 in December of the same year.[12]

Poverty and inequality, important contributors to the spread of AIDS, are clearly exacerbated by structural adjustment programs (SAPs) and other aspects of globalization. Malnutrition, closely linked to poverty, is also a major contributor to the crisis.[13] In a vicious cycle, HIV/AIDS contributes to famine and malnutrition as communities rely on smaller numbers of able-bodied and healthy workers to produce food and agricultural skills. Knowledge often is not passed from one generation to the next due to the loss of parents.[14]

Women are particularly vulnerable to the disease. They are often dependent on partners economically, and in weak positions to negotiate condom use. In times of economic hardship and job scarcity, poor women may see no alternative but to turn to sex as an income source.[15] By engaging in casual or non-monogamous sex, a woman can perhaps afford to pay rent, buy groceries, and send her children to school. Poor men often migrate far from home in search of work and have no other partners than casual or professional sex workers.

Finally, untreated illnesses and sexually transmitted diseases (STDs) render a person more vulnerable to HIV infection. While heterosexual intercourse is considered to be the major form of HIV transmission in sub-Saharan Africa, some researchers have pointed to needle reuse and poor sterilization in medical settings as also being important.[16] Clearly, providing adequate care is very difficult in settings that are strapped for resources.

Big Pharma Denies Drugs to the World's Poor

In 2002, the WHO estimated that six million people with HIV/AIDS would qualify for highly active antiretroviral therapy on clinical grounds.[17] Yet in the same year, only an estimated 50,000 to 60,000 were receiving the medicines. Activist pressure will raise that number to almost 500,000 by the end of 2004, but the pandemic cannot slow or stabilize as millions die every year. Because the vast majority of those living with HIV/AIDS are in poor countries, they still do not have access to these life-saving medicines.[18]

At the same time, people in whiter, wealthier nations have been living longer, healthier lives by taking antiretrovirals. Corporate greed, racist trade policies, the negligence of wealthy governments has created a global medical apartheid—a system of power and economics that threatens civilization.

The pharmaceutical industry plays an integral role in maintaining the health-wealth gap. As a result, pharmaceuticals are by far the most profitable companies in the US, heading up Fortune 500 lists year after year.[19] (Drug companies spent more in the 2000 and 2002 US elections than either the Republican or Democratic parties.)[20] And the US, home to most of the world's major pharmaceutical companies, has some of the longest-standing patent monopolies on pharmaceuticals in the world. Yet long patent restrictions prohibiting price competition from generic manufacturers have not always been the case for the rest of the world.

In 1995, the WTO agreement on Trade Related Aspects of Intellectual Property (TRIPS) established rules for enforcing patent monopolies for products and manufacturing processes (including pharmaceuticals).[21] By prohibiting competition from generic drug manufacturers for at least 20 years from the date of patent filing, the new monopolies all but eliminated the potential to access affordable treatments for HIV and other life-threatening illnesses in the developing world. At the invitation of the US Trade Representative (USTR), pharmaceutical manufacturers, as well as biotech and chemical companies, crafted much of the language on patents and intellectual property that was adopted in international trade agreements, guaranteeing high profits at the expense of millions of sick people in developing countries.

The Uruguay Round of GATT negotiations that led to the TRIPS rules were launched in 1986 when patent holders in wealthy countries pressed the USTR on the impact of counterfeit goods. Prior to this, patents were systematized internationally under the Paris Agreement on intellectual property (1883) and the Stockholm Agreement (1967). The 1995 TRIPS agreement goes much further than previous ones by requiring all prospective or current WTO members to set up 20-year patents in all industrial fields (including pharmaceuticals) for both products and manufacturing processes. It also set deadlines for these countries to achieve the necessary changes in their domestic patent legislation.[22] Prior to TRIPS, many countries had limited or no patent restrictions on pharmaceuticals.

The TRIPS negotiations were highly polarized. The negotiating position of the US during talks leading up to the TRIPS agreement was weighted heavily toward strict patent obligations supported by industry.[23] The negotiating team included advisors from the pharmaceutical industry lobby (IFPMA) and the Intellectual Property Committee, a coalition of 13 major US companies. Many of the companies on the Intellectual Property Committee had major pharmaceutical holdings, including Bristol-Myers Squibb, Johnson and Johnson, Monsanto, DuPont, Merck, and Pfizer.[24]

The US and European Community (EC) insisted on greater protections for intellectual property benefitting corporations in the North, squashing resistance from a group of developing countries attempting to safeguard the ability to build local infant industries (including pharmaceuticals) that would be undermined by strict universal intellectual property privileges.

Even though protectionist measures were common in Western Europe and the United States during their industrialization phases, the drive by developing countries to enable local industry were dismissed as "protectionist."[25] In Europe, pharmaceuticals were denied patent protection in some countries until the 1960s and 1970s to promote development of local industry—and to control drug prices. By denying such strategies to developing countries, the rich had effectively cut the rungs off the development ladder before the poor were able to climb it.

As Monsanto representative James Enyart told *Les Nouvelles*, a French journal,

> Industry has identified a major problem in international trade. It crafted a solution, reduced it to a concrete proposal and sold it to our own and other governments… We went to Geneva where we presented (our) document to the staff of the GATT [General Agreement on Tariffs and Trade] Secretariat. What I have described to you is absolutely unprecedented in GATT . . . the industries and traders of world commerce have played the role of patients, the diagnosticians and the prescribing physicians."[26]

TRIPS Safeguards Allow for Access to Medicines

While the TRIPS agreement (and the WTO) is heavily weighted toward commercial interests, impoverished countries were successful in winning safeguards that, when utilized, can mitigate the negative effects of extensive pharmaceutical patents. Foremost among these safeguards are *compulsory licensing* and *parallel importing*.

Compulsory licensing allows governments to grant licenses permitting a company or public agency to manufacture a patented product without the authorization of the patent holder. TRIPS permits compulsory licensing only under certain circumstances, including public health emergencies, or more flexibly for public, non-commercial use. Under a compulsory license, compensation must be provided to patent owners. A government could issue a compulsory license to compel a multinational pharmaceutical company with a patented product to license the drug to a domestic company. The domestic firm would then manufacture the drug for sale in its own country under a generic name, and pay a "reasonable royalty" to the patent holder. The amount of the royalty is not prescribed by TRIPS, and the patent holder need not deem the compensation reasonable or adequate.

A modest but growing number of countries are locally manufacturing medicines that were not under domestic patent before TRIPS compliance deadlines. Brazil, India, and Thailand are foremost in AIDS pharmaceuticals, and China launched limited local manufacture in 2003. Unfortunately, under threat of retaliation from the US, *no developing country has yet issued a compulsory license*. Ironically, with no hue and cry, the US has issued compulsory licenses on many goods, ranging from infrared goggles for military usage to a device called the "backsaver," which benefits tow truck operators.[27]

Parallel importing consists of purchasing proprietary drugs from a third party in another country, rather than directly from the manufacturer, taking advantage of the fact that pharmaceutical companies sometimes charge significantly lower prices in one country than in another. For instance, in Britain, where parallel importing is common, GlaxoSmithKline's Retrovir (also known as AZT) is listed for £125, but consumers can purchase the same proprietary drug imported from other European countries for as little as £54.[28] Importing a product from one country and pursuing resale, without authorization of the original seller, allows the buyer to search for the lowest world price.

The Medicines Act in South Africa: Activists Turn the Heat Up

Almost all nations have had to pass new intellectual property laws to conform to the new TRIPS rules. In 1996 under President Nelson Mandela, the South African Parliament adopted the WHO's "essential drugs list" (EDL), consisting of medicines critically required for the prevention and management of 90 to 95 percent of the common conditions in the country. To ensure EDL availability, parliament passed amendments to the Medicines and Related Substances Control Act in 1997. The "Medicines Act" included measures to make essential medicines more accessible and affordable through compulsory licensing and parallel importing.

A report leaked from the US State Department detailed an extensive pressure campaign waged by the Clinton/Gore Administration to force South Africa to repeal the offending provisions of the Medicines Act. The State Department report confirmed the extent to which multiple governmental resources have been brought to bear on the issue—often coordinated by the US offices of the US-South Africa Binational Commission, a new government body created to manage our relations with the new South Africa:

> All relevant agencies of the US government—the Department of State together with the Department of Commerce, its US Patent and Trademark Office, the Office of the United States Trade Representative, the National Security Council and the Office of the Vice President—have been engaged in an assiduous, concerted campaign to persuade the government of South Africa to withdraw or modify [the Medicines Act]. [29]

The State Department report explained how "US government agencies have been engaged in a full court press with South African officials from the departments of Trade and Industry, Foreign Affairs, and Health" to pressure them to change the law. Vice President Gore, as co-chair of the US-South Africa Bi-national Commission, raised the issue repeatedly with South Africa's Deputy President.

South Africa refused to repeal the law. As punishment, the Congress withheld certain trade benefits, limiting South Africa's access to US markets. The USTR threatened further trade sanctions by putting South Africa on the special "301 Watch List" of countries receiving heightened scrutiny regarding trading practices.[30] The US government also enlisted the French, Swiss, and German presidents to raise the issue with top South African officials.

Yet in April 1999, US groups wrote to Vice President Gore about the South Africa dispute, pointing out that every request for consultation by the public health community had been rebuffed. They asked for a reversal of US policy, and strongly objected to the administration's frequent and false public assertions that the South African initiatives were not permitted under the WTO TRIPS accord, and that the US refused to bring its concerns to the WTO under its dispute resolution framework.

In June, 1999, AIDS activists from several US ACT UP chapters, following the lead of a gay and lesbian direct action group, organized numerous protests during Gore's presidential campaign events, including disruptions at most of the stops on his initial campaign announcement tour. Concurrently, South African activists began mounting pressure with actions targeting US embassies.

The activists continued to meet with the administration, making clear that the punishments being dealt Vice President Gore would not let up until the sanctions were lifted and South Africa was declared TRIPS-compliant. Under a firestorm of negative publicity, the vice president began to signal in early July that US policy might change. His campaign director waded through a police line at a large protest of a Gore fundraiser in Philadelphia to hand the activists a letter that had been sent to the Congressional Black Caucus. The letter stated that the administration would no longer oppose compulsory licensing or parallel importing of medicines, so long as the South African provisions were applied in a manner consistent with TRIPS.[31] South African treatment activists received a similar message in follow-up meetings with US Embassy officials after a demonstration.

The letter equivocally implied that South Africa may be out of compliance with the TRIPS agreement, and was based on an unacceptably narrow reading of the trade rules, so activists continued targeting Gore's campaign. Facing disruptions and a threatened occupation of his campaign headquarters, Gore directed the USTR to end the dispute with South Africa. Shortly before newly elected South African President Thabo Mbeki was scheduled to make an appearance with Vice President Gore in the US, a new agreement was announced on September 17, 1999 that indicated that the US now deemed the South African Medicines Act compliant with the TRIPS agreement.[32] The US also removed South Africa from the "301 Watch List."

Energized by the victory, activist groups maintained pressure to expand this decision for South Africa to other impoverished countries. But the dramatic climb-down by the USTR still did not open the way for implementation of the Medicines Act. Thirty-nine multinational drug companies filed a lawsuit against President Mandela in 1998, tying the law up in South African courts for almost a year. With an organized response by the Treatment Action Campaign (TAC) of South Africa and a global day of solidarity actions by activists around the world, the pharmaceutical manufacturers finally withdrew the lawsuit in 2001.[33]

New Challenges, New Victories

In June 2001, after being appointed by President Bush to head the US Agency for International Development (USAID), Andrew Natsios told the House International Relations Committee that resources for global AIDS should be reserved for prevention and not treatment. Natsios, who is in charge of most US foreign assistance programs, stated that Africans "do not have a western sense of time," and thus would not be capable of taking a schedule of pills.[34] Aside from being racist and uninformed about newer, simpler drug regimens, his comments illuminated a deeply held policy by the global health establishment: It is not "cost-effective" to treat the poor.

Paul Farmer, founder of Partners in Health, argues that this logic is flawed because preventive efforts have shown less than impressive results in isolation. "The belief that treatment may be reserved for those in wealthy countries whereas prevention is the lot of the poor might be less repugnant if we had highly effective preventive measures."[35] And with few exceptions, AIDS prevention in the absence of treatment has limited effectiveness.

Meaningful disease prevention is predicated on strategies that require a significant percentage of at-risk populations to know if they have an infectious illness. However, without treatment, there is little incentive for those in resource-poor countries to seek HIV testing. Indeed, without the ready availability of essential drugs, the only outcome of a positive test result is to suffer several years of stigma and violence while awaiting one's death. In the most resource-poor settings in Africa, where access to treatment has been denied to millions, it is estimated that fewer than five percent of HIV-infected individuals actually know their status.

The benefits of many health and development initiatives are greatly magnified where treatment is made available. For example, in 1994, the World

Bank estimated that by 2000 Brazil would have 1.2 million HIV-positive people.[36] In 1997, in response to organized efforts by the gay and lesbian community and people living with AIDS in Brazil, the government began to provide free medicine to the sick in every part of the country. New clinics were built in remote areas as well as in cities. As a result, the World Bank's 1994 prediction did not come true. Brazil was able to reduce rates of AIDS death *and rates of new HIV infection* by 50 percent in three years.[37] The incidence of other diseases has declined as well; for instance, TB in HIV-positive patients also dropped. The decline in hospitalizations from opportunistic infections between 1997 and 1999 saved the Brazilian Health Ministry over $400 million.[38]

How was this successful program possible? The government of Brazil manufactured domestic copies of drugs that were under patent protection in wealthier nations. And the ability to provide a comprehensive health package which responded to the needs of the public justified the expense of building and staffing new clinics. Hundreds of thousands of lives have been saved, and Brazil presents a highly successful model for other developing nations.[39]

When treatment is available, caregivers who may have been unable to save dying patients for want of medicines, are re-energized. Likewise, politicians in developing countries can stop hiding from the epidemic when they have the resources to offer life-saving medication to their citizens. Furthermore, stigma is reduced when disease is known to be treatable, and destructive social interpretations of the disease—that it is a form of witchcraft, or a CIA form of bioterrorism, or that it can be cured by having sex with a virgin—are diminished as soon as successful medical interventions are demonstrated. Concurrently, citizens begin to demand medicine when a trickle of availability is detected. In countries like Brazil and Thailand, demands for medicine by activists with AIDS have generated tremendous social benefits.

The Global Fund to Fight AIDS, Tuberculosis, and Malaria Offers Hope

Large-scale generic drug competition, when fully realized, creates economies of scale in manufacturing and raw materials to drive down the costs of triple-combination therapies. However, the poorest nations—those struggling with debt repayments, decimated workforces, and only able to muster a few dollars per capita for health spending—remain unable to take advantage of reduced drug costs.

In 1999, international AIDS activists began to assess the modestly funded bilateral assistance agencies and programs operated by wealthy nations. Even cursory research revealed wide duplication, inefficiencies in reporting requirements, and deeply held race-based belief systems that justified prevention-only interventions in poor countries. Most rich-country aid also had dangerous political strings attached to it; for example, the USAID is legally required to only purchase products manufactured in the US, where cost-effective generic medicines for AIDS are not yet available.[40] The unwritten but strong prohibition against use of generic medicines applies even when the "Buy-American" clause is waived.

Clearly, to attract the new funding necessary for more effective treatment and prevention (while minimizing the impact of US foreign policy) a new multilateral vehicle was needed. So in early 2000, activists began calling for a global bulk drug procurement and distribution system, sponsoring meetings to build support for the proposal before the Okinawa G8 summit and the International AIDS Conference in Durban, South Africa, later that year. Working with activists, US Representative Barbara Lee and US Senator John Kerry established a preliminary legislative framework for a global trust fund to fight AIDS.

After the Okinawa summit, Representative Lee's bill creating a new entity to fight global AIDS wound its way through US Congress. By late 2000, the bill had been passed by Congress, but had not been implemented due to the difficulty of creating a new multilateral body seen as originated by the US.

The idea of a trust fund initially generated opposition from the pharmaceutical industry and traditional aid agencies. Drug companies opposed measures to create a large scale buyer able to leverage prices for countries or groups of countries because they would threaten Big Pharma's company-by-company, country-by-country, drug-by-drug negotiations, recently launched in response to threats of competition from generics. Additionally, many development organizations based in donor countries had grave concerns about threats to agency contracts funded by USAID and other bilateral aid agencies, and some USAID recipients publicly complained about the impossibility of providing AIDS treatment in developing countries.

But the activists persevered. In late 2000 and early 2001, activists from Health GAP (Global Access Project) and Médecins Sans Frontières (MSF) worked quietly to insert proposals for bulk procurement and distribution of generic medicines into the framework of the Trust Fund, and into a new European Commission proposal addressing HIV/AIDS, TB and malaria. Simultaneously, Health GAP built support within UNAIDS and the WHO for a new multilateral framework for AIDS funding, while working with officials in the office of UN Secretary General Kofi Annan.

By April 4, 2001, the fight gained new allies when the Harvard Center for International Development released a consensus statement signed by over 100 academics and development experts proposing an "HIV/AIDS Prevention and Treatment Trust Fund."[41] On April 26, Annan gave an electrifying speech at the meeting of the Organization of African Unity in Abuja, Nigeria, calling for the creation of a Global AIDS Fund.

> We must put care and treatment within everyone's reach. Even a year ago, few people thought that effective treatment could be brought within reach of poor people in developing countries. Those already infected with HIV were condemned to be treated like lepers in earlier times...
>
> However, now there has been a worldwide revolt of public opinion. People no longer accept that the sick and dying, simply because they are poor, should be denied drugs which have transformed the lives of others who are better off...This crisis is so grave that developing countries must face it by exploiting all options to the full—including the production and importation of "generic" drugs...The war on AIDS will not be won without a war chest, of a size far beyond what is available so far.... At a minimum, we need to be able to spend an additional seven-to-ten billion dollars a year on the struggle against HIV/AIDS in the world as a whole, over an extended period of time.
>
> I propose the creation of a Global Fund, dedicated to the battle against HIV/AIDS and other infectious diseases.[42]

Within days after the extensive media coverage of the speech, world leaders stepped forward to applaud the Secretary General's call to arms. A significant victory seemed at hand. But people with AIDS and activists were handed a tragic setback two weeks after the Abuja address when President Bush delivered a speech announcing that the US would contribute a meager $200 million to the fund. Furthermore, in his speech, Bush attempted to define the Global Fund as one that "emphasizes prevention" and "respects intellectual property rights."[43]

By making the first contribution to the Global Fund, President Bush appeared to be a world leader. In reality, President Bush dealt a tremendous blow to efforts to win a multilateral ten billion dollar-a-year war chest. Contributions from other donor countries were not pegged to meet real needs, but instead to simply be nominally less-stingy than the US. By the July 2001 G8 Summit in Genoa, the fund had been expanded to address HIV/AIDS, TB, and malaria, and all of the world's richest nations could muster less than $2 billion spread over three or more years. The world's long-overdue response to AIDS was starved of resources before it could be launched.

Today, the Global Fund is constantly threatened with bankruptcy and its success or failure still hangs in the balance.[44] Stinginess and US aversion to multilateralism has played a significant role in its underfunding, and the resistance of aid bureaucrats to treatment has slowed new contributions from rich countries which have much better foreign aid records than the US, such as the UK, Sweden, the Netherlands and Denmark. Given the enormous loss of life and the economic and political destabilization caused by HIV/AIDS, something must change, now.

Dismantling Medical Apartheid: A Call for Action

As you read this chapter, trade negotiators, CEOs, and politicians are coming up with new tricks that may further limit access to treatment. At the same time, the strength of the AIDS activist community is rapidly growing and public regard for the pharmaceutical industry is in steep decline.

For example, one significant battle was fought at the WTO ministerial meetings in Doha, Qatar. In 2001, the "Doha Declaration on TRIPS and Public Health" confirmed that governments have the right to override patents and authorize the manufacture of cheap generic medicines. But pressure from pharmaceutical companies became a barrier to access. After Doha, the WTO's TRIPS Council was relentlessly pressured by the US Government and pharmaceuticals to limit compulsory licensing for developing countries to strictly defined "national emergencies." The TRIPS Council was also encouraged to limit the ability of member countries to import generics from other countries with existing manufacturing capacity under compulsory license.

In December, 2002, the US government was the lone voice arguing that the Doha Declaration apply only to a few diseases, and that in all other cases the poorest and smallest countries should be required to build expensive new factories instead of purchasing drugs from India or Thailand. In the end, the US was able to win a new interpretation of TRIPS, limiting the rights of poor countries to gain access to generics and increasing the power of the WTO to administer intellectual property rules in formerly sovereign nations.

Partially in response to Doha, AIDS activists campaigned for a new Presidential AIDS Initiative, and in 2003 the Bush Administration pledged $15 billion for global AIDS over five years.[45] However, only $10 billion of that is new, and much of that is earmarked for future spending. The bilateral Bush program also comes with tremendous political baggage, including funding requirements for disproven abstinence-only prevention measures, a strong aversion to TRIPS-legal generics, and a two year roll-out delay while millions die and the Global Fund remains in dire need of new funds.

And thousands of loosely coordinated US activists are pushing to make global AIDS an issue in upcoming elections in order to double the Bush pledge; ramp up contributions to the Global Fund; drop the debt of the poorest countries; and roll-back the new and more limited TRIPS agreement.

Working for HIV/AIDS treatment access offers opportunities to bridge North-South divides, and design new models of development based on collaboration and solidarity. For example, pressure by activists has resulted in favorable reinterpretations of WTO rules on affordable generic medicines. With the removal of major barriers to generic competition in 2000, the cost of a year's supply of AIDS medications fell from $15,000 per person to $350 per person. Since then, generic prices have fallen even more and will soon be available for $140 per person per year.[46] Activists have also forced multinational corporations with major workforces in sub-Saharan Africa such as Anglo Gold and Coca-Cola to launch workplace AIDS treatment programs.

But there is a long road ahead. In spite of a crushing epidemic in the South that threatens the future of the globe, privileged activists in the North too often include AIDS issues as an afterthought—if at all. Similarly, many public health advocates and professionals have not been willing to take on the pharmaceuticals and other corporations. Indeed, labor and environmental activists have been much more visible than health organizations in campaigns against corporate-centered globalization.

However, AIDS activists have been able to consistently win the groundbreaking victories that have turned the tables on multinationals, and wealthy governments. Together we must demand that wealthy countries pay a fair share to the Global Fund, so that treatment can be made available to anyone who needs it. We must pressure the World Bank for debt cancellation, so that national governments will be able to invest their own resources in health services and essential medicines. And we must insist that policymakers encourage, rather than block, the production and importation of affordable life-saving generic medicines by poor countries.

Activists from the North and South can work together to resist the attempts by corporate elites and wealthy governments to deny millions of poor people the right to health, while pressuring governments of the South to adopt aggressive "pro-poor" agendas. By directly and creatively confronting power, we can secure global health and democracy.[47]

MOBILIZING FOR HEALTH

The principles behind corporate-centered globalization and profit-based approaches to health services are in direct conflict with the belief that everyone has a right to health care. Around the world, activists are fighting unjust policies that limit access to water, food, shelter, and health care. However, with the exception of AIDS activists and the newly-formed People's Health Movement, health activists have been conspicuously absent from organized protests of IMF, World Bank, WTO policies.

We conclude *Sickness and Wealth* by acknowledging that we cannot wait for experts to make just decisions about people's health. We have learned from our experiences with structural adjustment programs, health sector reform, unfair trade agreements, and irrational wars that health and social justice are not priorities for those in power. Furthermore, with a few excpetions international agencies with global health on their agendas (like UNDP, UNICEF, and WHO) are not putting globalization on trial.

However, people's movements around the world have stepped into this void. There are countless efforts underway to make health a human right. Chapter 13 describes some of the many organizations and movements that are working to advocate for health and social justice and to confront globalization. And the resource guide in the section provides contact information for some of these groups, as well as recommendations for further reading and advocacy tools.

Corporate-centered globalization has created more poverty and less health. Creating a more just and healthy world will be difficult, but as more people join the struggle our job will become easier, and more productive.

Chapter 13

THE STRUGGLE FOR PEOPLE'S HEALTH

ALEJANDRO CERÓN, ABHIJIT DAS, AND MEREDITH FORT

While many people—in poor and wealthy countries—feel isolated in their struggles for health and social justice, most are fighting the same forces. Communities around the world are confronting the privatization of critical services, lack of access to medical care and essential drugs, and the ongoing imposition of Washington Consensus policies.

This chapter highlights just a handful of the thousands of organizations working to resist and overturn harmful policies. These varied approaches and experiences demonstrate that there is not one path for all health activists to follow—there are many ways to effect change. Furthermore, working for health and justice does not require complex or technical knowledge, but engagement, commitment, and creativity. Progress has come through identifying and fighting injustice; creating alternatives to the corporate health model; supporting global people's movements based in the South; and participation in solidarity efforts, locally and globally.

Finally, whether you live in Washington, DC, or Mozambique, it is also key to remember that effective advocacy requires participation at all levels—lobbying policy makers, creating and implementing alternatives, marching in the streets, researching and producing newsletters, and providing care directly to people in need.

Resisting Injustice

Viable, informed resistance to injustice is critical to every movement. Successful liberation struggles in South Africa and India were the results of sustained and sophisticated actions. Large protests in Seattle shut down World Trade Organization (WTO) meetings in 1999, bringing public attention to the complete one-sidedness of corporate-centered globalization. And similar protests around the world—at the Genoa G8 Summit in 2001, or in Miami at Free Trade

Agreement of the Americas (FTAA) meetings—dramatically show that civil society has been left out of discussions about how, when, and why to "globalize."

This visible activism makes a difference. In 2000, a Bechtel subsidiary that had taken control of the water system in Bolivia's third largest city, Cochabamba, hit water users with huge price increases. The company doubled and tripled water rates for the poor. After massive popular protests, which were violently repressed by government troops, Bechtel left the country. Although the company is currently suing the government for $25 million—claiming as an "expropriated investment" the millions it had hoped to make in profits—the ability of people to face down a corporate giant is impressive and hopeful.

As described in Chapter 12, Brazilian AIDS activists called public attention to the desperate need for more treatment, and their work led to universal access to AIDS treatment in 1997. This Brazilian model is now known throughout the world.

Creating Original Alternatives

Health care providers and public health workers, especially, are in special positions to be strong advocates in the struggle for health, and direct service work is valuable and provides constant reminders of the need for change. Yet in many places, health care providers have not participated in the struggle for justice. They're often part of the problem. When doctors lobby for higher salaries or are silent when international financial institutions coerce governments to make life-and-death decisions based on profit, they have forfeited their influence, and for some, their credibility.

However, some health care workers are working with others to bring about political change, building on traditions of resistance. For instance, Brazilian educator Paulo Freire pioneered new approaches in consciousness-raising and community education in the 1960s, and these principles have been used in health programs, especially in Central and South America.

In El Salvador, doctors and other health care workers have been working with community organizations, laborers, unions, and students to fight the privatization of health care and work for a more equitable health care system since 1999. On the front lines of this struggle are the Social Security Hospital Workers' Union (STISSS), and the Social Security Doctors' Union (SIMETRISSS). Through walkouts, protests, takeovers, and other controversial actions, the unions have paralyzed the Social Security hospital system, tending only to emergencies. As a result, these unions achieved major gains, such as an agreement with the government to prevent the privatization of two hospitals in 2000. Nevertheless, the El Salvadoran "State Guarantee to Health" is constantly under attack by neoliberal policymakers.

If change is to happen, we must continue to develop positive alternatives that *transform power relations* in addition to resisting injustice. We should begin by clarifying the principles and values that propel our work, and by reclaiming concepts that are being coopted by international financial institutions (IFIs), like community participation, equity, and democracy.

India's Navdanya movement shows how responses to globalization push activists to develop new strategies, as well as models of what might work. Navdanya, or the "nine seeds" movement for biodiversity conservation and farmers' rights, was launched in the early 1990s by the Research Foundation for Science, Technology, and Ecology, Vandana Shiva's organization. In response to the growing vulnerability of communities to monoculture food production and corporate monopolies, Navdanya facilitates seed conservation and the exchange of traditional seed varieties by local groups and communities. It has also initiated a national network of community seed banks and on-farm conservation programs. Finally, Navdanya works with farmers' organizations to protect farmers' rights by crafting national and international legislation.

Another example of a successful grassroots effort is the Instancia Nacional de Salud (National Health Advocacy Platform) in Guatemala, whose work is also described in Chapter Five. The Instancia is comprised of about 30 different organizations, and is working for an inclusive, comprehensive health system which incorporates the principles of gender and ethnic equity, as well as the right to health. In 2002, the Instancia developed an alternative proposal for primary care that is being carried out in Guatemala. (See Chapter Five for more on health care and activism in Guatemala.)

In designing alternative models like these, we must clarify the principles and values that direct and inform us. And we must work toward alternatives and strategies that actually transform power relations. *Alternatives to Economic Globalization*, a book by the International Forum on Globalization (IFG) that is the result of years of input from many progressive thinkers, puts forth solid recommendations for alternative economic and global systems.[1] The authors advocate sustainable, inclusive systems and structures that emphasize local needs and production over global trade and call for these publically held environmental resources to be off limits to corporate interests.

Gonoshasthaya Kendra (GK), or the People's Health Center of Bengal, was founded in 1972 to provide primary health care services for rural communities. The center has participated in efforts to improve access to medicines, encouraged women's health and empowerment, and supported community-based initiatives. Used as model of comprehensive primary health care in the Alma-Ata Declaration in 1978, GK continues to be used as an example. The center provides comprehensive care in a low-income setting, supported by the labor of paramedics and village health workers. The institution also runs programs in education, nutrition, agriculture, and employment generation and produces basic medicines at Gono Pharmaceuticals factory. As a result of these continued efforts, infant and maternal mortality in the area have fallen to about half of Bangladesh's national average.[2]

The Rise of Global Movements:
The People's Health Assembly and World Social Forum

The efforts of global health activists coalesced at an historic meeting in December 2000 in Savar, Bangladesh. More than 1,400 health care providers, advocates, and others from 90 countries came together for a People's Health Assembly hosted by the primary health are organization, GK. At this first assembly, a charter demanding the fulfillment of a promise made 22 years before at Alma-Ata was drafted. In fact, the People's Health Charter goes beyond the Alma-Ata Declaration, incorporating other concerns such as the acknowledgment that economic globalization has become a key impediment to achieving health.[3] (See Chapter Three for an excerpt from the People's Health Movement Charter.)

The People's Health Movement (PHM), which has continued since the assembly, is a coalition of individuals and organizations from around the world dedicated to challenging the prevailing system of "free market" health care that is not serving the world's poor. The PHM is working to reestablish health and equitable development as top priorities in local, national, and international policymaking. The PHM also recognizes the importance of confronting the international financial institutions (IFIs) who control the purse strings, as well as the necessity of holding agencies like the World Health Organization (WHO) accountable.

On a broader level, thousands of groups working for social justice—including fair and safe working conditions, just wages, sustainable resource use, fair trade alternatives, the redistribution of land, and farmer's rights—have come together for the last three years at the World Social Forum (WSF). The WSF, launched in 2001 in Porto Alegre, Brazil, began as a counterpoint to the World Economic Forum, a gathering of corporate executives, economic ministers, and political leaders that has come together each year since 1971 in the Swiss resort town of Davos. (Porto Alegre is a city in the southernmost province of Brazil where the pro-leftist Workers'

Party has been in power since 1989. The city is an example of a participatory democracy that is governed by local people through an open budget process.) The WSF provides an open, supportive meeting place where debate and idea exchange can take place, where organizations can formulate proposals to promote human-centered development as an alternative to the current economic and social order. In addition to the annual WSF, regions and countries have begun to hold preparatory and simultaneous forums to involve more people in the process.

What is key about these movements is they are defined by people in the developing world on their own terms. They are not headquartered in North America or Europe, with the traditional top-down approach to international development. They are breaking ground by setting up new ways to organize and collaborate. Of course such efforts face challenges, but as momentum and involvement increase, these movements may bring us closer to global democracy.

Working Locally and Globally in Solidarity

Through global solidarity, people in the North and people in the South have an opportunity to convert traditional, paternalistic relationships to equal partnerships. For example, activists with Democracy Center in San Francisco—where Bechtel is headquartered—and the people of Cochabamba, Bolivia, have worked together to call attention to the situation in Bolivia while highlighting Bechtel's legal action against the country.

Similarly, global health activists must bring attention to the wrongdoings of the US government and its impact on people's health. Many groups, such as the California-based Filipino/American Coalition for Environmental Solutions (FACES) with local chapters in other cities, are working in solidarity with people living in the Philippines. FACES was formed in 1999 to support Filipino activists working with those affected by the environmental contamination of former US military bases. Throughout the Philippines, many have died or fallen ill to diseases related to toxic waste exposure. In December 2002, FACES, 38 Filipinos, and a nonprofit group, Arc Ecology, filed a suit against the Department of Defense requiring the US military to conduct environmental assessments at the former bases.

Coalition work helped to win an important victory in November 2001 at the ministerial meeting in Doha, Qatar. Groups such as Médicins Sans Frontières (MSF), Health Action International, and the Health GAP Coalition were present at the meeting to support developing country leaders and representatives from (led by the African group of countries) concerned about the health of their populations. At the meeting, the declaration on trade-related aspects of intellectual property rights (TRIPS) and public health was passed. The Declaration states that the TRIPS agreement should not prevent WTO members from protecting public health, and it emphasized the importance of access to medicines. TRIPS ensured that the rich countries (mainly the US, EU and Japan) had to back down on patent protection, and respect the right of developing countries to provide low-cost generics to their populations. These and other efforts demonstrate the importance of working across borders.

Saying that change is incremental and takes time makes the struggle for health no less pressing. Confronting power is never easy, and as activists, sometimes we are required to take the path of most resistance. But as social commentator Jim Hightower reminds us, "Even a dead fish can go with the flow."

Although 21st century robber barons can take away our money and livelihoods, together we can still resist and work to build a better world. It is in our collective hands to mobilize and educate others, think creatively, and bridge the global health divide.

SHALL WE LEAVE IT TO THE EXPERTS?

MARY ANNE MERCER

Not many years ago, "the experts" assured us that globalization would benefit rich and poor nations alike, peasants as well as dot-com millionaires. The rising tide of free trade would promote economic prosperity, which would trickle down and bring about gradual improvements in the lives and health of the world's poor. To the extent that we allowed the experts to keep us informed, however, we were sadly misled. And to the extent that we allowed them to make decisions, to guide the process, we found that their interests were not necessarily the same as ours. Arundhati Roy vividly describes our contemporary dilemma:

> What's hard to reconcile oneself to, both personally and politically, is the schizophrenic nature of [globalization]....In the lane behind my house, every night I walk past road gangs of emaciated laborers digging a trench to lay fiber-optic cables to speed up our digital revolution. In the bitter winter cold, they work by the light of a few candles. It's as though the people of India have been rounded up and loaded onto two convoys of trucks (a huge big one and a tiny little one) that have set off resolutely in opposite directions. The tiny convoy is on its way to a glittering destination somewhere near the top of the world. The other convoy just melts into the darkness and disappears.[1]

The critical question about globalization, implicit in every chapter of this book, is "Does it promote social justice?" To date, testify our authors, it has mostly done the opposite. We know that the current economic globalization has produced a small but growing number of extremely wealthy persons, wealthier than at any other time in history. But it has not produced a concurrent growth in the fortunes of those least well-off.

What of globalization's benefits? Increased speed in communications, transportation, and other transactions across nations and regions is often how the benefits of globalization are characterized. Direct benefits from better international communication cannot be denied. The spread of the lethal SARS virus that killed thousands in 2003 was no doubt hastened by the ease of international travel, but so also was its containment assisted by an efficient system of transglobal communication among public health authorities. The potential benefits of a speedy response to dramatic international events and infectious disease outbreaks are real, particularly to those in the developed countries. But the simple reality is that the bulk of the population in today's world is not primarily oppressed by fears of Ebola outbreaks, SARS, or even natural disasters. Their children still succumb to measles and malaria, the women die in childbirth, the men suffer from tuberculosis, just as those in the rich countries did a century ago. Among the important health problems for most of the world, only AIDS is a new disease, and it might be argued that the sluggish international response to AIDS in the underdeveloped world contributed to its terrible dominance in many countries today.

Some of the same technologies that are being used to increase the rate of return on global capital can also be harnessed for progressive social change. Perhaps the brightest example of how speedier communication can invigorate activism is the organizing potential of the Internet. Originally designed by nuclear scientists and the military, it has been used to mobilize people much more rapidly than phone trees, direct mailings, and fliers. When the US government was gearing up for a war against Iraq, an antiwar network rapidly organized, turning out almost a million people in the US on February 15th, 2003, achieving in six months what had taken organizers four years to do during the Vietnam War.[2] Beyond the US borders, the mobilization was even more impressive; millions of people around the world organized through e-mail and Web communication to mobilize the largest protest in history.

Yet we also know that for the great bulk of immediate problems facing the world's poor, the Internet is either unknown or an irrelevant curiosity, and its benefits untested. The speed with which international financial transactions can take place may simply mean that their local currency can lose half its value faster than ever before, perhaps overnight, or that their jobs as state employees can be dissolved in a matter of days or weeks. Speed is not a good in itself; it may simply bring what it will faster than before. The real focus in analyzing the effects of globalization must be on what changes, not how quickly change comes.

If our goal is to improve health, those within the health sector must move outside classrooms, laboratories, and hospital walls to embrace a broader approach to health. We cannot be "neutral" as the health care industry reaps huge profits and restricts people's access to treatment and care.

Globalizing the Struggle for Health

What, then, should be the response of those who want to change the current directions of this globalized world? To Noam Chomsky, the answer to that question is not new: "Being alone, you can't do anything. All you can do is deplore the situation. But if you join with other people . . . . millions of things are possible, depending on where you want to put your efforts."[3] Whatever the response, it will almost certainly involve not working alone but organizing others to join in the effort.

Movements to promote fair trade and global justice have won many small and several large victories in the struggles thus far. In 1998 the proposed Multilateral Agreement on Investment (MAI), which would have granted corporations equal international standing, with nation-states, was scuttled as a result of intensive grassroots education and political pressure.[4] The famous "Battle of Seattle" in 1999 brought together tens of thousands of activists from around the world to express public protest against the corporate-sponsored plans and policies of the World Trade Organization. That historic event proved beyond doubt that people of both North and South do care, and are willing to show they care, about the future of this planet and its people. Today, each successive round of trade negotiations is faced with a formidable range of protests and demands from consumer groups, environmental activists, organized labor, and others demanding a place at the negotiating table.

The influential Jubilee movement that pressed for canceling the debts of the poorest countries began in churches, in response to an understanding of the shocking burden of debt. After several years of Jubilee's grassroots education and activism, some of the most heavily indebted poor countries were granted a reduction in their debt.

Smaller victories of "people power" are also cause for celebration. Citizens of Vieques Island in Puerto Rico succeeded in 2003 in stopping the US Navy from using their island as a bombing range. In Bolivia, a proposed pipeline to transport natural gas through Chile to the Pacific coast appears to be stalled because of strong protests from the indigenous population. All through Europe, resistance to the use of genetically altered foods is growing and has been successful in bringing about outright bans of such foods in some areas. Where people care about an issue and are willing to take action to back up their concerns, change is possible.

The health community has had only a limited voice in discussions about globalization to date, but health workers and agencies have tremendous potential to further globalize the struggle for health. AIDS activists have set a good example of what can be accomplished through social action and persistence. The People's Health Movement presents a good opportunity to participate in a global solidarity movement for health. As health care becomes further privatized in the US and abroad, there is an increased need and ample opportunities for mobilization. Linking health to other efforts such as the environmental and economic justice campaigns can multiply the potency of each struggle. Very important efforts are underway to develop alternatives to the global economic structure (e.g., fair trade, supporting local economies) at the meetings of the World Social Forum. Chapter Fourteen describes a few of the efforts underway and the Resource Guide at the end of this book lists some of the groups that are working for health and justice.

Those concerned about health need to work with movements that are proposing alternative models for globalization, even though the precise structures for these alternatives may not yet be fully defined. Words matter: we might begin by clarifying global justice and human development as essential determinants of health, and refusing to use the term anti-globalization. We must show the powerful corporate interests that they must answer to the public for all they do, or do not do, to affect the health of the public. We need to think of ways to show the world the ugliness of the current world order, to build on the growing skepticism about where this planet is headed, and to talk of globalizing health as an alternative.

We suggest two key principles for those involved in promoting global health. The first is to *promote equity* as the central focus of efforts, going beyond health services to recognize that it is mostly broader conditions of life that provide more or less opportunity for achieving health—water, land, housing, health care, food security, work, dignity.

The second is to press for the provision of *health care as a fundamental universal human right*, as agreed by all countries that signed the 1948 Universal Declaration of Human Rights. Such a movement would seek to revive the concept of comprehensive primary health care as it was proposed in 1978 at Alma-Ata. Both principles demand that health care not be a commercial product, to be bought and sold in the marketplace. Both will require, in the longer run, deep changes in the basic economic and political systems that currently define our lives.

Time and again, health has been declared a basic human right. The 1948 Universal Declaration of Human Rights states, "Everyone has the right to a standard of living adequate for the health and well-being of himself and of his family, including food, clothing, housing, and medical care and necessary social services."[5] The International Covenant on Economic, Social, and

Cultural Rights, adopted by the UN in 1977, recognizes the right of everyone to enjoy "the highest attainable standard of physical and mental health."[6] In 1978, the goal of Health for All by the year 2000 was laid out at the Alma-Ata conference and every participating country, including the US, signed on to make it a reality through comprehensive Primary Health Care.[7] The WHO Ottawa conference on Health Promotion held in 1986 put forth a charter highlighting the fundamental conditions and resources that are prerequisites to health, including "peace, shelter, education, food, income, a stable eco-system, sustainable resources, social justice, and equity."[8]

Within those principles lies a broad array of actions or objectives that those working to improve health might aim to address. Any one individual or group can focus on only a limited set of issues. The aim must be to contribute to a network of like-minded activists who, together, can make a difference. The following are likely to be key areas for the immediate future:

1. Promote equity in the global economic system, probably the most central concern. A wide range of initiatives is under way for such efforts as restricting the power of transnational corporations and multilateral lending institutions, restructuring trade policies to promote fair trade, canceling the debt of the poorest countries, and taxing international transactions (the "Tobin Tax").

2. Restrict or ban international trade in industries whose products are designed or destined to kill, such as military hardware, including land mines, and tobacco.

3. Promote national responsibility for the provision of health care to all. In both North and South, resist privatization of health care and support national health care systems.

4. Assure that food, clean water, and other basic needs are seen as basic human rights and protected from profit-oriented exploitation.

5. Redesign and enforce an international essential drug policy that will regulate prices for the supply of, and research on drugs so that basic medicines can be provided to all who need them.

6. Include worker health and well-being whenever issues of industrial production or trade are discussed. Continue the international pressure to ban sweatshop labor and promote fair trade practices.

7. Demand environmental protection for this planet earth, requiring control of toxic wastes, clean and reduced energy use, and other similar measures.

Whatever the issue, strategically there is a critical need for intra-national and international solidarity—North-South, North-North, and South-South.

Solidarity means struggling together, as well as celebrating together when gains are made, small or large. People from many walks of life must be inspired to move out of their "comfort zones" and step into other worlds, to see the reality of globalization as it affects the lives and health of people today. We need above all to globalize dissent, resistance, and the demand for accountability. We need to envision and project a new reality that will move the globe towards a more just system.

And in the words of Arundhati Roy, we cannot leave it to the experts.

GLOSSARY: TERMS AND ORGANIZATIONS

Alma-Ata Conference	International conference on Primary Health Care held in 1978
ANC	African National Congress
APL	Adaptable Program Loan
Bretton Woods System	A system of rules, institutions, and procedures regulating the international political economy, comprised of the World Bank and the IMF
Bureau of Western Hemisphere Affairs	Branch of US Department of State designed to promote US interests throughout the Americas
CDC	Center for Disease Control and Prevention
CIA	Central Intelligence Agency
DDT	Dichlorodiphenyltrichloroethane
EPZ	Export Processing Zone
ESAF	Enhanced Structural Adjustment Facility
ESAP	Economic Structural Adjustment Program
FTAA	Free Trade Area of the Americas
GATS	General Agreement on Trade in Services
GATT	General Agreement on Tariffs and Trade
GDP	Gross Domestic Product
GNP	Gross National Product
GOBI	Growth monitoring, Oral rehydration, Breastfeeding, Immunization

FTAA	Free Trade Area of the Americas
HAI	Health Alliance International
HIPC	Heavily Indebted Poor Countries
HIV/AIDS	Human Immunodeficiency Virus/Acquired Immune Deficiency Syndrome
HSR	Health Sector Reform
IADB	Inter-American Development Bank
IFI	International Financial Institution
IMF	International Monetary Fund
IMR	Infant Mortality Rate
Life expectancy	The probable lifespan of a newborn based on mortality rates for the year of its birth
MCH	Maternal and Child Health
MOH	Ministry of Health
NGO	Non-Governmental Organization
OECD	Organization for Economic Co-operation and Development
OPEC	Organization of the Petroleum Exporting Countries
PAHO	Pan American Health Organization
PHA	People's Health Assembly
PHC	Primary Health Care
PHM	People's Health Movement
SAL	Structural Adjustment Loan
SAP	Structural Adjustment Program
SPHC	Selective Primary Health Care
STD	Sexually Transmitted Disease
SWAP	Sector Wide Approach Program

TB	Tuberculosis
TRIPS	Trade Related Aspects of Intellectual Property Rights
UN	United Nations
UNDP	United Nations Development Programme
UNICEF	United Nations International Children's Fund
USAID	United States Agency for International Development
USDA	United States Department of Agriculture
USTR	United States Trade Representative
Washington Consensus	The neoliberal agenda commonly associated with globalization
WHA	World Health Assembly
WHO	World Health Organization

Also see the Trade Agreement Timeline in Chapter 7 for more information on some of these terms.

RESOURCE GUIDE

This listing provides a sample of groups working on health and social justice issues worldwide. We have attempted to include organizations with varied focuses, including economic justice, women's health and rights, access to basic treatment and care, community development, and environmental justice.

Alternative Information and Development Centre (AIDC)
http://www.aidc.org.za/aboutaidc.htm
E-mail: info@aidc.org.za
129 Rochester Road, Observatory 7925, Cape Town, South Africa
Tel: 011-27-214475770; Fax: 011-27-214475884
AIDC is a nongovernmental organization working in the context of globalization, together with popular organizations and social movements in South and southern Africa, for economic justice and social transformation.

Associacion Latinoamericana de Medicina Social (ALAMES)
http://users.movinet.com.uy/~alames/
E-mail: alames@psi.uba.ar
Secretaria Ejecutiva, C.C.N° 18 Suc. 26 (1426),
Correo Argentino, Buenos Aires, Argentina
Tel/Fax: 011-54-1147752891
ALAMES is a social, academic, and political movement working to orient the fields of public health and social medicine to resolve the historical and social determinants of the health-disease process.

Canadian Centre for Policy Alternatives (CCPA)
http://www.policyalternatives.ca
E-mail: ccpa@policyalternatives.ca
CCPA National Office
Suite 410, 75 Albert Street, Ottawa, ON K1P 5E7, Canada

Tel: 613-563-1341; Fax: 613-233-1458
By undertaking and promoting research on issues of social and economic
justice, the Canadian Centre for Policy Alternatives offers support to
activists and progressive working on a range of issues, including health care.

Center for Policy Analysis on Trade and Health (CPATH)
http://www.cpath.org/
E-mail: info@cpath.org
98 Seal Rock Drive, San Francisco, CA 94121-1437
Tel: 415-933-6204; Fax: 415-831-4091
CPATH is a nonprofit organization dedicated to protecting human health
and expanding access to health care, water, and other vital human services.

CIVICUS: World Alliance for Citizen Participation
http://www.civicus.org
South Africa: CIVICUS House, 24 Pim Corner, Quinn Street, Newtown
Johannesburg 2001, South Africa
Tel: 011-27-118335959; Fax: 011-27-118337997
US: 1112 16th Street NW, Suite 540
Washington DC, 20036
Tel: 202-331-8518; Fax: 202-331-8774
CIVICUS is an international alliance dedicated to strengthening and
promoting a worldwide community of informed, inspired, committed
citizens.

Consumers International (CI)
http://www.consumersinternational.org
E-mail: consint@consint.org
24 Highbury Crescent, London, N5 1RX, UK
Tel: 011-44-2072266663, Fax: 011-44-2073540607
CI supports, links, and represents consumer groups and agencies,
campaigning at the international level for policies which respect consumer
concerns.

The Council of Canadians/Les Conseil des Canadiens
http://www.canadians.org
502-151 Slater Street, Ottawa, ON K1P 5H3, Canada
Tel: 800-387-7177

Founded in 1985, the Council of Canadians is a powerful citizens' watchdog organization, working specifically to shelter socialized medicine, public pensions, and Canada's water and wilderness.

Dag Hammarskjold Foundation
http://www.dhf.uu.se
E-mail: secretariat@dhf.uu.se
Övre Slottsgatan 2, SE-753 10 Uppsala, Sweden
Tel: 011-46-18102772; Fax: 011-46-18122072
The foundation organizes development seminars, conferences, and workshops.

The Democracy Center
http://www.democracyctr.org
E-mail: info@democracyctr.org
Bolivia: Casilla 5283, Cochabamba, Bolivia
Tel: 011-591-415644767; Fax: 011-591-978831269
US: PO Box 22157, San Francisco, CA 94122
The Democracy Center was founded in San Francisco in 1992 to strengthen the advocacy work of nonprofit and community groups in California, as well as NGOs in a variety of countries around the world.

Development Alternatives with Women for a New Era (DAWN)
http://www.dawn.org.fj/
E-mail: admin@dawn.org.fj
PO Box 13124, Suva, Fiji
Tel/Fax: 011-679-314770
DAWN is a network of women scholars and activists from the global South who engage in feminist research and analysis and are committed to working for economic justice, gender justice and democracy. DAWN works globally and regionally on globalization, political restructuring and social transformation, and sexual and reproductive health and rights.

Doctors for Global Health
http://www.dghonline.org/
E-mail: development@dghonline.org
PO Box 1761, Decatur, GA 30031
Tel/Fax: 404-377-3566

DGH is a private, not-for-profit organization promoting health, education, art, and other human rights throughout the world.

Doctors Without Borders/Médecins Sans Frontières (MSF)
http://www.msf.org
Rue de la Tourelle, 39, 1040 Bruxelles, Belgium
Tel: 011-32-22801881; Fax: 011-32-22800173
MSF is a private, nonprofit organization that seeks to deliver emergency aid to victims of armed conflict, epidemics, and natural and manmade disasters, and to others who lack health care due to social or geographical isolation.

Essential Information
http://www.essential.org
E-mail: jrichard@essential.org
PO Box 19405, Washington DC 20036
Tel: 202-387-8034; Fax: 202-234-5176
Essential Information is a nonprofit, tax-exempt organization involved in a variety of projects to encourage citizens to become active and engaged in their communities. The organization publishes the monthly magazine *Multinational Monitor* (http://multinationalmonitor.org) which tracks corporate activity.

50 Years Is Enough Network
http://www.50years.org
E-mail: info@50years.org
3628 12th Street NE, Washington DC 20017
Tel: 202-463-2265
50 Years is Enough calls for the immediate suspension of policies and practices of the International Monetary Fund and the World Bank which have caused poverty, inequality, and damage to the world's environment.

Filipino/American Coalition for Environmental Solutions (FACES)
http://www.facessoluctions.net
E-mail: info@facessolutions.net
PO Box 2597, El Cerrito, CA 94530
Tel: 866-206-9067, ext. 3905
FACES was formed in 1999 to support the efforts of Philippine activists working with communities affected by the environmental contamination of

former US military bases in the Philippines, where many have died from or fallen ill to diseases related to toxic waste exposure.

Focus on the Global South
http://www.focusweb.org
E-mail: admin@focusweb.org
c/o CUSRI, Chulalongkorn University, Bangkok 10330, Thailand
Tel: 011-66-22187363-65; Fax: 011-66-22559976
Focus on the Global South is a program of progressive development policy research and practice, dedicated to regional and global policy analysis and advocacy work with an emphasis on North-South issues.

Food First—Institute for Food and Development Policy
http://www.foodfirst.org
E-mail: foodfirst@foodfirst.org
398 60th Street, Oakland, CA 94618
Tel: 510-654-4400; Fax: 510-654-4551
Established more than 25 years ago, Food First is a member-supported nonprofit organization working to eliminate the injustices that cause hunger. Food First examines the root causes of hunger and creates value-based solutions to hunger and poverty around the world.

Global Exchange
http://www.globalexchange.org/
2017 Mission Street, No. 303, San Francisco, CA 94110
Tel: 415-255-7296; Fax: 415-255-7498
Global Exchange is a human rights organization dedicated to promoting environmental, political, and social justice around the world. Founded in 1988, Global Exchange strives to increase global awareness among the US public while building international partnerships around the world.

The Global Justice Center
http://www.global.org.br/index.php
E-mail: global@global.org.br
Av. N. S. de Copacabana, 540/402, 22020-000, Rio de Janeiro, RJ, Brazil
Tel: 011-55-2125477391; Fax: 011-55-2125493599
Global Justice Center promotes social justice and human rights in Brazil through documentation and distribution of reports on rights abuse, as well the use of international mechanisms to protect human rights.

Gonoshasthaya Kendra (GK)/Peoples Health Center
PO Mirzanagar, Via Savar Cantonment, Dhaka–1344, Bangladesh
GK was founded in 1972 to provide primary health care services for rural communities. Used as a case study for the Alma-Ata Declaration, GK continues to be a wonderful example of how comprehensive primary health care can be provided in a low-income setting with an emphasis on the role of paramedics and community health workers. The institution has expanded to include education, nutrition, agriculture, employment, the production of basic medicines at Gono Pharmaceuticals factory, and women's emancipation. In 1992, the organization received the Right Livelihood Award.

Greenpeace International
http://www.greenpeace.org/
E-mail: supporter.services@int.greenpeace.org
Ottho Heldringstraat 5, 1066 AZ Amsterdam, Netherlands
Tel: 011-21-31205148150; Fax: 011-21-31205148151
Greenpeace has a presence in 40 countries across Europe, the Americas, Asia, and the Pacific and focuses on the most crucial worldwide threats to biodiversity and the environment.

Health Alliance International (HAI)
http://depts.washington.edu/haiuw/
E-mail: hai@u.washington.edu
HAI Headquarters, 1107 NE 45th Street, Suite 427, Seattle, WA 98105
Tel: 206-543-8382; Fax: 206-685-4184
HAI is a nonprofit organization committed to improving the health and welfare of disenfranchised peoples and working toward a more equitable delivery of health services worldwide. HAI provides technical and material assistance to government and community institutions to evaluate, strengthen, and sustain effective health services, as well as focus on changing the inequitable conditions that contribute to poor health.

Health Global Access Project (Health GAP)
http://www.healthgap.org/
E-mail: info@healthgap.org
4951 Catharine Street, Philadelphia, PA 19143
Tel: 215-474-9329; Fax: 215-474-9329

Health GAP is an action-oriented advocacy organization created in 1999 by US-based AIDS and human rights activists, public health experts, fair-trade lawyers, economists, and concerned individuals dedicated to expanding access to AIDS treatment and care worldwide.

Health Wrights

http://www.healthwrights.org
E-mail: healthwrights@igc.org
PO Box 1344, Palo Alto, CA 94302
Tel: 650-325-7500; Fax: 650-325-1080
Health Wrights is a nonprofit organization committed to advancing the health, basic rights, social equality, and self-determination of disadvantaged persons and groups.

The Hesperian Foundation

http://www.hesperian.org
E-mail: hesperian@hesperian.org
1919 Addison Street, suite 304, Berkeley, CA 94704
Tel: 510-845-1447; Fax: 510-845-9141
The Hesperian Foundation is a nonprofit publisher of books and newsletters focusing on community-based health care. The foundation's philosophy is that health is a fundamental human right, and it promotes self-determination by creating accessible and appropriate health care resources.

Instancia Nacional de Salud/National Health Advocacy Platform

E-mail: insgua@hotmail.com
3a Ave. 3-7a, San Lucas, Sacatepequez, Guatemala
Tel/Fax: 011-502-8308557
The Instancia is a coalition of more than 30 grassroots organizations dedicated to working toward an inclusive, comprehensive approach to health based on the principles of primary health care. It was formed in 1997 after the Guatemalan government adopted neoliberal health sector reform.

International People's Health Council (IPHC)

http://www.iphcglobal.org/
E-mail: info@iphcglobal.org
Apartado no. 6152, Managua, Nicaragua
Fax: 011-505-2662225

IPHC is a worldwide coalition of people's health initiatives and socially progressive groups and movements committed to working for the health and rights of disadvantaged people—and ultimately of all people. The IPHC views health in the broadest sense, including physical, mental, social, economic, and environmental well-being.

International Forum on Globalization
http://www.ifg.org
E-mail: ifg@ifg.org
1009 General Kennedy Avenue no. 2, San Francisco, CA 94129
Tel: 415-561-7650; Fax: 415-561-7651
The International Forum on Globalization advocates equitable, democratic, and ecologically sustainable economics. It was formed in response to the present worldwide drive toward a globalized economic system dominated by supranational corporate trade and banking institutions that are not accountable to democratic processes or national governments.

Kabissa: Space for Change in Africa
http://www.kabissa.org
E-mail: info@kabissa.org
1519 Connecticut Avenue NW, suite 200, Washington DC 20036
Tel: 202-265-6116; Fax: 202-441-8964
Kabissa uses technology to strengthen nonprofit organizations working to improve the lives of people in Africa, emphasizing access to Internet services, training opportunities, and channels for networking.

Landless Workers Movement/Movimento Sem Terra (MST)
http://www.mstbrazil.org/
E-mail: semterra@mst.org.br
Friends of the MST, c/o Global Exchange
2017 Mission Street, no. 303,
San Francisco, CA 94110
Tel: 415-255-0795; Fax: 415-255-7498
The Brazilian MST is the largest social movement in Latin America, and one of the most successful grassroots movements in the world. Less than 3 percent of Brazil's population owns two-thirds of its arable land, and thousands of peasants, urban poor, and other activists are pressuring the Brazilian government for land reform.

Medact

http://www.medact.org
E-mail: info@medact.org
601 Holloway Road, London, N19 4DJ
Tel: 011-44-02072722020; Fax: 011-44-02072815717
Medact is an organization of health professionals challenging social and
environmental barriers to health—including violent conflict, poverty, and
environmental degradation.

Navdanya and the Research Foundation
for Science, Technology, and Ecology

http://www.vshiva.net
E-mail: rfste@vsnl.com
A-60, Hauz Khas, New Delhi, India 110016
Tel: 01-91-1126968077 or 01-91-1126853772; Fax: 01-91-1126856795
As an effort of the Research Foundation for Science, Technology, and
Ecology, Vandana Shiva launched Navdanya, or the "nine seeds"
movement for biodiversity conservation and farmers' rights, in the early
1990s in order to facilitate seed conservation and the exchange of
traditional seed varieties by local groups and communities.

OneWorld International

http://www.oneworld.net
E-mail: justice@oneworld.net
Second Floor, River House
143-145 Farringdon Road, London, EC1R 3AB, UK
Tel: 011-44-02072391400; Fax: 011-44-02078333347
OneWorld works for equitable and sustainable distribution of wealth
among the world's population and supports human rights legislation and
governance structures which permit local communities control over their
own affairs.

Oxfam

http://www.oxfam.org.uk/
E-mail: enquiries@oxfam.org.uk
Oxfam Supporter Services, Oxfam House, 274 Banbury Road
Oxford, OX2 7DZ, UK
Tel: 011-44-08703332700

Oxfam International is a confederation of 12 organizations working in more than 100 countries to find lasting solutions to poverty and injustice.

Partners In Health (PIH)/Institute for Health and Social Justice
http://www.pih.org
E-mail: info@pih.org
641 Huntington Avenue, First Floor, Boston, MA 02115
Tel: 617-432-5256; Fax: 617-432-5300
PIH is a nonprofit organization that works in Latin America, the Caribbean, Russia, and the United States and draws on Boston-based resources to tackle varied and chronic health crises in poor communities.

People's Global Action/Action Mondiale des Peoples (PGA)
http://www.agp.org
E-mail: agpweb@lists.riseup.net
c/o Canadian Union of Postal Workers
377 Bank Street, Ottawa, ON Canada K2P 1X9
People's Global Action is a coalition of activists opposed to "free trade" and World Trade Organization policies.

People's Health Movement
http://www.phmovement.org
E-mail: secretariat@phmovement.org
People's Health Movement Secretariat c/o Community Health Cell no. 367, Srinivasa Nilaya, Jakkasandra I Main, I Block, Koramangala, Bangalore-560 034, India
Tel: 011-91-8051280009; Fax: 011-91-8025525372
The People's Health Movement is an international coalition of individuals and grassroots organizations dedicated to challenging the prevailing systems of health care that are failing to serve most of the world's poor.

Physicians for Human Rights
http://www.phrusa.org
100 Boylston Street, Suite 702
Boston, MA 02116
Tel: 617-695-0041; Fax: 617-695-0307
Physicians for Human Rights is an organization that promotes health by protecting human rights. Along with much other work, it seeks to realize the right to the highest attainable standard of health. Its Health Action

Campaign seeks to bring the resources needed to end the pandemic and to deploy them in a manner consistent with human rights, including developing health systems that recognize human rights for all.

Physicians for a National Health Program
http://www.phnp.org
E-mail: phnp@aol.com
29 East Madison Street, suite 602, Chicago, IL 60602
Tel: 312-782-6006; Fax: 312-782-6007
Physicians for a National Health Program is a not-for-profit organization of health care professionals that support universal health care.

Positive Futures Network (PFN)
http://www.futurenet.org/index.htm
E-mail: yes@futurenet.org
PO Box 10818, Bainbridge Island, WA 98110-0818
Tel: 206-842-0216; Fax: 206-842-5208
Founded in 1996, PFN is an independent, nonprofit organization dedicated to supporting people's active engagement in creating a just, sustainable, and compassionate world.

Prayas: Initiatives in Health, Energy, Learning, and Parenthood
http://www.prayaspune.org/
E-mail: info@prayaspune.org
Amrita Clinic, Athawale Corner, Karve Road Corner, Deccan Gymkhana, Pune-411 004, India
Tel: 011-91-202544 1230; Tel/Fax: 011-91-2025420337
Prayas is a nongovernmental, nonprofit, public charitable trust in India. Members of Prayas are professionals working to protect and promote the public interest.

Public Citizen
http://www.citizen.org/
1600 20th Street NW, Washington, DC, 20009
Tel: 202-588-1000
Public Citizen is a national nonprofit consumer advocacy organization founded more than 30 years ago to represent consumer interests through the promotion of consumer rights, democratic accountability in government, socially and economically just trade policies, safe and

affordable health care, environmental protection, and sustainable energy resources.

Public Services International (PSI)
http://www.world-psi.org/
E-mail: psi@world-psi.org
BP 9, F-01211 Ferney-Voltaire Cedex, France
Tel: 011-33-0450406464; Fax: 011-33-0450407320
PSI is an international trade union federation for public sector unions. Since 1907, PSI has organized many different occupations: health workers, firefighters, workers in public utilities, child care workers, civil servants, judges, food inspectors, social workers, etc. Some of the PSI affiliates are million-strong trade unions, able to influence the national social policy of their countries.

Results
http://www.results.org
E-mail: results@results.org
440 First Street NW, suite 450, Washington DC 20001
Tel: 202-783-7100; Fax: 202-783-2818
Results is a grassroots organization whose mission is to end hunger and the worst aspects of poverty and empower individuals to exercise their personal and political power.

Society for Community Health Awareness, Research, and Action (SOCHARA)
http://www.sochara.org
E-mail: chc@sochara.org
No. 367, Srinivasa Nilaya, First Block, Jakkasandra, Koramangala, Bangalore-560 034, India
SOCHARA is a health policy, training, and research group actively involved with community health action in India. Since 2003, SOCHARA has served as secretariat for the People's Health Movement.

Social Watch
http://www.socwatch.org
E-mail: socwatch@socialwatch.org
Jackson 1136, Montevideo 11200, Uruguay
Tel: 011-598-24196192; Fax: 011-598-24119222

Social Watch is an international NGO watchdog network monitoring poverty eradication and gender equality. The international secretariat of Social Watch is hosted by the Third World Institute in Montevideo, Uruguay.

Society for International Development (SID)
http://www.sidint.org/
E-mail: info@sidint.org
Via Panisperna, 207, 00184 Rome, Italy
Tel: 011-39-064872172, Fax: 011-39-064872170
SID is a global network focused on sustainable and democratic development. SID has over 3,000 individual members in 125 countries, 55 institutional members, and 65 local chapters.

STISSS Salvadoran Health Worker's Union/Sindicato de Trabajadores del Seguro Social
E-mail: stisss@groups.msn.com
http://groups.msn.com/stisss/
Tercera Calle poniente N
1225, San Salvador, El Salvador
Tel/Fax: 011-503-221-0503
Unions, peasant groups, and students mobilizing to prevent the privatization of health care in El Salvador.

Teaching Aids at Low Cost (TALC)
http://www.talcuk.org
E-mail: info@talcuk.org
PO Box 49, St. Albans, Herts, AL1 5TX, UK
Tel: 011-44-01727853869; Fax: 011-44-01727846852
TALC promotes the health of children and advances medical knowledge and teaching internationally by providing and developing educational material, particularly for sub-Saharan Africa and Asia.

Third World Network
http://www.twnside.org.sg/
E-mail: twnet@po.jaring.my
121-S, Jalan Utama, 10450, Penang, Malaysia
Tel: 011-60-42266728 or 011-60-2266159; Fax: 011-60-42264505
Third World Network is an independent, nonprofit international network

of organizations and individuals involved in issues relating to development, the third world, and North-South issues.

Treatment Action Campaign (TAC)
http://www.tac.org.za/
E-mail: info@tac.org.za
PO Box 74, Nonkqubela 7793, South Africa
Tel: 011-27-217883507; Fax: 011-27-217883726
TAC's main objective is to campaign for greater access to treatment for all South Africans, by raising public awareness and understanding about issues surrounding the availability, affordability, and use of HIV treatments. TAC campaigns against the belief that AIDS is a death sentence.

The Union of Palestinian Medical Relief Committees (UPMRC)
http://www.upmrc.org
E-mail: mrs@upmrc.org
PO Box 51483, Jerusalem, Israel
Tel: 011-972-25833510; Fax: 011-972-25830679
UPMRC is a grassroots, community-based Palestinian health organization. UPMRC was founded in 1979 by a group of Palestinian doctors and health professionals seeking to supplement the decayed and inadequate health infrastructure caused by years of Israeli military occupation.

United for a Fair Economy
http://www.stw.org
E-mail: info@faireconomy.org
37 Temple Place, second floor, Boston, MA 02111
Tel: 617-423-2148; Fax: 617-423-0191
United for a Fair Economy focuses on developing media capacity for the education of individuals and other groups committed to understanding the widening gap between the rich and the poor, both domestically and globally.

Wemos Foundation
http://www.wemos.nl/
Ellermanstraat 15, 1099 BW Amsterdam, Netherlands
Tel: 011-31-20688388; Fax: 011-31-204686008
Wemos works on access to baby food and pharmaceuticals, as well as broader issues related to women's health.

Women's Global Network for Reproductive Rights
http://www.wgnrr.org/
E-mail: office@wgnrr.nl
Vrolikstraat 453-D, 1092 TJ Amsterdam, Netherlands
Tel: 011-31-206209672; Fax: 011-31-206222450
Women's Global Network for Reproductive Rights is an autonomous
network of groups and individuals which supports reproductive rights and
self-determination for women.

World Social Forum (WSF): "Another World Is Possible"
http://www.forumsocialmundial.org.br
Email: fsminfo@forumsocialmunidal.org.br
Rua General Jardim, 660, 8° andar, sala 81,
Cep 01223-010, São Paulo–SP, Brazil
Tel/Fax: 011-55-113258-8914
The World Social Forum was launched in 2001 in Porto Alegre, Brazil, to
provide an open, supportive meeting place for democratic debate and the
exchange of ideas where social movements can formulate proposals that
promote human-centered development as alternatives to the current global
economic and social order.

CONTRIBUTORS

Stephen Bezruchka has worked as a physician for more than 30 years in the US, Canada, and Nepal. He teaches in the International Health Program at the University of Washington School of Public Health and Community Medicine. His academic work focuses on the weaknesses of the US health system and the declining health of Americans relative to those in other countries. He also works in rural Nepal to improve surgical services. His email address is sabez@u.washington.edu.

Patrick Bond is a professor at the University of the Witwatersrand Graduate School of Public and Development Management in South Africa, and visiting professor at York University's Department of Political Science in Toronto. His recent books include *Against Global Apartheid* (Zed Press, 2003); *Elite Transition* (Pluto Press, 2003); *Zimbabwe's Plunge* (Merlin Press, 2003); *Unsustainable South Africa* (Merlin Press, 2002); *Fanon's Warning* (Africa World Press, 2002); and *Cities of Gold, Townships of Coal* (Africa World Press, 2000). He is also associated with the Municipal Services Project. His email address is pbond@sn.apc.org.

Joseph Brenner is a director of the Center for Policy Analysis in San Francisco, which sponsors policy research and analysis on trade and health. He also directs the Center for Policy Analysis on Trade and Health, a project of the Center for Policy Analysis, and explores the links between international trade agreements, human services, and health. He is an experienced community organizer. His email address is jebrenner@cpath.org.

Alejandro Cerón is a Guatemalan physician dedicated to rural health work in that country. He is currently coordinating the implementation of the inclusive primary health care proposal, developed by the activist organization Instancia Nacional de Salud (National Health Advocacy Platform), in one of the two

Guatemalan sites with the Clinica Maxeña, an innovative medical facility based out of a Catholic mission. His email address is maceron1@yahoo.com.

Abhijit Das is a women's health and rights advocate from India. For more than 15 years, he has served as an obstetrician and gynecologist in Indian rural health projects. He works with the voluntary organization Sahayog Society for Participatory Rural Development, an NGO working on issues related to development, the rights of the marginalized, and women's health in Almora, India. Das is also involved in promoting the implementation of the International Conference on Population and Development Program of Action in India. His email is abhijit@sahayogindia.org.

Paul Davis has a long history as an AIDS activist, working primarily with ACT UP Philadelphia, and more recently with the Health GAP (Global Access Project) Coalition, a group working to guarantee access to HIV/AIDS treatment. He is director of government relations with the Health GAP Coalition, where he lobbies the US government to contribute in a meaningful way in the global fight against AIDS. His email address is pdavis@healthgap.org.

Meredith Fort is a health policy activist and public health practitioner. She has participated in grassroots health efforts in Guatemala since 1997, and she is currently working with the Instancia Nacional de Salud (National Health Advocacy Platform) to help implement the alternative primary health care proposal in rural Guatemala. In the US, she worked on efforts for treatment access, debt cancellation, and alternatives to neoliberal trade agreements. Her email address is meredithfort@yahoo.com.

Oscar Gish was a health economist and member of the University of Washington International Health Program faculty from 1990 to his death in 2004. He also taught at the University of Sussex and at the University of Michigan, and worked for the World Health Organization. He published six books, as well as numerous reports and articles. Dr. Gish lived and worked in more than 50 countries, including Tanzania, Ethiopia, and Indonesia.

Steve Gloyd is executive director of Health Alliance International (HAI), professor of health services, and director of the International Health Program at the University of Washington School of Public Health and Community Medicine. He is a family practice physician whose international work includes direct service and program support in Africa and Latin America. His academic areas of interest are the political economy of international health, research methods for developing countries, the effectiveness of health systems, and political and economic barriers to primary health care. His email address is gloyd@u.washington.edu.

Timothy Holtz is a founding member of Doctors for Global Health (DGH), a social justice and health nonprofit. He has worked in India with the Centers for Disease Control and Prevention (CDC) and was an active participant in the public health response to the World Trade Center disaster in September 2001. He is an adjunct professor of international health at the Rollins School of Public Health at Emory University and currently works as a medical epidemiologist for the Centers for Disease Control in Atlanta, Georgia. His email address is tholtz@igc.org.

Evelyne Hong is a member of Third World Network, an independent international network of organizations and individuals involved in issues relating to trade, development, the Third World, and North-South issues that publishes *Third World Resurgence* and *Third World Economics*. As an activist, she is chiefly concerned with health, development, and environmental issues. She has written several books and articles on women, indigenous people, health, development, and the environment. She is also an active participant in the People's Health Movement.

Celia Iriart is a researcher and professor at the Department of Family and Community Medicine at the University of New Mexico. She is a member of the health policy group of the Argentinean Workers Central (Central de Trabajadores Argentinos, or CTA)—an organization of labor unions based in Buenos Aires. She also works collaboratively with several groups (unemployed movements, physicians and health workers, human rights and grassroots organizations) in Argentina, Brazil, Uruguay, Chile, Ecuador, and the US. Her email address is iriart@unm.edu.

S. Patrick Kachur is a medical epidemiologist whose work has concentrated on implementation research for community-level initiatives to improve malaria prevention and treatment. Over the past decade he has worked in more than a dozen countries. He currently lives and works in Tanzania.

Emerson Mehry is professor of postgraduate education in the Department of Preventive and Social Medicine in the Faculty of Medical Sciences at the University of Campinas, Brazil. He was a founding member of the Brazilian Center for Health Studies, and has also worked for the journal *Salud em Debate* (*Health in Debate*) and the Laboratory of Planning and Administration in Preventive and Social Medicine at the University of Campinas. His research focuses on health policy, institutional analysis, and health services.

Mary Anne Mercer is a public health practitioner specializing in the delivery of maternal and child health care services, including the response to HIV/AIDS, in developing countries. She directed a technical support program at Johns Hopkins University for NGOs implementing programs for HIV/AIDS prevention in Africa. She is currently deputy director of Health Alliance International, and a faculty member in the International Health Program at the University of Washington School of Public Health and Community Medicine. Her email address is mamercer@u.washington.edu.

Joia Mukherjee trained in Infectious Disease, Internal Medicine, and Pediatrics at Massachusetts General Hospital, and has a Master's in Public Health from the Harvard School of Public Health. She has been involved in health care access and human rights issues since 1989 in the United States, Africa, Latin America, the Caribbean, and the countries of the former Soviet Union. Since 1999, Dr. Mukherjee has served as the Medical Director of Partners In Health, an international medical charity with clinical programs in Haiti, Peru, Mexico, Russia, and Boston.

Ellen Shaffer is a director of the Center for Policy Analysis on Trade and Health in San Francisco. She is an assistant clinical professor in the Department of Clinical Pharmacy at the University of California, San Francisco. She has worked for many years in the US on national health care reform and patients' rights. Her email address is ershaffer@earthlink.net.

Vandana Shiva is founder and director of the Research Foundation for Science, Technology, and Natural Resource Policy. She received the Right Livelihood Award in 1993. She is author of more than 300 papers in leading journals and numerous books, including *Water Wars* (South End Press, 2002); *Stolen Harvest: The Hijacking of the Global Health Supply* (South End Press, 2000); and *Biopiracy* (South End Press, 1997). Her email address is vshiva@vsnl.com.

Juan Carlos Verdugo is a Guatemalan physician who is cofounder of the Instancia Nacional de Salud (National Health Advocacy Platform). He is directing the implementation of the primary health care proposal in Guatemala and is a country representative of Medicus Mundi Navarra, an NGO working toward health care development in Latin America and Africa. He is also a university docent and a health systems policy analyst. His email address is juansil@terra.com.gt.

Howard Waitzkin is professor and codirector of the Division of Community Medicine at the University of New Mexico. He teaches in internal medicine and family practice. His research has focused on comparative international health policy and psychosocial issues in primary care. He is also an important advocate for improved health care access in the US and has been a lead critic of managed care in Latin America.

Seiji Yamada is a physician practicing and teaching in Honolulu, Hawaii. He is associated with Hawaii/Pacific Basin Area Health Education Center, the University of Hawaii Office of Medical Education, and the Division of Ecology and Health. He is actively involved in the movement for peace and demilitarization. His email address is seiji@hawaii.edu.

INTRODUCTION: GLOBALIZATION AND HEALTH

1   Devinder Sharma, "WTO and Agriculture: Zero-Tolerance for Farm Subsidies," *AgBioIndia Bulletin*, February 12, 2003, http://www.agbioindia.org/archive_m.asp?id=171&mo=2&yr=2003.

2   Forum of Farmers Organizations on Globalization and Agriculture, "Farmers' Suicide and Farmers' Rights Resolution," New Delhi, May 30, 1998, http://www.earthisland.org/eijournal/fall98/wr_fall98cotton1.html.

3   Sarah Grusky, "Hospitals Become Jails in Ghana," *Drop the Debt: Jubilee USA Network-Newsletter*, Winter 2002.

4   Alexander Irwin, Joyce V. Millen, and Dorothy Fallows, *Global AIDS: Myths and Facts, Tools for Fighting the AIDS Pandemic* (Cambridge, MA: South End Press, 2002), xvii.

5   Cover photograph of *Sickness and Wealth* was taken in Kathmandu, Nepal, in 1997 by Hartmuch Schwarzbuch.

6   Branko Milanovic, *Can We Discern the Effect of Globalization on Income Distribution? Evidence from Household Budget Surveys*, World Bank Policy Research Working Paper 2876 (Washington, DC: World Bank, 2002).

7   Branko Milanovic, *The Two Faces of Globalization: Against Globalization as We Know It* (Washington, DC: World Bank, 2002), http://www.worldbank.org/research/inequality/pdf/naiveglob2.pdf.

8   Andrew Simms, "Going Down in History," *New Internationalist*, no. 342 (2002): 20.

9   Barbara Rylko-Bauer and Paul Farmer, "Managed Care or Managed Inequality? A Call for Critiques of Market-Based Medicine," *Medical Anthropology Quarterly* 16, no. 4 (2002): 476–502.

10 Families USA, *Going without Health Insurance* (Washington, DC: Families USA Foundation, 2003), http://www.familiesusa.org/site/DocServer/Going_without_report.pdf?docID=273.

CHAPTER ONE: HOW ECONOMIC INEQUALITY AFFECTS HEALTH

1   United Nations Development Program, *Human Development Report 1999* (New York: Oxford University Press, 1999).

2   Jim Yong Kim and Joyce V. Millen, eds., *Dying for Growth: Global Inequality and the Health of the Poor* (Monroe, ME: Common Courage Press, 2000).

3   Ibid.

4   C. AbouZhar et al., *Maternity and Morality in 2000: Estimates Developed by WHO, UNICEF, and UNFPA* (Geneva: WHO, 2001).

5   UNICEF, *State of the World's Children 2004* (New York: UNICEF, 2004).

6   George Kennan, *State Department Policy Planning Study #23* (Washington, DC: US Department of State, 1948).

7   WHO, *World Health Report 2004* (Geneva: WHO, 2004), annex table 4, http://www.who.int/whr/2004/annex/topic/en/annex_4_en.pdf.

8   Ibid.

9   OECD, *OECD Health Data 2003*, "Tobacco Consumption—% of Population Who Are Daily Smokers," http://www.oecd.org/dataoecd/12/9/2957450.xls.

10 M. A. Corrao et al., eds., *Tobacco Control: Country Profiles* (Atlanta: American Cancer Society, 2000).

11 R. G. Wilkinson, *Unhealthy Societies: The Afflictions of Inequality* (London: Routledge, 1996).

12 Ibid.

13 I. Kawachi, B. P. Kennedy, and R. G. Wilkinson, eds., *The Society and Population Health Reader*, vol. 1, *Inequality and Health* (New York: New Press, 1999).

14 Wilkinson, *Unhealthy Societies*.

15 Amartya Sen, interview by David Barsamian, *Alternative Radio*, KGNU, Boulder, CO, April, 2001.

16 UNICEF, *State of the World's Children 2004*.

17 UNDP, *Human Development Report 1999*.

18 Kim and Millen, *Dying for Growth*.

19 Ibid.

20 Ibid.

21 United for a Fair Economy, *The Growing Divide: Inequality and the Roots of Economic Insecurity* (Boston: United for a Fair Economy, 2003), http://www.faireconomy.org/econ/workshops/workshop_pdfs/GD_Charts 1.0.pdf.

22 J. E. Stiglitz, "The Broken Promise of NAFTA," *New York Times*, January 6, 2004, sec. A.

23 Ibid.

24 Ibid.

25 Ibid.

26 R. E. Scott, *The High Price of "Free" Trade: NAFTA's Failure Has Cost the United States Jobs across the Nation*, Economic Policy Institute Briefing Paper no. 147 (Washington, DC: Economic Policy Institute, 2003), http://www.epinet.org/briefingpapers/nafta01/nafta-at-7.pdf.

27 Ibid.

28 Ibid.

29 R. G. Wilkinson, "How Can Secular Improvements in Life Expectancy Be Explained?" in *Health and Social Organization: Towards a Health Policy for the Twenty-first Century*, ed. D. Blane, E. Brunner and R. G. Wilkinson (London: Routledge, 1996).

30 M. Weisbrot et al., *The Scorecard on Globalization, 1980–2000: Twenty Years of Diminished Progress* (Washington, DC: Center for Economic and Policy Research, 2001).

31 Ibid.

32 Ibid.

33 L. Mogford, "Structural Determinants of Infant Mortality in Sub-Saharan Africa" (diss., University of Washington, 2003).

34 Ibid.

35 M. McKee and V. Shkolnikov, "Understanding the Toll of Premature Death among Men in Eastern Europe," *British Medical Journal* 323, no. 7320 (2001): 1051–55.

36 P. Walberg et al., "Economic Change, Crime, and Mortality Crisis in Russia: Regional Analysis," *British Medical Journal* 317, no. 7154 (2001): 312–18.

37 N. G. Bennett et al., "Demographic Implications of the Russian Mortality Crisis," *World Development* 26, no. 11 (1998): 1921–37.

38 E. M. Andreev et al., "The Evolving Pattern of Avoidable Mortality in Russia," *International Journal of Epidemiology* 32, no. 3 (2003): 437–46; WHO, *World Health Report 2004*.

39 Robert Conquest, *The Great Purge: A Reassessment* (New York, Oxford University Press, 1990).

40 R. W. Franke and B. H. Chasin, *Kerala: Radical Reform as Development in an Indian State* (Oakland, CA: Institute for Food and Development Policy, 1994).

41 G. Parayil, ed., *Kerala: The Development Experience* (London: Zed, 2000).

42 Ibid.

43 Kilian Crawford, "Nation's Health Depends on Equity, Not Wealth," *Georgia Straight* (Vancouver), June 8, 2000.

44 C. Hertzman, "The Case for an Early Childhood Development Strategy," *Canadian Journal of Policy Research* 1 (2000): 11–18.

45 J. L. McClain, *Japan: A Modern History* (New York: Norton, 2002).

46 Ibid.

47 Ibid.

48 Jimmy Carter (Lecture by the Nobel Peace Prize Laureate, Oslo, December 10, 2002), http://www.nobel.no/eng_lect_2002b.html.

CHAPTER TWO: THE LEGACY OF COLONIAL MEDICINE

1 Rangar Nurske, *Problems of Capital Formation in Underdeveloped Countries* (Oxford: Oxford University Press, 1953) 63.

2 United Nations Development Program, *Human Development Report 2001* (New York: Oxford University Press, 2001), http://hdr.undp.org/reports/global/2001/en/pdf/completenew.pdf.

3 R. Leys, "Migrant Labour and Population Growth in Lesotho," in *Report on the National Population Symposium*, ed. A. M. Monyake. The symposium was held in Masaru, Lesotho, June 11–13, 1974.

4 Keith Griffin, "Underdevelopment in History," *The Political Economy of Development and Underdevelopment*, 2nd ed. (New York: Random House, 1973), 85.

5 New York City Department of Health, "Infant Mortality by Prominent Causes in New York City," *Weekly Reports of the Department of Health* 21, no. 50 (December 17, 1932): 396.

6　Walter Rodney, *How Europe Underdeveloped Africa* (Washington, D.C.: Howard University Press, 1974).

7　In fact, in some cases, the introduction of medical missionaries preceded the coming of the imperial flag. For example, the famous explorer Dr. Livingtsone ("I presume") was a medical doctor.

8　In older, now unusually expanded regional and district hospitals in Africa, the former European ward is now often reserved (on a nonsegregated basis) for "Grade I" patients.

9　Hostile, that is, not because of so-called tropical diseases but because of the poor socioeconomic conditions of the masses and the related low sanitary standards which allowed (and continue to allow) these diseases to flourish.

10　Disease control (as opposed to eradication) programs were reborn in the 1990s; for example, the Global Fund to Fight AIDS, Tuberculosis, and Malaria. See http://www.theglobalfund.org/en/.

11　No federal-level ministry of health even existed in the US until the early 1950s, and in many respects, the Department of Health and Human Services is still inferior to similar agencies in other parts of the worlds.

CHAPTER THREE: THE PRIMARY HEALTH CARE MOVEMENT MEETS THE FREE MARKET

1　Gill Walt and Patrick Vaughan, *An Introduction to the Primary Health Care Approach in Developing Countries: A Review with Selected Annotated References* (London: Ross Institute, 1981), 8.

2　David Werner and David Sanders, *Questioning the Solution: the Politics of Primary Health Care and Child Survival* (Palo Alto, CA: WealthWrights, 1997), 16.

3　Debabar Banerji, "A Fundamental Shift in the Approach to International Health by WHO, UNICEF, and the World Bank," *International Journal of Health Services* 29, 2 (1999): 227–59.

4　WHO, "Declaration of Alma-Ata," in *Report on the International Conference on Primary Health Care* (Geneva: WHO, 1978).

5　Ibid.

6　Werner and Sanders, *Questioning the Solution*, 19.

7　David A. Tejada de Rivero, "Alma-Ata Revisited," *Perspectives in Health Magazine* 8, no. 2 (2003).

8　J. A. Walsh and K. S. Warren, "Selective Primary Health Care: an Interim Strategy for Disease Control in Developing Countries," *New England Journal of Medicine* 301 (1979): 967–74.

9　J. P. Unger and J. Killingworth, "Primary Health Care: A Critical Review of Methods and Results," *Social Science and Medicine* 22, no. 10 (1986): 1001–3.

10　Oscar Gish, personal communication with author, February 2, 2004.

11　Jan Swasthya Sabha, *Whatever Happened to Health for All by 2000?* Towards the People's Health Assembly, book 2 (Chennai, India: Jan Swasthya Sabha, 2000), 22.

12　Werner and Sanders, *Questioning the Solution*, 24–25.

13　Oscar Gish, "Selective Primary Health Care: Old Wine in New Bottles," *Social Science and Medicine* 16 (1982): 1049–63.

14　Banerji, "A Fundamental Shift," 239.

15 John Summa, "Killing Them Sweetly," *Multinational Monitor* 9, no.11 (1988), http://multinationalmonitor.org/hyper/issues/1988/11/mm1188_10.html.

16 "Welcome Back, Boycotter: Milk Is Murder," *Mother Jones* (August 1997) 6, http://www.motherjones.com/commentary/columns/1997/08/index6.html.

17 Anita Hardon, "Consumers versus Producers: Power Play Behind the Scenes," in *Drugs Policy in Developing Countries*, ed. Najmi Kanji et al. (London: Zed Books, 1992).

18 John Braithwaite and Peter Drahos, *Global Business Regulation* (Cambridge: Cambridge University Press, 2000).

19 Ibid.

20 S. M. Carter, "Mongoven, Biscoe and Duchin: Destroying Tobacco Control Activism from the Inside," *Tobacco Control* 11 (2002): 112–18.

21 Sarah Boseley, "Sugar Industry Threatens to Scupper WHO," *Guardian*, April 21, 2003.

22 Kelly D. Brownell and Marion Nestle, "The Sweet and Lowdown on Sugar," *New York Times*, Op-Ed, January 23, 2004.

23 World Bank, *Financing Health Services in Developing Countries: An Agenda for Reform* (Washington, DC: World Bank, 1987).

24 World Bank, *World Development Report: Investing in Health* (Washington, DC: World Bank, 1993).

25 Ibid.

26 Ibid.

27 Malaysian Medical Association, *Medical Journal of Malaysia*, April 2000.

28 Ibid.

29 Kamran Abbasi, "The World Bank and World Health: Healthcare Strategy," *British Medical Journal* 318 (1999): 933–36.

30 Ibid.

CHAPTER FOUR: THE IMPACT OF STRUCTURAL ADJUSTMENT PROGRAMS

1 Note that most of the decline in the infant mortality rate (IMR) preceded the economic liberalization of China that began in 1978. The IMR has continued downward but at a distinctly slower pace, to 36 per 1,000 live births by 1995. See O. Ahmad, A. Lopez, and M. Inoue, "The Decline in Child Mortality: A Reappraisal," *Bulletin of the World Health Organization* 78 (2000): 1175–91.

2 Godfrey Gunatilleke, ed., *Intersectoral Linkages and Health Development: Case Studies in India (Kerala State), Jamaica, Norway, Sri Lanka and Thailand* (Geneva: World Health Organization, 1984), 20–23.

3 Ibid.; Government of Kerala, *Economic Review 1999* (Thiruvananthapuram, India: State Planning Board, 2000), 25.

4 UNICEF, UNICEF statistics, "Child Mortality: Infant Mortality Rate," www.childinfo.org/cmr/revis/db1.htm.

5 Soon thereafter another organization, the General Agreement on Tariffs and Trade (GATT), which set the rules for global trade and the opening of economies, was formed.

6 Richard Swift, "Squeezing the South: 50 Years Is Enough," *New Internationalist* 257 (July 1994).

7   OPEC, *General Information 2002* (Vienna: OPEC Secretariat, 2002), www.opec.org.

8   Federal Deposit Insurance Corporation, "The LDC Debt Crisis," in *History of the Eighties—Lessons for the Future* (Washington, DC: Federal Deposit Insurance Corporation, 1997), 191–210, www.fdic.gov/bank/historical/history.

9   Judith Randel, Tony German, and Deborah Ewing, eds., *The Reality of AID 2000: An Independent Review of Poverty Reduction and Development Assistance* (London: Earthscan Publications, 2000), 3.

10 Salih Booker, "To Help Africa Battle AIDS, Write Off Its Debt," *Los Angeles Times*, May 20, 2002.

11 Jeff Rudin, "Odious Debt Revisited," *Jubilee South,* October 30, 2002, www.jubileesouth.org/news/EPFVuVkkFlkCCnpoKE.shtml.

12 Ibid.

13. In the late 1980s, World Bank missions in Zaire inspected schools and imposed the closing of those with too few students overall or with classes of less than 40 students. Dr. Cecile De Sweemer, personal communication with the author, April 2003.

14 Arthur MacEwan, "Economic Debacle in Argentina: The IMF Strikes Again," *Foreign Policy in Focus*, January 2, 2002, www.fpif.org.

15 Stephanie Black, *Life and Debt,* Tuff Going Pictures Production, 2001.

16 William Easterly, *The Effect of IMF and World Bank Programs on Poverty* (Washington, DC: World Bank, 2000).

17 Ibid.

18 This became particularly apparent to me during several visits to a large public hospital in Cote d'Ivoire in the early 1990s, after several years of SAPs in that country. In an area with enormous unmet health needs, most of the pediatric beds were empty. I asked a nurse at the hospital why, and he said that ever since the government began charging for basic drugs, people have had to take their children from the hospital.

19 Observed by author.

20 Ibid.

21 Ibid.

22 Ibid.

23 Giovanni Andrea Cornia, Richard Jolly, and Frances Stewart, eds., *Adjustment with a Human Face: Protecting the Vulnerable and Promoting Growth*, 2 vols. (Oxford: Clarendon Press, 1987).

24 Kwesi Owusu, Sarah Clarke, Stuart Croft, and John Garrett, *Through the Eye of a Needle: The Africa Debt Report—a Country by Country Analysis* (London: Jubilee 2000 Coalition, 2000), http://www.jubileeplus.org/analysis/reports/africa.pdf.

25 Nigerian president Olusegun Obasanjo described his country's debt after the G8 summit held on Okinawa in August 2000. "Leaders of Indebted Nations Hold London Debt Summit," Jubilee 2000 Coalition, http://www.jubilee2000uk.org/jubilee2000/news/london180800.html.

26 Oxfam, *Debt Relief and the HIV/AIDS Crisis in Africa: Does the Heavily Indebted Poor Countries (HIPC) Initiative Go Far Enough?* Briefing Paper no. 25, June 2002, http://www.oxfam.org/eng/pdfs/pp0206_no25_debt_relief_and_the_HIV_crisis.pdf.

27   Mozambican Ministry of Health, *Health Care Expenditure Report* (Maputo, Mozambique: Government of Mozambique, Mozambique, 2002).

28   Gorik Ooms, "How IMF Policies Block the Global Fund," Third World Network, December 2002, http://www.twnside.org.sg/title/5260c.htm.

29   William Finnegan, "The Economics of Empire," *Harper's Magazine*, May 2003, 41–54.

CHAPTER FIVE: HEALTH SECTOR REFORM IN GUATEMALA

1   World Bank, *Financing Health Services in Developing Countries: An Agenda for Reform* (Washington, DC: World Bank, 1987), 1.

2   Ibid., 3–6. World Bank economists wrote, "[These changes] will increase the resources available to the government health sector, allow for more spending on underfunded programs, encourage better quality and more efficiency, and increase access for the poor…Encourage well-designed health insurance programs to help mobilize resources for the health sector while simultaneously protecting households from large financial losses…Encourage the nongovernment sector (including nonprofit groups, private physicians, pharmacists, and other health practitioners) to provide health services for which consumers are willing to pay…Decentralize planning, budgeting, and purchasing for government health services, particularly the services offering private benefits for which users are charged."

3   World Bank, *Investing in Health* (Washington, DC: World Bank, 1993).

4   Jim Yong Kim et al., "Sickness amidst Recovery: Public Debt and Private Suffering in Peru," in *Dying for Growth*, 127–53 (see chap. 1, n. 2).

5   Nuria Homedes, "Managing Externally Financed Projects: The Integrated Primary Health Care Project in Bolivia," *Health Policy and Planning* 16, no. 4 (2001): 386–94.

6   John Gershman and Alec Irwin, "Getting a Grip on the Global Economy," in *Dying for Growth*, 11–43 (see chap. 1, n. 2).

7   Banco Interamericano de Desarrollo, *Programa sectorial de salud Guatemala*, internal document, 1993.

8   UNDP, *Guatemala: The Contrasts of Human Development; Human Development Report*, (Guatemala: UNDP, 1998).

9   UNDP, *Guatemala: The Inclusive Force of Human Development; Human Development Report* (Guatemala: UNDP, 2000).

10   World Bank, *Financing Health Services*, 38.

11   John Fiedler, "Latin American Health Policy and Additive Reform: The Case of Guatemala," *International Journal of Health Services* 15, no. 2 (1985): 275–99.

12   *Rector* is the word that is used by the IADB and the MOH for the new prescribed role of the state within the reorganized framework of the health sector under Health Sector Reform. As rector, the Ministry of Health is to oversee and regulate the sector and shift its previous responsibilities of health care service delivery and administration over to the private sector. *Rector* can be translated as director, chair, or steering role. Throughout the chapter we will use the word *director* instead of *rector*.

13   Guatemala's health ministry is known as the Ministry of Public Health and
     Social Welfare (MSPAS) but for purposes of simplicity, we will refer to it here
     as the Ministry of Health (MOH).

14   A health system organizes care at three levels. The primary level is basic care
     for the population—the first contact between people and health services. The
     secondary level is care of a greater complexity that employs various medical
     specialties. The tertiary level is care that requires hospitalization at a medical
     center for diverse treatments.

15   Ministry of Public Health and Social Welfare (MSPAS), *Guia para el calculo de
     recursos y presupuesto de una jurisdiccion, usando como modelo una jurisdiccion de 10,000
     habitantes* (Guatemala: MSPAS, 1997).

16   Juan Carlos Verdugo, *Análisis de la implementación del modelo de primer nivel de
     atención del sistema integral de atención en salud (SIAS) en Guatemala* (Guatemala:
     Instancia Nacional de Salud, 2000).

17   Meredith Fort, "Assessment of the Guatemalan Health Sector Reform at the
     Primary Care Level" (Master's Thesis in Public Health, University of
     Washington School of Public Health and Community Medicine, 2002).

18   The Health Sector Reform extends beyond any single administration's time in
     office. And given that reforms require 10 years to consolidate, the
     administrations are considered to be changing actors inside a historical analysis
     of the HSR.

19   Although the government did not change the overall reform effort, among the
     principal problems were the extreme politicization of the Ministry of Health
     and the corruption and financial abandonment of the ministry (growing debts
     with private care providers that seriously limited SIAS implementation)
     because of the prioritizing of other spending, such as on the military.

20   Personal communication with government health officials, 1996.

21   Juan Carlos Verdugo, "Neoliberalismo y política de salud en Guatemala"
     (Master's Thesis in Social Medicine, Universidad Autónoma Metropolitana
     Unidad Xochimilco, Mexico, 1995).

22   Ana García and Laura Lerner, "El discurso neoliberal en las pol'ticas sociales:
     aportes para una discusión," *Cuadernos Médicos Sociales*, no. 58 (1991): 34–45.

23   The monitoring system—HACyA, which stands for Qualification, Award,
     Certification and Accreditation—was part of the effort to transfer
     responsibility for primary care from departmental- and district-level health
     authorities to the field.

24   Evelyne Brodking and Dennis Young, "El sentido de la privatización: ¿Que
     podemos aprender del análisis económico y político?" in *La privatización y el
     estado benefactor*, ed. Sheila Kamerman and Alfred Kahn, 27–39 (Mexico: Fondo
     de Cultura Economica, 1993).

25   Ana Diez and Hugo Spinelli, "El sistema de salud de Estados Unidos:
     Paradigma a imitar o espejismo?" *Cuadernos Médicos Sociales* 63 (1993): 8–16.

26   S. Woolhandler and D. V. Himmelstein, "The Deteriorating Administrative
     Efficiency of the US Health Care System," *New England Journal of Medicine* 324
     (1991): 1253–58.

27   According to the World Health Organization, in 2000 there were 470,606
     recorded cases of cervical cancer worldwide. Of those, 19 percent surfaced in

"more-developed" countries, while 81 percent of cases took place in the "less-developed" countries. See www-dep.iarch.fr/globocan/globocan.html.

28 Instancia Nacional de Salud, *Hacia un primer nivel de atención en salud incluyente: bases y lineamientos* (Guatemala City, Guatemala: Instancia Nacional de Salud, 2002).

CHAPTER SIX: MANAGED CARE IN LATIN AMERICA

1 Henry Kissinger quoted in Sam Gindin, "Social Justice and Globalization: Are they Compatible?" *Monthly Review* 54, no. 2 (2002): 1–11.

2 John Williamson, "What Washington Means by Policy Reform," in *Latin American Adjustment: How Much Has Happened?* ed. John Williamson (Washington, DC: Institute for International Economics, 1990).

3 Roberto Feletti and Claudio Lozano, *Reestructuración capitalista y endeudamiento externo latinoamericano* (Buenos Aires: Instituto de Estudios sobre Estado y Participación IDEP/CTA, 1997).

4 Celia Iriart, Francisco Leone, and Mario Testa, "Las políticas de salud en el marco del ajuste," *Cuadernos Médico Sociales*, 71 (1995): 5–21.

5 World Bank, *World Development Report: Investing in Health* (Washington, DC: World Bank, 1993).

6 Pereira Bresser and C. Luiz, "Reforma administrativa do sistema de saúde: Criação das organizaçoes sociais" (Technical Colloquium Preceding the 25th Annual Meeting of CLAD's Board of Directors, Buenos Aires, Argentina, August 23–26, 1995).

7 Interview with anonymous official, 1998.

8 Howard Waitzkin and Celia Iriart, "How the United States Exports Managed Care to Developing Countries," *International Journal of Health Services* 31, no. 3 (2001): 495–505.

9 Cristina Asa Laurell and Olivia López Orellano, "Market Commodities and Poor Relief: The World Bank Proposal for Health," *International Journal of Health Services* 26, no. 1 (1996): 1–18.

10 See Chapter 7.

11 Karen Stocker, Howard Waitzkin, and Celia Iriart, "The Exportation of Managed Care to Latin America," *New England Journal of Medicine* 340 (1999): 1131–36.

12 Milt Freudenheim and Clifford Krauss, "Dancing to a New Health Care Beat," *New York Times*, June 16, 1999, C1.

13 Louise Kertesz, "The New World of Managed Care," *Modern Healthcare*, November 1997: 114–20.

14 Suzanne Felt-Lisk and Sara Yang, "Changes in Health Plans Serving Medicaid: 1993–1996," *Health Affairs* 16, no.5 (1997): 125–33.

15 Robert Kuttner, "Must Good HMOs Go Bad? The Search for Checks and Balances," *New England Journal of Medicine* 338 (1998): 1558–63.

16 Results related to Latin American countries presented in this section are based on Celia Iriart et al., *Atención gerenciada: Su papel en la reforma de los distemas de salud en América Latina* (Geneva: WHO, 1999).

17 Ministerio de Salud y Acción Social, *Guía de establecimientos asistenciales de la republica Argentina* (Buenos Aires: Ministerio de Salud y Acción Social, 1995).

18 Artemio López, "La situación de la niñez en Argentina: Indicadores sanitarios y socioambientales, Evolución durante la convertibilidad," *Trabajo y Sociedad*, August–October 2000.

19 Ibid.

20 Celia Iriart, Emerson Elías Merhy, and Howard Waitzkin, "Managed Care in Latin America: The New Common Sense in Health Policy Reform," *Social Sciences and Medicine* 52 (1999): 1243–53.

21 M. J. Fisher, "Medical Care Plans Exit Medicare," *National Underwriter* 104, no. 28 (2000): 1–2; V. Lankarge, "Medicare HMO Withdrawals in 2001: A State-by-State List of Pullouts," Insure.com, http://info.insure.com/health/medicare/hmodrops01/index.html; L. McGinley and R. Winslow, "Major HMOs to Quit Medicare Markets," *Wall Street Journal*, June 30, 2000, sec. A.

CHAPTER SEVEN: TRADE AND HEALTH CARE

1 With his 1855 study explaining the source of a cholera outbreak that his London in 1854, Snow ushered in a new era in microbiology, germ theory, and epidemiology. His findings—that cholera was being spread by common use of a contaminated water pump—rocked the then-dominant miasma ("bad air") theory of cholera contagion. In 2003, a group of British physicians voted Snow "the greatest doctor ever" in a survey published in the magazine *Hospital Doctor*. See www.ph.ucla.edu/epi/snow/snowgreatestdoc.html.

2 J. Eisenberg, J. Bartram, and P. Hunter, "A Public Health Perspective for Establishing Water-Related Guidelines and Standards," in *Water Quality—Guidelines, Standards and Health: Assessment of Risk and Risk Management for Water-Related Infectious Diseases*, eds. L. Fewtrell and J. Bartram (Geneva: World Health Organization, 2001).

3 In 1999, the Interpress Third World News Agency (IPS) reported that WHO director Gro Harlem Brundtland claimed that the WHO budget has been reduced 20 percent in real terms over the last 20 years. See http://www.hartford-hwp.com/archives/27/067.html.
A paper written in 2000 by Professor Ilona Kickbusch of Yale University, entitled "The World Health Organization: Some Governance Challenges," asserts that WHO "has a very small regular budget (roughly US$800 million US for two years) and is highly dependent on voluntary donations...Its budget has been decreasing over the last 15 years." See http://www.yale.edu/gegdialogue/docs/who_governancechallenge.doc.

4 Board on International Health, Institute of Medicine, *America's Vital Interest in Global Health: Protecting Our People, Enhancing Our Economy, and Advancing Our International Interests* (Washington, DC: National Academy Press, 1997).

5 Interhemispheric Resource Center and the Institute for Policy Studies, "World Trade Organization," *Foreign Policy in Focus* 2, no. 14 (January 1997).

6 International Forum on Globalization, *Alternatives to Economic Globalization: A Better World Is Possible* (San Francisco: Berrett-Koehler Publishers, 2002).

7 Sarah Sexton, *Trading Health Care Away? GATS, Public Services and Privatisation*, Briefing 23: Trade and Health Care (Dorset, UK: Corner House, 2001).

8 "First Bananas, Then Beef Fuels US-EU Trade War," *World Socialist*, May 1999, http://www.wsws.org/articles/1999/may1999/wto-m14.shtml.

9   Lori Wallach and Michelle Sforza, *The WTO, Five Years of Reasons to Resist Corporate Globalization* (New York: Seven Stories Press, 1999).

10   Lori Wallach and Michelle Sforza, *Whose Trade Organization? Corporate Globalization and the Erosion of Democracy* (Washington, D.C.: Public Citizen, 1999).

11   United Nations Conference on Trade and Development, *Least Developed Countries Report, 2004: Linking International Trade with Poverty Reduction* (Geneva: UN, 2004), http://www.unctad.org/en/docs//ldc2004_en.pdf. While international trade has the potential to reduce poverty in less-developed nations, this is not happening. In practice, trade liberalization doesn't eliminate poverty because of three factors: weak trade performance, weak trade-growth linkages, and the association of export expansion with a form of economic growth that is not poverty reducing.

12   Joseph Stiglitz, "A Second Chance for Brazil and the IMF," *New York Times*, August 14, 2002.

13   Ibid.

14   WTO Secretariat and WHO, *WTO Agreements and Public Health: A Joint Study by the WHO and the WTO Secretariat* (Geneva: WTO Secretariat, 2002).

15   European Services Forum, *About ESF*, January 26, 1999. World trade in commercial services accounted for $1.57 trillion in 2002, up 6 percent from the year before, according to the WTO's international trade statistics for 2003. See http://www.wto.int/english/res_e/_e/its2003_e.pdf.

16   M. Ellis-Jones and P. Hardstaff, *Serving (Up) the Nation: A Guide to the UK's Commitments under the WTO General Agreement on Trade in Services* (London: World Development Movement, 2002).

17   European Commission, "Opening World Markets for Trade—the Text of the GATS," in *Info-Point on World Trade in Services*, http://gats-info.eu.int.

18   Under section 2 of the GATS guidelines, "General Obligations," members are not allowed to make preferential trade arrangements with other nations. Also, members cannot introduce legislation or policies that favor their domestic services or service suppliers, but rather, must leave them open to competition with international services and service suppliers. GATS member nations can tailor their coverage such that some service sectors (of around 160 possible sectors) are subject to these rules, while others may not be, in accordance with state agendas.

19   Ibid.

20   Maude Barlow, "A GATS Primer," Council of Canadians, http://www.canadians.org/documents/campaigns-gats_primer.pdf.

21   Celia Iriart, Howard Waitzkin, and Emerson Merhy, "International Trade Agreements, Health Care Systems and Social Movements in Latin America" (presentation, American Public Health Association annual meeting, Atlanta, October 24, 2001).

22   WHO statistics indicate that the US spends 13.9 percent of its GDP on health, the highest of all 192 WHO member states. See WHO, *World Health Report 2003* (Geneva: WHO, 2003), annex table 5, www.who.int/whr/2003/en/Annex5-en.pdf.

23 According to the WHO, the United States ranks 22nd in life expectancy at birth (69.3), just between Slovenia and Portugal. Among large and industrialized countries, Japan is first (75 years), followed by Sweden, Switzerland, Iceland, and Italy. See WHO, *World Health Report 2003*, 166–69, annex table 4: "Healthy Life Expectancy (HALE) in All Member States, 2002 Estimates," www.who.int/whr/2003/en-Annex4-en.pdf.

24 Canada's health care system is indeed heavily subsidized and is often referred to as "socialized medicine." Government spending accounts for about 70 percent of health dollars and private spending the other 30 percent. Canada spends 9.5 percent of its GDP on health, according to WHO's *World Health Report 2003*, annex table.

25 Canada ties with France for 10th place (72 years). See WHO, *World Health Report 2003*, 166–69.

26 Some recent articles on health tourism include: "Cuba Moves to Boost Health Tourism by Promoting in Europe," *Deutsche Presse-Agentur*, March 4, 2003; "Thailand Targets Higher Earnings from Health Tourism," *Global News Wire–Thai Press Reports*, June 24, 2003; "India Set to Cash In on Health Tourism," *Global News Wire–India Business Insight*, July 24, 2003; "Sand, sun, surf, and stethoscopes," *Xinhua*, March 26, 2004; and "Health Right Medicine for Tourism," *The Times of India*, April 20, 2004.

27 Sarah Sexton, "GATS, Privatisation and Health" (Presentation, "Service without Borders? Privatisation—GATS and the Consequences for Women," Cologne, May 2003).

28 Alliance for Responsible Trade, *Sector Analysis of the Free Trade Area of the Americas*, 2002, http://www.art-us.org.

29 S. Rogers, e-mail message to author, August 20, 2002.

CHAPTER EIGHT: MILITARISM AND THE SOCIAL PRODUCTION OF DISEASE

1 Dinesh D'Souza, "In Praise of American Empire," *Christian Science Monitor*, April 26, 2002.

2 Robert Fisk, "This Looming War Isn't about Chemical Warheads or Human Rights: It's About Oil," *Independent*, January 18, 2003.

3 Thomas L. Friedman, "A War for Oil?" *New York Times*, January 5, 2003, sec.4.

4 Mark Curtis, *Web of Deceit* (London: Vintage, 2003), 15–16, cited in Noam Chomsky, *Hegemony or Survival* (New York: Henry Holt & Co., 2003), 150.

5 Glenn Frankel, "US Mulled Seizing Oil Fields In '73," *Washington Post*, Jan 1, 2004, sec. A.

6 Noam Chomsky, *Understanding Power* (New York: The New Press, 2002), 74–75.

7 "Transformed? A Survey of the Defense Industry," *Economist*, July 20, 2002, 3–16.

8 Conn Hallinan, "War Is Good Business," *ZNet*, January 11, 2003, www.zmag.org/content/economy/halliman_business.htm.

9 Toni Gabric, "Noam Chomsky Interviewed," *Croatian Federal Tribune*, April 27, 2002, reprinted in *ZNET*, www.zmag.org/content/TerrorWar/chomskygab.cfm.

10 Noam Chomsky, "The Colombia Plan: April 2000," *Z Magazine*, June 2000, zmag.org/zmag/articles/chomsky.june2000.htm.

11 Jose Miguel Vivanco, testimony before the US Senate Foreign Relations Committee, April 24, 2002, Human Rights Watch, www.hrw.org/backgrounder/americas/colombia-testimonyouzu.htm.

12 Andres Sanchez, "Human Rights in Colombia" (based on a presentation given to a Witness for Peace Delegation, Bogota, July 2001), *ZNet*, www.zmag.org/CrisesCurrents/Colombia/ccjhr.htm.

13 George N. Lewis, Theodore A. Postol, and John Pike, "Why National Missile Defense Won't Work," *Scientific American* 281, no. 2 (1999): 22–27.

14 Stephen Weinberg, "Can Missile Defense Work?" *New York Review of Books*, February 14, 2002.

15 Theresa Hitchens, "Rushing to Weaponize the Final Frontier," *Arms Control Today*, September 2001.

16 Lawrence Kaplan, "Offensive Line," *New Republic*, March 12, 2001, 20.

17 "An American Dream," *Economist*, December 20, 2003, 25–26.

18 Noam Chomsky, "September 11th and Its Aftermath: Where Is the World Heading?" (speech, Chennai, India, November 10, 2001), www.hinduonnet.com/fline/fl1824/uc.htm.

19 John Cooley, *Unholy Wars* (London: Pluto, 1999), 230, cited in Chomsky, *Hegemony or Survival*, 111 (see n. 4).

20 Paul Richter, "US Works Up Plan for Using Nuclear Arms," *Los Angeles Times*, March 9, 2002.

21 Information on the fiscal year 2004 military budget comes from the Center for Defense Information, tkwww.cdi.org.

22 Ibid.

23 William Blum, "American Empire for Dummies," *ZNet*, October 21, 2002, www.zmag.org/content/ForeignPolicy/blum_empire.cfm.

24 Seymour M. Hersh, "Overwhelming Force," *New Yorker*, May 22, 2000, 49–82.

25 Beth Osborne Daponte, "A Case Study in Estimating Casualties from War and Its Aftermath: The 1991 Persian Gulf War," *PSR Quarterly* 3 (1993): 57–66.

26 Patrick Sloyan, "Iraqi Troops Buried Alive by US Army Assault Tactic on Trenches Kept a Secret," *Toronto Star*, Sept 12, 1991, sec. A.

27 For a full list of casualties see the *Guardian*, April 23, 2003, http://www.guardian.co.uk/Iraq/Story/0,2763,928043,00.html.

28 "Surveys Pointing to High Civilian Death Toll in Iraq," *Christian Science Monitor*, May 22, 2003.

29 Richard Garfield and Seiji Yamada, "Kalamaoka`aina Niheu, Pu`uhonua: Sanctuary and Struggle at Makua Hawaii" (unpublished manuscript).

30 Ibid.

31 Ibid.

32 Ibid.

33 Gregg K. Kakesako, "Makua Activists Fight the Army's Plan to Resume Training in the Valley," *Honolulu Star-Bulletin*, January 19, 2001.

34 Walden Bello, *People and Power in the Pacific* (London: Pluto Press, 1992), 25–26.

35 Filipino/American Coalition for Environmental Solutions,
    www.facessolutions.net.
36 A. Bleise, P. R. Danesi, and W. Burkart, "Properties, Use and Health Effects
    of Depleted Uranium (DU): A General Overview," *Journal of Environment
    Radioactivity* 64 (2003): 93–112.
37 United Nations Environment Programme, "Depleted Uranium Fact Sheet,"
    http://postconflict.undep.ch./dufact.html.
38 Laurence Carucci, *Nuclear Nativity: Rituals of Renewal and Empowerment in the
    Marshall Islands* (DeKalb, IL: Northern Illinois University Press, 1997).
39 Ruth Levy Guyer, "Radioactivity and Rights: Clashes at Bikini Atoll," *American
    Journal of Public Health* 91 (2001): 1371–76.
40 Seiji Yamada and Neal Palafox, "On the Biopsychosocial Model: Political
    Economic Perspectives on Diabetes in the Marshall Islands," *Family Medicine*
    33 (2001): 348–50.
41 Seiji Yamada, Anna Dodd, Tin Soe, Tai-Ho Chen, and Kay Bauman,
    "Diabetes Mellitus Prevalence in Out-Patient Marshallese Adults on Ebeye
    Island, Republic of the Marshall Islands, " *Hawaii Medical Journal* 63 (2004):
    47–53.
42 Mark E. Beatty et al., "An Outbreak of Vibrio Cholerae O1 Infections on
    Ebeye Island, Republic of the Marshall Islands, Associated with Use of an
    Adequately Chlorinated Water Source," *Clinical Infectious Diseases* 38 (2004):
    1–9.
43 Walter F. Roche and Willoughby Mariano, "Trapped in Servitude Far from
    Their Homes," *Baltimore Sun*, September 15, 2002.
44 "Marshalls Missile Range Owners Hire Washington 'Insider,'" *PINA Nius
    Online*, May 18, 2002, www.pinauius.org.
45 Janet Dibblin, *Day of Two Suns: US Nuclear Testing and the Pacific Islanders* (New
    York: New Amsterdam, 1988).
46 Richard Horton, "Public Health: A Neglected Counterterrorist Measure,"
    Lancet 358 (2001): 1112–13.
47 Jeffery Sachs, "Weapons of Mass Salvation," *Economist*, October 24, 2002, 72.

CHAPTER NINE: THE HIJACKING OF THE GLOBAL FOOD SUPPLY

1   Vandana Shiva, "The Crisis of Potato Growers in U.P.," *ZNet*, April 24, 2003,
    http://www.zmag.org/sustainers/content/2003-04/22shiva.cfm. One US
    dollar is worth approximately 47 Indian rupees. The quintal is equivalent to
    100 kilos, or 220 pounds.
2   Hope Shand, *Human Nature: Agricultural Biodiversity and Farm-Based Food Security*
    (Ottawa: Rural Advancement Foundation International, 1997).
3   RFSTE (Research Foundation for Science, Technology, and Ecology),
    Monsanto: Peddling Life Sciences or Death Sciences? (New Delhi: RFSTE, 1998)
4   *Wall Street Journal*, March 16, 1999.
5   Ibid.
6   Leora Broydo, "A Seedy Business," *Mother Jones*, April 7, 1998.
7   RFSTE, *Monsanto*.
8   "Let Nature's Harvest Continue!" *Third World Resurgence*, no. 97.

9   Geri Guidetti, *Seed Terminator and Mega-Merger Threaten Food and Freedom* (Jacksonville, OR: Ark Institute, 1998).

10   Monsanto's open letter on this issue is available at www.monsanto.com.

11   RFSTE, *Basmati Biopiracy* (New Delhi: RFSTE, 1998).

12   *Bija Newsletter*, no. 17, RFSTE, 1998; *Bija Newsletter*, no. 18, RFSTE, 1998.

13   Ronnie Cummins, "Monsanto Under Attack," *Food Bytes*, October 31, 1998, 2.

14   Rick Weiss, "Seeds of Discord: Monsanto's Gene Police Raise Alarm on Farmers Rights, Rural Tradition," *Washington Post*, February 3, 1999.

CHAPTER TEN: THE POLITICAL ROOTS OF SOUTH AFRICA'S CHOLERA EPIDEMIC

1   Kader Asmal, letter to the author, May 8, 1998.

2   J. Rome, "Water Pricing and Management"(World Bank presentation, South African Water Conservation Conference, South Africa, October 2, 1995). For more information on the role of the World Bank in South Africa see Patrick Bond, *Against Global Apartheid: South Africa Meets the World Bank, IMF and International Finance* (Cape Town: University of Cape Town Press, and London: Zed Press, 2003).

3   Statements from Dr. Chippy Olver to the *Mail & Guardian*, November 22, 1996.

4   The records cited are from a Ministry of Health news release of February 7, 2003. Although outbreaks were subsequently publicized in various sites, the Department of Water Affairs and Forestry stopped updating its daily Web site records on cholera. See http://www.dwaf.gov.za.

5   *Sunday Times*, October 9, 2001.

6   L. Veotte, "Restructuring Human Rights and Water Access to Vulnerable Groups" (South African Municipal Workers Union presentation, International Conference on Fresh Water, Bonn, Germany, December 2001).

7   Department of Health, *Health Sector Strategic Framework: 1999–2004* (Pretoria, *South African Department of Health, 1999).*

8   In KwaZulu-Natal, there were only 330 such officers in the civil service in 1999, a shortfall of 562; equivalent figures in the Eastern Cape were 228 officers, with a shortfall of 438. For more detail, see R. Stein, "Environmental Rights: Government Turns on the Indicators" (Unpublished paper, Wits University Law School, 2002).

9   *Sunday Times*, January 2002.

10   This point became a matter of fierce debate in *Sunday Independent Reconstruct* in early 1999. The article was followed by rebuttal letters from the bank's Mozambique officer. See Patrick Bond, "Mozambican Parliament Questions Debt Management," *Sunday Independent Reconstruct*, December 21, 1998; Phyllis Pomerantz, letter to the editor, *Sunday Independent Reconstruct*, January 24, 1999; and Patrick Bond and Joe Hanlon, letter to the editor, *Sunday Independent Reconstruct*, February 7, 1999.

11   B. Carty, "Whose Hand on the Tap? Water Privatization in South Africa," Canadian Broadcasting Corporation, February, 9 2003. See also J. Jeter, "South Africa's Dry Season," *Mother Jones*, December 2002; and J. Pauw, "Metered to Death: How a Water Experiment Caused Riots and a Cholera Epidemic," International Center for Investigative Journalism, Center for Public Integrity,

Washington DC, February 5, 2003,
http://www.icij.org/dtaweb/water/PrintReady.aspx?AID=6.

12 Carty, "Whose Hand on the Tap?"

13 Patrick Bond, *Unsustainable South Africa: Environment, Development, and Social Protest* (London: Merlin Press, 2002), chaps. 4–5.

14 R. Evans, *Death in Hamburg: Society and Politics in the Cholera Years, 1830–1910* (Harmondsworth, UK: Penguin, 2001), 568.

15 *Sunday Times*, October 9, 2001.

16 See the Municipal Services Project (M.P.) 2001 survey of Soweto household electricity bills and the joint Human Sciences Research Council and M.P. national household survey in 2001 (both at http://www.queensu.ca/msp). See also "Culture of Low Income Blamed for Arrears," *Business Day*, March 14, 2001. The article refers to the University of the Free State Center for Development Support's national study of household afford ability in 2000 sponsored by the US Agency for International Development, which found that "nine out of 10 low paying households gave unemployment, no income or too low an income as the main reasons for nonpayment." See also D. McDonald and J. Pape, *Cost Recovery and the Crisis of Service Delivery in South Africa* (Pretoria: Human Sciences Research Council and London: Zed Press, 2002); and A. Desai, *We Are the Poors* (New York: Monthly Review Press, 2002).

17 D. McDonald and J. Pape, *Cost Recovery and the Crisis of Service Delivery in South Africa*.

18 By way of definition, public goods can be observed and measured; they have two fundamental characteristics: "nonrival" consumption and "nonexclusion" from consumption. Consumption of a good or service is nonrival if its enjoyment by one person does not diminish the quantity available to others. Typical examples are a lighthouse or a national defense system. Likewise, the benefits of a clean environment and a hygienic public water system—reflecting a strong municipal water system and lifeline access to all—are enjoyed by all, regardless of how much water a particular individual consumes. In fact, the system must be accessible to all—that is, it must be nonexclusive—if it is to successfully prevent the spread of infectious disease."

19 M. Muller, "Reply to Bond," press release, April 18, 2001, 1–2.

20 D. Yach and D. Bradshaw, "Epidemiology: Key Concepts for the Child Health Practitioner," in *Child Health for All*, eds. M. A. Kibel and L. A. Wagstaff (Oxford: Oxford University Press, 1995), 422.

21 I. Mara, *Between Diarrheal Diseases and HIV/Aids Debates in South Africa* (Johannesburg: Group for Environmental Monitoring, 1996).

22 Sources include J. M. Pettifor and J. D. L. Hansen, "Malnutrition," in *Child Health for All* (see note 20); Y. Von Schirnding, D. Yach, R. Blignaut, and C. Mathews, "Environmental Determinants of Acute Respiratory Symptoms and Diarrhea in Young Colored Children living in Urban and Peri-Urban Areas of South Africa," *South African Medical Journal* 79 (1991): 457–61; S. A. Esrey, "Water, Waste and Well-Being: A Multi-country Study," *American Journal of Epidemiology* 143, no. 6 (1996); S. A. Esrey et al., "Drinking Water Source, Diarrhoeal Morbidity and Child Growth in Villages with Both Traditional and Improved Water Supplies in Rural Lesotho, Southern Africa," *American Journal of Public Health* 78, no. 11 (1998); S. Hutley, "The Impact of Inadequate

Sanitary Conditions on Health in Developing Countries," *World Health Statistics Quarterly* (2000): 118–26; L. Dikassa et al., "Maternal Behavioural Risk Factors for Severe Childhood Diarrhoeal Disease in Khinshasa, Zaire," *International Journal of Epidemiology* 22 (1993): 2; S. A. Esrey, R. G. Feachem, and J. M. Hughes, "Interventions for the Control of Diarrhoeal Diseases among Young Children: Improving Water Supplies and Excreta Disposal Facilities," *Bulletin of the World Health Organization* 63 (1985): 757–72; and B. Gunthe and J. Seager, *The Effect of Water Supply, Handling and Usage on Water Quality in Relation to Health Indices in Developing Communities* (Pretoria: Water Research Commission, 1996).

23   WHO, *Improving Health Outcomes of the Poor: The Report of Working Group 5 of the Commission on Macroeconomics and Health* (Geneva: WHO, 2001).

24   Ibid.

25   World Bank, *Sourcebook on Community Driven Development in the Africa Region: Community Action Programs: Africa Region* (Washington DC: World Bank, 2000), annex 2. The report was prepared by Calisto Madavo and Jean-Louis Sarbib." if that is accurate.

26   Nick Mathiason, "Left High and Dry by the Water Companies," *Observer*, March 16, 2003.

27   D. Hull, *Water Multinationals in Retreat* (London: Public Services International Research Unit, University of Greenwich, 2003).

28   Ibid.

CHAPTER ELEVEN: THE REGLOBALIZATION OF MALARIA

1   N. Mohr, *Malaria: Evolution of a Killer* (Seattle: Serif and Pixel Press, 2001).

2   See the malaria information page at the World Health Organization Web site, http://www.rbm.who.int/cmc_upload/0/000/015/372/RBMInfosheet_1.htm.

3   Ibid. Also see WHO, *Africa Malaria Report 2003,* ch. 1, p. 17, http://www.rbm.who.int/amd2003/amr2003/ch1.htm.

4   R. Carter and K.N. Mendis, "Evolutionary and Historical Aspects of the Burden of Malaria," *Clinical Microbiology Reviews* (October 2002) 564-594.

5   Ibid.

6   Ibid..

7   See the malaria information page at WHO Web site, http://www.rbm.who.int/cmc_upload/0/000/015/372/RBMInfosheet_1.htm.

8   Author calculation based on data from the Royal Society of Tropical Medicine and Hygiene.

9   See the malaria information page at WHO Web site, http://www.rbm.who.int/cmc_upload/0/000/015/372/RBMInfosheet_1.htm.

10   Ibid.

11   N. Levine, editor's preface to selections from *Malaria in the Interior Valley of North America* (Urbana: University of Illinois Press, 1964).

12   L.H. Hackett, *Malaria in Europe: An Ecological Study* (New York: Oxford University Press, 1937).

13   D.R. Gwatkin, M. Guillot, and P. Heuveline, "The Burden of Disease Among the Global Poor," *Lancet* 354 (1999): 586-589.

14   See WHO *World Health Report 2002,* http://www.who.int/whr/2002/en.

15   T.H. Holtz, et. al., "Care-seeking Behavior and Treatment of Febrile Illness in Children Under Five: A Household Survey in Blantyre District, Malawi," *Transactions of the Royal Society of Tropical Medicine and Hygiene* (forthcoming.)

16   P.J. Brown, "Culture and the Global Resurgence of Malaria," in *The Anthropology of Infectious Disease: International Health Perspectives,* eds. M.C. Inhorn and P.J. Brown (Amsterdam: Gordon and Breach, 1997).

17   W.H. McNeill, *Plagues and Peoples* (New York: Anchor Books/Doubleday, 1997).

18   Brown, "Culture and the Global Resurgence of Malaria."

19   M. Humphreys, *Malaria: Poverty, Race, and Public Health in the United States* (Baltimore: Johns Hopkins University Press, 2001).

20   Brown, "Culture and the Global Resurgence of Malaria."

21   Paul Farmer, *Infections and Inequalities: The Modern Plagues* (Berkeley: University of California Press, 1999).

22   J.L. Gallup and J.D. Sachs, *The Economic Burden of Malaria* (Cambridge: Center for International Development at Harvard University, 2000).

23   P. Olliaro, J. Cattari, and D. Wirth, "Malaria, the Submerged Disease," *Journal of American Medical Association* 275 (1996): 230-233.

24   Farmer, *Infections and Inequalities: The Modern Plagues.*

25   Gallup and Sachs, *The Economic Burden of Malaria.*

26   E. Gruenbaum, "Struggling with the Mosquito: Malaria Policy and Agricultural Development in Sudan," *Medical Anthropology* 7 (1983): 51-62.

27   R.M. Packard, "Agricultural Development, Migrant Labor, and the Resurgence of Malaria in Swaziland," *Social Science and Medicine* 22 (1986): 861-867.

28   G. Chapin and R. Wasserstrom, "Pesticide Use and Malaria Resurgence in Central America and India," *Social Science and Medicine* 17 (1983): 273-290.

29   W.F. Waters, "Globalization, Socioeconomic Restructuring, and Community Health," *Journal of Community Health* 26 (2001): 79-92.

30   F. Castro-Leal, et. al., "Public Spending on Health Care in Africa: Do the Poor Benefit?" *Bulletin of the World Health Organization* 78 (2000): 66-74.

31   S.R. Whyte, S. Van der Geest, and A. Hardon, *Social Lives of Medicines* (Cambridge: Cambridge University Press, 2002).

32   P.J. Brown, "Culture and the Global Resurgence of Malaria."

33   L. Roberts, M. Despines, "Mortality in the Democratic Republic of Congo," *Lancet* 353 (1999): 2249-2250.

34   R. Garfield, "Malaria Control in Nicaragua: Social and Political Influences on Disease Transmission and Control Activities," *Lancet* 354 (1999): 414-418.

35   R. Garfield, N. Low, J. Caldera, "Desocializing Health Care in a Developing Country," *Journal of the American Medical Association* 270 (1993): 989-993.

36   P.A. Phillips-Howard, et. al., "Efficacy of Permethin-Treated Bednets in the Prevention of Mortality in Young Children in an Area of High Perennial Malaria Transmission in Western Kenya," *American Journal of Tropical Medicine and Hygiene* 68 (Suppl. 4, 2003): 23-29.

37 T.H. Holtz et. al., "Insecticide-Treated Bednet Use, Anemia, and Malaria Parasitaemia in Blantyre District, Malawi," *Tropical Medicine and International Health* 7 (2002): 220-230.

38 C.A. Goodman, P.G. Coleman, and A.J. Mills, "Cost-Effectiveness of Malaria Control in Sub-Saharan Africa," *Lancet* 354 (1999): 378-385.

39 R.W. Snow, et. al., "Insecticide-Treated Bed Nets in Control of Malaria in Africa," *Lancet* 345 (1995): 1056-7.

40 WHO, *Scaling-up Insecticide-Treated Netting Programs in Africa: A Strategic Framework for Coordinated National Action* (Geneva: World Health Organization, 2002) 43.

41 P. Brentlinger, K. Sherr, M.A. Mercer, S. Gloyd, Letter to the Editor, *Lancet Infectious Diseases* 3 (2003): 467.

42 C. Curtis, et. al., "Scaling-up Coverage with Insecticide-Treated Nets Against Malaria in Africa: Who Should Pay?" *Lancet Infectious Diseases* 2 (2003): 30-33.

43 See the malaria information page at the World Health Organization Web site, http://www.rbm.who.int/cmc_upload/0/000/015/372/RBMInfosheet_1.htm.

44 M. Phillips, "World-Wide Fund to Fight Disease is Running Short," *Wall Street Journal,* May 7, 2003.

45 Ibid.

CHAPTER TWELVE: THE BATTLE AGAINST GLOBAL AIDS

1   Personal communication with author, April 2000. Swaziland's infection rate is now over 30 percent.

2   UNAIDS and WHO, *AIDS Epidemic Update* (Geneva: UNAIDS and WHO, 2003), http://www.unaids.org/html/pub/publications/irc-pub06/jc943-epiupdate2003_en_pdf.pdf.

3   Ibid.

4   John Donnelly, "World's AIDS Crisis Worsening, Report Says: Disease Spreading Fast in Sub-Saharan Africa," *Boston Globe,* June 16, 2002.

5   Lewis Machipisa,"Government Rejects UN Report on Life Expectancy," *Inter Press Service,* June 6, 2001.

6   "Zimbabwe City Wants Double Burials Due to AIDS," *Reuters,* July 12, 2001. Also see Grant Ferrett, "AIDS-Hit Zimbabwe Promotes Cremation," BBC News, December 1, 2000. http://www.news.bbc.co.uk/1/hi/world/africa/1049421.stm. Prior to the double-burial proposal, the Harare City Council suggested cremation, which is considered taboo in parts of Africa, as a solution to crowded burial sites.

7   Alexander Irwin, Joyce V. Millen, and Dorothy Fallows, *Global AIDS: Myths and Facts; Tools for Fighting the AIDS Pandemic* (Cambridge, MA: South End Press, 2003), 7.

8   UNAIDS and WHO, *AIDS Epidemic Update.*

9   UNAIDS, "Report on Global HIV/AIDS Epidemic," (presentation, Fourteenth International Conference on AIDS, Barcelona, July 7–12, 2002), www.unaids.org/barcelona/presskit/embargo_html.htm.

10 Stephen H. Lewis (Keynote Speech, Alternative Summit, Calgary, Canada, June 22, 2002).

11 Ines Perin and Amir Attaran. "Trading Ideology for Dialogue: An Opportunity to Fix International Aid for Health?," *Lancet* 361 (2003): 1216–19.

12 Results, *User Fees on Primary Health and Education,* fact sheet, 2001, http://sept.globalizethis.org/docs/wbuserfees.pdf.

13 Alison Katz, "AIDS, Individual Behaviour and the Unexplained Variation," *African Journal of AIDS Research* 1 (2002): 125–42.

14 Oxfam International, *Crisis in Southern Africa,* Briefing Paper no. 23, June 2002.

15 G. Brooke, Claude Schoepf, and Joyce V. Millen, "Theoretical Therapies, Remote Remedies: SAPs and the Political Ecology of Poverty and Health in Africa," in *Dying for Growth* (see chap. 1, n. 2), 91–125.

16 Devon Brewer, "Mounting Anomalies in the Epidemiology of HIV in Africa: Cry the Beloved Paradigm," *International Journal of STD & AIDS* 14 (2003): 144–47.

17 Scott Hammer et al., "Scaling Up Antiretroviral Therapy in Resource Limited Settings: Guidelines for a Public Health Approach," WHO, April 22, 2002, www.who.int/medicines/organization/par/edl/access-hivdrugs.shtml.

18 UNAIDS and WHO, *AIDS Epidemic Update.*

19 The industry ranked number one in all three of *Fortune* magazine's profitability measures in 2002. See http://www.fortune.com for more information.

20 Tom Hamburger, "Drug Industry Raises Spending For Ads, Lobbyists to Fight Critics," *Wall Street Journal Interactive Edition,* September 22, 2000, http://wsj.com/archive. See also Public Citizen, http://www.publiccitizen.org/congress/reform/drug_industry/articles.

21 WTO TRIPS online, www.wto.org/wto/english/tratop_e/trips_e/trips_e.htm.

22 For most countries, the deadline for revising (or creating) WTO-compliant patent legislation was January 2000,with a second tier for developing countries in 2005. At the WTO Ministerial in Doha, an extension to the deadline for the poorest countries until 2015 was negotiated. However, the US government has pressed some countries to change their legislation in advance of this deadline. Additionally, the Trade Promotion Authority bill (aka "fast-track") signed by President Bush in August 2002 requires the United States Trade Representative to attempt to accelerate TRIPS compliance in bi- and multilateral trade negotiations.

23 Chakravarthi Raghavan, *Recolonization: GATT, the Uruguay Round, and the Third World* (London: Atlantic Highlands, 1990) 118.

24 In 1990 the *Multinational Monitor* noted that "trade negotiators from the US, working with the Reagan and Bush administrations, including individual companies, as well as industry groups like the Pharmaceutical Manufacturers Association (PMA) and the Intellectual Property Committee (IPC), a coalition of 13 major US companies, including IBM, DuPont, General Motors, Merck and Co. and Pfizer, have strongly lobbied the Reagan and Bush administrations on intellectual property issues. The IPC claims to have 'played a key advisory role, at USTR's request, in developing the official US proposal on intellectual property that the US Government tabled before the GATT TRIPS working groups in October 1987.' The industry lobby group adds that its 'close relationship with USTR and Commerce has permitted the IPC to shape the US proposals and negotiating positions during the course of the

negotiations.'" Robert Weissman, "GATT Patent Plunder: TRIPping the Third World," *Multinational Monitor*, November 1990.

25 There is concern, especially in developing countries, that domestic industrial policies— limits on foreign competition, technology-transfer requirements etc., all aimed to help build local infant industries (including the pharmaceutical sector) and shield local companies from head-on competition with multinational firms, ultimately in order to build up the local economy so it can produce reliable and high-quality goods and services for the local population—may be declared "protectionist" and illegal under the current WTO international trade regime. Similarly, by not covering industries with patent privileges, these industries have greater flexibility to explore innovations such as developing new production processes so local firms can produce goods more cheaply and compete with more-established industry players.

26 Kristen Dawkins, *Gene Wars: The Politics of Biotechnology* (New York: Seven Stories Press, 1997.)

27 James Love and Michael Palmedo, *Examples of Compulsory Licensing of Intellectual Property in the United States*, Background Paper no. 1, Consumer Project on Technology, September 29, 2001 www.cptech.org/ip/health/cl;/us-cl.html.

28 GlaxoSmithKline's list price from January 2000.

29 US Department of State, "U. S. Government Efforts to Negotiate the Repeal, Termination or Withdrawal of Article 15(C) of the South African Medicines and Related Substances Act of 1965," Consumer Project on Technology, February 5, 1999, www.cptech.org/ip/health/sa/stdept-feb51999.html.

30 The S. 301, Super 301, and Special 301 provisions are successive amendments to the US Trade Act of 1974, authorizing the USTR to use coercive powers in trade negotiations to secure stated objectives from various trade partners. "Under S. 301, domestic producers and other interests could petition the USTR about 'unfair' trading practices of foreign countries [and] the USTR could aggressively negotiate with the foreign country concerned to comply with US demands and failing a satisfactory conclusion impose unilateral tariff and non-tariff barriers to imports from the countries concerned. The USTR also had powers to self-initiate some cases under S. 301, particularly with respect to intellectual property protection." Raghavan, *Recolonization: GATT*, 85.

31 Al Gore to James E. Clyburn, Consumer Project on Technology, June 25, 1999, www.cptech.org/ip/health/sa/vp-feb-25-99.html. In the letter, Gore endorses the use of compulsory licensing and parallel imports of pharmaceutical drugs in South Africa.

32 United States Trade Representative, press release, September 17, 1999, www.ustr.gov/releases/1999/09/99-76.html

33 Even after external pressures were greatly lessened, the Mbeki government in South Africa continued to resist the demands of people with AIDS for universal access to treatment. In spite of strong support from former president Mandela, the struggle for access to treatment continues in a country with one of the highest AIDS rates in the world.

34 John Donnelly, "Prevention Urged in AIDS Fight; Natsios Says Fund Should Spend Less on HIV Treatment," *Boston Globe*, June 7, 2001.

35 Paul Farmer et al., "Community-Based Approaches to HIV Treatment in Resource-Poor Settings," *Lancet* 358 (2001): 404–9.

36 Tina Rosenberg, "Look at Brazil," *New York Times Magazine*, January 28, 2001, http://www.nytimes.com/library/magazine/home/20010128mag-aids.html

37 Ibid.

38 Ibid.

39 Ibid.

40 Mary Anne Mercer of Health Alliance International in discussion with the author, June 2004.

41 "Consensus Statement on Antiretroviral Treatment for AIDS in Poor Countries by Individual Members of the Faculty of Harvard University," Harvard School of Public Health, April 4, 2002, http://www.hsph.harvard.edu/bioethics/pdf/consensus_aids_therapy.pdf.

42 Kofi Annan (address, African Summit on HIV/AIDS, Tuberculosis and Other Infectious Diseases, Abuja, Nigeria, April 26, 2001), excerpts available at www.un.org/News/Press/docs/2001?SGSM7779R1.doc.htm.

43 George W. Bush (remarks by the president during the announcement of the proposal for the Global Fund to Fight HIV/AIDS, Malaria and Tuberculosis, the White House, Washington, DC, May 11, 2001), www.whitehouse.gov/news/releases/2001/05/20010511-1.html.

44 Gauatam Naik, "In AIDS Fight, Ambitious Goals Meet Hard Realities," *Wall Street Journal*, July 1, 2004. "President Bush pledged $15 million over five years for AIDS and related programs overseas in his State of the Union Address in 2003...but [the US] is far from its goal of treating two million people by 2008...One reason for the slow progress, according to critics: the Bush administration is blocking access to cheaper versions of AIDS drugs and insisting on rules that favor big pharmaceutical companies."

45 The Office of the President of the US, "President Delivers the State of the Union Address," news release, January 28, 2003, www.whitehouse.gov/news/releases/20030128-19.html.

46 Medecins Sans Frontieres, Campaign for Access to Essential Medicines, briefing note, February 2004. In the fall of 2003, the Clinton Foundation announced that it had negotiated prices with a number of generic companies and producers of raw materials to make triple-drug therapy available for as low as $140 per person per year (for the fixed-dose combination of d4T40mg/3TC/NVP).

47 Ideas and wording were derived from Salih Booker and Wiliam Minter, "Global Apartheid," *Nation*, July 9, 2001.

CHAPTER THIRTEEN: THE STRUGGLE FOR PEOPLE'S HEALTH

1 International Forum on Globalization, *Alternatives to Economic Globalization* (San Franciso: Berrett-Koehler Publishers, 2002).

2 The Right Livelihood Award, Roll of Honor, "Gonoshasthaya Kendra," 1992. See http://www.rightlivelihood.se/recip/gk.htm.

3 See People's Health Movement Web site, www.phmovement.org

4 "Rolling Thunder: The Other America, Dissent in the Super-Rogue State," *New Internationalist*, November 2002, 351.

CONCLUSION: SHALL WE LEAVE IT TO THE EXPERTS?

1   Arundhati Roy, *Power Politics* (Cambridge, MA: South End Press, 2001), 2–3.

2   Jennifer Lee, "How Protesters Mobilized So Many and So Nimbly," *New York Times*, February 23, 2003.

3   Noam Chomsky, *Secrets, Lies, and Democracy* (Tucson, AZ: Odonian Press, 1994).

4   Tony Clarke and Maude Barlow, *MAI: Mulitlateral Agreement on Investment and the Threat to Canadian Security* (Toronto: Stoddart Publishing, 1997).

5   Article 25, Universal Declaration of Human Rights, adopted by UN General Assembly resolution 217A (III), December 10, 1948.

6   Article 12, International Covenant on Economic, Social, and Cultural Rights, adopted by UN General Assembly, January 3, 1976.

7   "Alma-Ata Declaration" (see chap. 3, n. 4)

8   WHO, "Ottawa Charter for Health Promotion" (First International Conference on Health Promotion, Ottawa, November 17–21, 1986), http://www.euro.who.int/AboutWHO/Policy/20010827_2.

INDEX

A

ACT UP, 151
Action Program on Essential Drugs,
    31–32
activism. *See* opposition movements
Adjustment with a Human Face, 3, 51
Aetna, 72–73, 76
Afghanistan, 97–99
African Growth and Opportunity
    Act (AGOA), 92
African National Congress (ANC),
    119, 177
Agreement on the Application on
    Sanitary and Phyto-Sanitary
    Standards (SPS), 81
agriculture: agreements, 81;
    biopiracy, 109–16; export model
    of, 6, 20, 58, 107–9, 112, 117,
    138; genetically altered foods,
    169; monoculture, 108–10, 163;
    potatoes, 107–8, 114–17; price
    deregulation, 108–9, 116–17;
    Roundup Ready technology,
    115–16; seed patents, 6, 110–12,
    114
ague. *See* malaria
AIDS. *See* HIV/AIDS
Alaska, 98
Albania, 99
Albrecht, Josef, 114
Algeria, 20

Alma-Ata Declaration, 5, 9, 28–31,
    35, 82, 164, 170–71. *See also*
    Health for All
Alternatives to Economic Globalization,
    163
American empire, 96, 98–99
American International Group
    (AIG), 72–73
Andean Pact, 91
Andean Sub-regional Integration
    Agreement, 93
Andean Trade Preference Act
    (ATPA), 91
Annan, Kofi, 52, 155
Anti-Ballistic Missiles (ABMs),
    97–98, 101, 103
Anti-Diarrhoeal Core Advocacy
    Group, 127
Antigua, 90
apartheid, 47, 103, 126–27, 147,
    156–57
Arc Ecology, 165
Argentina, 3, 49, 71–76, 91, 129–30
Asgrow Seed, 115
Asia-Pacific Economic Cooperation
    (APEC), 91
Asmal, Kader, 120, 124
Astra/Zeneca, 110
Aventis, 110

B

Bahrain, 93, 99
Balkans, 100
ballistic missile defense, 97–98, 101, 103
Bamako Initiative, 52, 146
Bangladesh, 27, 35, 37, 44, 164
Barbados, 90
barefoot doctor program, 27, 44
Basmati rice, 112–13
Basutoland, 19
"Battle of Seattle," 3, 161, 169
Baucum, Scott, 115
Bechtel, 98, 129–30, 162, 165
bed nets, 136, 141, 143
Bezruchka, Stephen, 5
Bikini Atoll, 101
biopiracy, 109–16
Bissio, Roberto, 2
Biyela, B.B., 121, 123–24
Boeing, 96, 98
Bolivia, 3, 91, 93, 129–30, 162–66, 169
Bond, Patrick, 6, 84, 120
Bosnia, 99
Botswana, 145
Brazil, 72–73, 83, 87, 91, 149, 152–53, 162, 164
Brenner, Joseph, 6, 79
Bretton Woods agreements, 9, 45, 81, 90, 128
Bristol-Myers Squibb, 148
British Guyana, 90
British Society for Plant Breeders, 114
Burma, 22
Burundi, 131
Bush, George W., 152, 155
Business Day, 124

C

California Senate Joint Resolution, 40, 88
California, 88, 98, 101, 165
Cambodia, 97
Camdessus, Michel, 4
Canada, 3, 15, 17, 86–87, 91–92, 116
Canada-US Free Trade Agreement, 91
Caribbean Basin Initiative (CBI), 93
Caribbean Community and Common Market (CARICOM), 91
Caribbean Free Trade Association (CARIFTA), 90–91
Carter, Jimmy, 17
Centers for Disease Control and Prevention (CDC), 134
Central American Common Market (CACM), 90
Central American Free Trade Agreement (CAFTA), 93
Cerón, Alejandro, 7, 161
Chernobyl nuclear accident, 103
child mortality, 164
Chile, 73, 75, 87, 91, 93, 96, 169
China, 15, 27, 44, 53, 86
Chissano, Joaqim, 124
chloroquine, 132, 134–36, 140, 142
cholera, 6, 75, 121–28
Chomsky, Noam, 97–98, 169
Ciba-Geigy, 110
CIGNA, 72–73, 76
Coca-Cola, 2, 157
Cochabamba water war, 3, 91, 93, 129–30, 162–66
Colombia, 75, 91, 93, 97
colonialism, 5, 19–26

Common Market of the South (See also MERCOSUR, Southern Cone Common Market), 72, 91

Comprehensive Health Care System (SIAS), 60–66

compulsory licensing, 149–51, 156

Congo, 140

Consultative Group on International Agricultural Research, 111

Convention on Biological Diversity (CBD), 113

cost recovery, 57, 80, 86, 122–24, 129, 146, 162

Costa Rica, 16, 93

Country Assistance Strategy, 120

Croatia, 99

Cuba, 16, 27, 86–87

currency devaluation, 45, 48–50, 76, 95, 108, 116

Curtin, Mike, 130

D

dams, 2, 45, 57, 122, 134, 138, 143

Das, Abhijit, 161

Davis, Paul, 6, 145

DDT, 135–36, 139

de León Carpio, Ramiro 62

debt: in Argentina, 49, 76–77; cancellation of, 157, 169; exports and, 48–49; infant mortality rates and, 16; relief, 52–54, 124, 157, 169; SAPs and, 45–53

Delta and Pine Land Company, 110

Democracy Center, 165

Democratic Convergence Front, 77

dengue fever, 75

development, economic: colonialism and, 20–24, 45; neoliberal approaches to, 33, 43–45, 53–55, 59, 70, 84, 138–40; people-centered, 3, 27–28, 37–41, 44–45, 119, 164–65, 170; SPHC and, 29–31

diabetes, 102

diarrhea, 32, 65, 75, 119, 122–23, 127–28, 132–33

Dickenson Bay Agreement, 90

Disability Adjusted Life Years (DALYs), 34

disease: social causes of, 13, 18, 28–31, 37–41, 44–45, 99–104, 133–36; treatment models, 4–5, 19–27, 31, 40, 45, 63, 69–78. *See also individual diseases, especially* cholera, HIV/AIDS, malaria

Dlamini, Phetsile, 145

Doctors Without Borders, 154, 165

Doha Declaration, 156, 165–66

donors (financial), 24–25, 29–31, 40, 45–47, 134, 138, 141–42, 154–55

drugs: Bamako Initiative, 52; chloroquine, 132, 134–36, 140, 142; costs, 2, 52, 150, 157; essential, 31–32, 40, 52, 81, 150, 152, 157, 171; generic, 147–49, 153–57, 166; HIV/AIDS medicines, 147–50, 157; Medicines Act, 150–52; patents, 81, 147–49, 153; resistance to, 134–36

DuPont, 110, 148

Duvalier family, 47

E

Ebeye Island, 101–3

ecological issues: deregulation and, 85, 88, 95; globalization and, 25–26, 134–35, 157, 163, 171; groups, 127, 163, 165; health and, 38–39, 134–36, 139; pollution, 2–3, 95, 100–101, 116, 121–28, 165; privatization and, 79, 81, 84, 163; terminator technology and, 110–12, 115; unfunded and underfunded efforts, 65–66, 82, 122, 127

The Economic Burden of Malaria, 136

Ecuador, 91, 93

education: community, 128, 162–64, 169; non-priority of, 63, 67, 70; trade agreements and, 16, 48, 70, 85, 92; universal, 16–17, 30, 39, 44, 54, 77

Egypt, 22

El Salvador, 90, 93, 162–63

elder discrimination, 4, 74–76

electricity, 50, 59, 77, 83, 102, 120, 122, 126

Enewetak Atoll, 101

Enhanced Structural Adjustment Facility (ESAF), 52

Enron, 83

Enyart, James, 149

epidemics, 75, 119–25, 131, 133, 135, 145–47

equity: economic development and, 14–15, 43–45, 53–54, 65; free market and, 27, 31, 35; health care and, 9–13, 16–18, 27, 53, 58, 64, 139; income gaps and, 3–5, 13–17, 19, 33, 44, 80, 126; PHM Charter and, 37–41; power relations and, 163, 171; UNICEF and, 31

essential drugs, 31–32, 40, 52, 81, 150, 152, 157, 171

European Economic Community (EEC), 90

Evans, Richard, 125–26

The Expert Consultation of Diet, Nutrition and the Prevention of Chronic Diseases, 33

exports: agricultural, 20, 58, 107–9, 112, 138; debt and, 48–49; exploitation of poor countries and, 2, 10, 46, 95, 107, 116, 143; globalization focus on, 10, 95, 107–8, 116, 143; land use shifts and, 20, 107; oil, 46, 96; pesticide use and, 138, 143; services market and, 84; water, 88

EXXEL Group, 72–73

F

famine, 16, 107, 109–10, 146

Farmer, Paul, 152

fertility regulation, 24, 40–41

FFF program (family planning, food supplements, female education), 30

Filipino/American Coalition for Environmental Solutions (FACES), 165

Financing Health Services in Developing Countries: An Agenda for Reform, 33, 57

food: famine, 16, 107, 109–10, 146; formula feeding, 31–32; genetically altered, 169; potatoes, 107–8, 114–17; security, 6, 51, 116; subsidization of basic, 16, 49. *See also* agriculture

Food and Agriculture Organization (FAO), 33
Ford Foundation, 29
Fort, Meredith, 7, 68, 161, 196
Framework Convention on Tobacco Control (FCTC), 32
France, 86, 91
free market: at expense of social services, 43–44, 49–50, 58, 69–70, 125; growth *vs.* development argument and, 14–18, 25, 33, 43, 53, 75, 125; health care and, 34–36, 60–61, 133, 137, 139, 164
free trade: infant formula and, 32; national governments restricted by, 2, 50, 79, 82; questionable benefits of, 3–4, 107, 126, 167; results of NAFTA decade, 15; treaties and agreements, 72, 77, 87, 90–93; unbalanced agreements, 2, 5, 14–15, 87; Washington Consensus principles, 80
Freire, Paulo, 162
FTAA (Free Trade Area of the Americas), 77, 79–80, 87–88, 92–93

G
G7/G8 summits, 91–92, 154–55
Gallup, John, 137
GATS (General Agreement on Trade in Services), 79–81, 84–88, 92
GATT (General Agreement on Tariffs and Trade), 81, 90, 92, 148–49
General Dynamics, 96

Georgia, 99
Gerber, 82
Germany, 91, 114, 125
Ghana, 22
Gish, Oscar, 5, 19
GlaxoSmithKline, 150
Global Exchange, 52, 183
Global Fund to Fight AIDS, Tuberculosis, and Malaria, 53, 142, 153–57
globalization: definitions, 1, 14, 18–20, 69–70, 95–96, 113; environmental issues and, 25–26, 134–35, 157, 163, 171; exploitive effects of, 19–20, 167; export focus of, 10, 95, 107–8, 116, 143; as impediment to health, 6, 105, 131–39, 143, 164; inequality increase due to, 5, 11, 18. *See also* neoliberal economic theory; privatization; regulation/deregulation
Gloyd, Steve, 5, 43
GOBI child survival strategy, 30–31
Gono Pharmaceuticals, 164
Gonoshasthaya Kendra (GK), 163–64. *See also* People's Health Center of Bengal
Gore, Al, 150–51
governments: decisions overturned by trade agreements, 14–15, 54, 79–80, 82–85, 88–89, 113, 156; enforcement and control by, 58, 63, 97–98; public sector services and, 54–55, 80, 84, 86; reduction of, 48–50, 58, 63, 69–72, 79–84, 86, 88–89, 162; regulation of vital services by, 40, 65, 79–89,

108–9; restricted by free trade agreements, 2, 50, 79, 82

Greenpeace, 103

Groenewald, Pam, 127

Group for Environmental Monitoring, 127

Group of Eight (G8), 92, 154–55

Group of Seven (G7), 91, 154

Guantanamo Bay camp, 97

Guatemalan Republican Front (FRG), 62

Guatemala, 6, 57–68, 82, 90, 93, 96, 163

Guidetti, Geri, 111

Gulf Wars, 98–100

H

Haiti, 47

Hall, David, 130

Halliburton, 96

Harvard Center for International Development, 136, 155

Hawaii, 100, 102–3

health: determinants of, 11–16, 26, 29, 51, 171; ecological issues and, 38–39, 134–36, 139; as a fundamental human right, 5, 9, 28–31, 35–37, 39–41, 45, 68, 170–71; reproductive, 24, 40–41. *See also* disease; health care; health care systems

Health Action International, 165

Health Alliance International, 5

health care services: barriers to use of, 57, 71, 74–75, 80, 86, 146; expenditures per capita, 4, 53, 60; financing, 33–36, 53, 71, 86, 146; as fundamental human right, 5, 9, 28–31, 35–37, 39–41,

45, 170–71; traditional practitioners of, 20–21, 27, 40, 86; workers and salaries, 50–51

health care systems: exclusions, 34, 74–76, 86, 137, 154; infrastructure, 65–67; managed care, 25, 34–36, 40, 69–78, 86, 137, 154; models of, 4–6, 19–27, 31, 40, 58, 67, 69–78, 86; privatization of, 25, 34–36, 38, 40, 59, 69–76, 87–88, 162, 171; public sanitation and, 12, 21–22, 49, 54, 60, 80, 125–28; reforms, 57–68, 70–80

Health for All, 5, 10, 28, 31, 35–37, 45, 171. *See also* Alma-Ata Declaration; People's Health Movement

Health GAP (Global Access Project), 6, 154–55, 165

health insurance, 4, 25, 34–36, 40, 69–76, 86

Hightower, Jim, 166

HIPC Initiative (Heavily Indebted Poor Countries), 52–53, 124

HIV/AIDS: activism, 162; apartheid/racism and, 47, 103, 126–27, 147, 156–57; drugs for, 147–50, 152–57; economic causes of epidemic, 145–47; global trust fund for, 53, 142, 153–57; infection rates, 145, 153; prevention, 150–54, 156

Holtz, Timothy, 131

Honduras, 90, 93

Hong, Evelyne, 5, 27

Hong Kong, 44

Horton, Richard, 104

human rights: clean water as, 121–24, 128–30; demands for basic, 170–71; health care as, 5, 9, 28–31, 35–37, 39–41, 45, 68, 170–71; sanitation as, 29
Hungary, 99

I

IADB (Inter-American Development Bank), 55, 58, 60–65
IFIs (international financial institutions), 62–63, 66, 70–72, 86, 146, 162, 164, 168. *See also* Inter-American Development Bank; International Monetary Fund; World Bank
IFPMA (International Federation of Pharmaceutical Manufacturers' Associations), 148
illiteracy, 18, 20, 23, 25
IMF. *See* International Monetary Fund (IMF)
immunization, 29–30, 51–52, 65, 75, 83, 141
imports, 48–49, 81–82, 102, 116, 149–51, 156
income disparities, 3–5, 13–17, 19, 33, 44, 80, 126
India: AIDS medicines from, 149, 156; Basmati rice and, 112–13; Bengal famine, 107; cash crops in, 107–9, 116–17; equity health care service models, 16–17, 27, 44–45; GOBI in, 30; malaria eradication programs in, 135; Navdanya movement, 163; and Pakistan conflict, 98; patent law

overruled by WTO, 113; on terminator technology, 111
Indonesia, 47, 116
Infant Formula Marketing Code, 31–32
infant mortality, 11–13, 15–17, 20
Innovation in Public Health prize, 61
Inouye, Daniel, 100
insecticide use, 2, 110, 133–36, 138–39, 141–43
Instancia Nacional de Salud, 6, 61, 67–68, 163
insurance, health, 4, 25, 34–36, 40, 69–76, 86. *See also* managed care
intellectual property: compulsory licensing, 149–51, 156; Doha Declaration, 156, 165–66; GATT and, 148; parallel importing and, 150–51; patents and, 148; pharmaceuticals as, 147–50, 155–56; seed as, 110–16; TRIPS agreement, 81, 112–13, 116, 147–51, 156–57, 166; WTO and, 112, 147, 156
Intellectual Property Committee, 148
Inter-American Development Bank (IADB), 55, 58, 60–65
International AIDS Conference (Durban), 154
International Bank for Reconstruction and Development, 45. *See also* World Bank
International Code of Marketing of Breastmilk Substitutes, 31–32

International Covenant on
Economic, Social, and Cultural
Rights (UN), 170
International Federation of
Pharmaceutical Manufacturers'
Associations (IFPMA), 148
International Forum on
Globalization (IFG), 163
International Managed Care
Advisors (IMCA), 73
International Medical Group (IMG),
72
International Monetary Fund (IMF):
Camdessus and, 4; on health
care, 4–5, 86, 146; Milanovic
and, 3–4; neoliberal philosophy
of, 2, 45–47, 55, 81, 95; SAPs
and, 43, 48–53, 59–60, 70, 95,
146; Stiglitz and, 3
International Trade Organization
(ITO), 81
Investing in Health, 33–34, 57, 65, 70
Iowa, 115
Iran, 90
Iraq, 90, 96–97, 99–100, 103
Iriart, Celia, 6, 69, 89, 197
ISAPRE (Instituciones de Salud
Previsional) managed care, 74
Israel, 93
Italy, 3, 91

J
Jamaica, 22, 49–50, 142
Japan, 12–13, 17, 86, 91, 99–100,
104
Johnson and Johnson, 148
Jordan, 86, 93
Jubasi, Mawande, 122
Jubilee movement, 47, 52, 169

K
Kachur, S. Patrick, 6, 131
Kasrils, Ronnie, 124
Kazakhstan, 99
Kellogg Brown and Root, 96
Kentucky, 115
Kenya, 22
Kerala (India), 16–17, 44, 53
Kerry, John, 154
Keynes, John Maynard, 46
Kohl, Helmut, 45
Korea, 15, 97–98
Kosovo, 99
Kuala Lumpur, Malayasia, 35
Kuwait, 90, 99
Kwajalein Atoll, 101–3
Kyoto World Water Forum, 129
Kyrgyzstan, 99

L
labor: activists, 86, 95, 129, 157, 162,
169; cheap, native, 1, 19–20, 58,
95, 102, 146; child, 83;
movements and unions, 17, 20,
49, 77–78, 95, 121–22, 162;
standards, 51, 81–83, 85, 171;
underemployment, 25, 50;
unemployment, 17, 25, 50, 70,
76–78, 126; wages and benefits,
50, 61, 66, 76–78
Lancet, 104
Landless Workers Movement
(MST), 77
Laos, 97
Latin American Free Trade
Agreement (LAFTA), 90
Latin American Integration
Association (LAIA/ALADI), 91
Lee, Barbara, 154

Leipzig Conference on Plant
    Genetic Resources, 114
Leipzig Global Plan of Action, 113
Les Nouvelles, 149
Lesotho, 19
Lewis, Stephen, 146
Liberia, 140
Life and Debt, 50
life expectancies, 11–13, 15–17, 145
lifeline water, 54, 120–25, 128–29
literacy, 18, 20, 23, 25
Livingstone, Frank, 135
Lockheed Martin, 96, 98

M
Macedonia, 99
Mahler, Halfdan, 28
MAI (Multilateral Agreement on
    Investment), 92, 162
Mail & Guardian, 120
Mâkua Valley, Oahu, Hawaii, 100
malaria: chloroquine, 132, 134–36,
    140, 142; combating, 24, 30, 39,
    53, 60, 132, 134–37, 139–40,
    142; global fund to fight, 53,
    142, 153–57; insecticide
    resistance, 134–35; in Nicaragua,
    140–41; pesticide overuse,
    138–39; reglobalization of, 6,
    105, 131–39, 143; in US, 133–36
Malaysia, 3, 35
managed care: exclusions, 34, 74–76,
    86, 137, 154; HMOs, 4–6, 25,
    69–78; profitability of, 34–36,
    40, 73–76. *See also* health care
    systems
Mandela, Nelson, 150, 152
Mara, Ibinibini, 127
Marcos, Ferdinand, 47

Marshall Islands, 95, 98, 101–4
Marshall Plan, 45
maternal mortality, 164
Mathiason, Nick, 129
Mauritius, 103, 142
Mbeki, Thabo, 151
McDonald's, 109, 117
Médecins Sans Frontières (MSF),
    154, 165
Medicaid, 65, 74
medical care. *See* health care; health
    care systems
Medicare, 65, 74, 76
medicines. *See* drugs
Medicines and Related Substances
    Control Act (South Africa),
    150–52
Mercer, Mary Anne, 5
Merck and Co., 148
MERCOSUR (Common Market of
    the Southor or Southern Cone
    Common Market), 72, 91
Merhy, Emerson, 6, 69
Mestrallet, Gerard, 130
Metalclad Corporation, 88
Mexico, 15, 27, 87, 92–93, 110
Middle East Free Trade Area
    (MEFTA), 93
Milanovic, Branko, 3–4
militarism, 6, 95–104
Millennium Summit, 52
Mobuto, Sese Seko, 47
monoculture, 108–10, 163. *See also*
    agriculture
monopolies: medicine, 81, 147–49,
    153; seed, 108–15, 163
Monsanto, 110–12, 115–16, 148–49
Montevideo Treaties, 90, 91
Morocco, 93

Morrissey, Megan, 94
mortality rates, 11–13, 16–17, 20,
    133, 164
Mozambique, 30, 50–51, 53, 124,
    129, 141, 161
Muller, Mike, 124, 127
Multilateral Agreement on
    Investment (MAI), 92, 169
Myanmar, 22

N
NAFTA (North American Free
    Trade Agreement), 14–15, 79,
    87–88, 92–93
Namibia, 146
National Academy of Sciences, 80
National Advancement Party (PAN),
    60
National Health Advocacy Platform
    (Instancia), 6, 61, 67–68, 163
National Security Council, 150
NATO (North American Treaty
    Organization), 90
Natsios, Andrew, 152
Navajo people, 103
Navdanya movement, 163
neoliberal economic theory: cost
    recovery in, 57, 80, 86, 122–24,
    129, 146, 162; defined, 2;
    development and, 33, 43–45,
    53–55, 59, 70, 84, 138–40;
    disease and, 137; export focus,
    108–9; growth and, 14–15,
    43–44, 59, 125; on health care,
    4–5, 25, 34–36, 40, 69–76, 86,
    137, 146; IMF and, 2, 45–47, 55,
    81, 95; WTO and, 2, 108. *See also*
    free market; free trade;
    privatization; trade agreements

Netherlands, 156
nets, insecticide-treated, 136, 141,
    143
New York City, 20
Nicaragua, 30, 90, 93
Nigeria, 22, 52, 155
Northrop Grumman, 96
Novartis, 110
Nqayi, Samson, 123

O
Okinawa, 100
Oliver, Melvin, 111
Olver, Chippy, 120
Oman, 99
OPEC (Organization of Petroleum
    Exporting Countries), 90
opposition movements: Bolivia
    water wars, 3, 89, 93, 129–30,
    162–66; Chomsky on, 169;
    against IMF, 52; Jubilee
    movement, 47, 52, 169; labor
    movements, 20, 49, 77, 162;
    against MAI, 92, 169; against
    NAFTA, 3, 93, 156, 159, 161;
    against privatization of health
    care, 162; against Suez water,
    130; worldwide, 52, 77–78, 88,
    96, 103, 148, 166, 169–72;
    against WTO, 3, 93, 156, 159,
    161, 169
Organization for Economic
    Cooperation and Development
    (OECD), 90
Organization of African Unity, 155
Ottawa Conference on Health
    Promotion, 171
Oxfam, 52

P

Pakistan, 98–99
Pan-American Health Organization (PAHO), 61
Paraguay, 91
parallel importing, 150–51
Paris Agreement on Intellectual Property, 148
patents: intellectual property, 112, 113; pharmaceuticals, 81, 147–49, 153; rice, 112–13; seed, 6, 110–12, 114. *See also* Trade Related Aspects of Intellectual Property Rights
People's Health Center of Bengal, 163–64
People's Health Charter, 37–41, 164
People's Health Movement (PHM), 35–41, 164, 170
Pepsico, 2, 108, 117
Peru, 91, 93
pesticides, 2, 110, 133–36, 138–39, 141–43
Pfizer, 148
pharmaceutical industry, 4, 81, 147–50, 152–57
Philippines, 27, 100, 165
Pioneer Hi-bred, 110
Plant Variety Act, 115
polio, 24, 75
pollution, 2–3, 95, 100–101, 116, 121–28, 165. *See also* ecological issues
Population Council, 29
Portugal, 86
potato growers, 107–8, 114–17
prefabricated programs. *See* vertical organizations
Presidential AIDS Initiative, 156

prevention: AIDS, 150–56; breastmilk as, 32; cholera, 80, 125–26; curative care and, 23, 67; education, 29, 65, 80; essential drugs list, 150; immunization, 29–30, 51–52, 65, 75–76, 83, 141; malaria, 80, 132–34, 137–38, 141–42; PHC definitions, 29; social policy and, 44–45, 65, 70, 75
Primary Health Care (PHC) movement, 28–31, 35–41, 170
privatization: cost recovery and, 57, 80, 86, 122–24, 129, 146, 162; ecological issues and, 79, 81, 84, 163; of electricity, 59, 77; government roles reduced by, 70, 79, 82–84; of health care systems, 25, 34–36, 38, 40, 59, 69–76, 86–88, 162, 171; trade agreements and, 79; of water, 79, 84, 120–24, 128–30; World Bank and, 10, 70–71, 86, 129–30. *See also* neoliberal economic theory; regulation/deregulation
prostitution, 100, 102, 147
Prudential, 72
Public Citizen's Global Trade Watch, 86
public goods, 35, 55, 70, 72, 123, 126–27, 138–39, 143. *See also* human rights
public sector. *See* governments
public services. *See* education; electricity; governments; health care systems; privatization; sanitation; water
Public Services International, 86, 130

Puerto Rico, 103, 129, 169

Q

Qatar, 99

R

racism, 47, 103, 147, 152

Raytheon, 96

Reagan, Ronald, 45, 81

Reagan Ballistic Missile Defense Test Site (RTS), 101–3

regulation/deregulation: prices, 108–9, 116–17, 119–29, 162–66; of sanitation, 84, 121–22; of service industry, 84; of vital services, 40, 65, 79–89, 108–9; of water, 84, 119–29, 162–66. *See also* privatization

reproductive health, 24, 40–41

resistance, drug, 134–36

resistance, insecticide, 134–36, 139, 142–43

resource guide, 179–89

rice, 102, 109–13

RiceTec, Inc., 112–13

right to health care, 5, 9, 28–31, 35–37, 39–41, 45, 170–71

Rockefeller, David, 91

Rockefeller Foundation, 24, 29

Roll Back Malaria (RBM), 142, 157

Ronald Reagan Ballistic Missile Defense Test Site (RTS), 101–3

Rongelap Island, 101

Roome, John, 120

Roundup Ready technology, 115–16

Roy, Arundhati, 167, 172

Rural Advancement Foundation International (RAFI), 109, 111, 116

Russia, 92, 145

S

Sachs, Jeffrey, 104, 137

Sachs Commission, 128

San Luis Potosí, Mexico, 87

Sanders, David, 127

Sandoz, 110

sanitation: as basic human right, 29; deregulation of, 84, 121–22; public health and, 12, 21–22, 49, 54, 60, 80, 125–28

SAPs (structural adjustment programs): destabilizing effects of, 45–53; government role reduced by, 69–72; health and, 10, 52–53, 70–71, 146; International Monetary Fund (IMF) and, 43, 48–53, 59–60, 70, 95, 146; purpose of, 1, 43–45, 54, 69, 95; World Bank and, 48–54, 59, 69–71

SARS virus, 167–68

Saudi Arabia, 90, 99

schistosomiasis, 24, 27

Schlesinger, James, 96

Schmeiser, Percy, 116

Scotland, 114–15

Seattle, 3, 161, 169

secrecy, 62, 71, 79, 87–88, 162

seed: conservation, 163; diversity *vs.* monoculture, 109–10; law, 110–16; monopolies, 108–15, 163; patents, 6, 110–16; technology, 111. *See also* agriculture

Seed Act, 114

Selective Primary Health Care (SPHC), 29–36, 61, 82

semantics, creative, 87–88, 109, 116, 120, 124

Sen, Amartya, 3, 13
sex trade, 100, 102, 147
Shaffer, Ellen, 6, 79
Shand, Hope, 109, 116
Shezi, David, 122–23
Shiva, Vandana, 6, 107
SIAS (Comprehensive Health Care System), 60–66
Sierra Leone, 140
Singapore, 44
slave trade, 19, 47
Slovenia, 86
smallpox, 24
smoking, 12–13
Snow, John, 80
Social Security Doctors' Union (SIMETRISSS), 162
Social Security Hospital Workers' Union (STISSS), 162
social stratification, 13–14
Social Watch (Uruguay), 2
Solomon Islands, 132
Sourcebook on Community Driven Development in the Africa Region—Community Action Programs (World Bank), 129
South Africa, 27, 47, 84, 103, 119–29, 150–54, 161, 177
South African Municipal Workers Union (SAMWU), 121–22
South Korea, 44, 53, 97
Southern Cone Common Market (MERCOSUR), 91
Soviet Union, 16, 92, 97–98, 145
Spain, 47
special campaigns, 24–25, 30–31, 40
SPHC (Selective Primary Health Care), 29–36, 61, 82
Sri Lanka, 16, 22, 27, 44, 53

Stalin, Josef, 16
STDs (sexually transmitted diseases), 147
Stiglitz, Joseph, 3, 83
Stockholm Agreement, 148
structural adjustment programs (SAPs). *See* SAPs
subsidization: defined, 66, 83; of foodstuffs, 16, 49; GATS rules and, 85; of profitable business, 96, 108; of social services, 44, 49–50, 58, 80, 87, 120–25, 128–29; unbalanced, 2, 14–15, 83; of water, 120–25, 128–29. *See also* tariffs; taxes
Suez (corporation), 123, 125, 129–30
sugar industry, 33
Suharto, 47
suicide, 2, 107, 116
Sun Belt Water, Inc., 87
Sunday Times, 121–22
Surinam, 132
Swaziland, 145
Sweden, 17, 86

T
Taiwan, 44, 53–54, 142
Tajikistan, 99
Tanzania, 22, 27
tariffs: GATT, 81, 90, 92, 148–49; removal of, 49, 58, 79, 81, 91–93; value of, 83; water, 120, 123–25, 129
taxes, 5, 17, 66–67, 83, 108, 171. *See also* subsidization; tariffs
Technical Barriers to Trade (TBT) agreement, 81
Tejada de Rivero, David, 29

"terminator technology," 110–12, 115

Thailand, 3, 100, 149, 153, 156

Thatcher, Margaret, 81

Third World Network, 5

301 Watch List, 151–52

Tobacco Company Strategies to Undermine Tobacco Control Activities at the World Health Organization, 32–33

tobacco industry, 32–33

Tobago, 22

Tobin Tax, 171

trade agreements: farm crisis and, 107–9, 116–17; food supply and, 82; government decisions overturned by, 79–80, 82–83, 113; government role reduced by, 48–50, 58, 63, 80–84, 86, 88–89, 162; health and, 148; purposes of, 82–83; timeline of, 90–93; unbalanced, 2, 5, 14–15, 87. *See also* intellectual property; *specific agreements*

Trade Promotion Authority bill, 88

Trade Related Aspects of Intellectual Property Rights (TRIPS), 81, 112–13, 116, 147–51, 156–57, 166

Treatment Action Campaign of South Africa, 152

Treaty of Asunición, 91

Treaty on European Union, 91

Trilateral Commission, 91

Trinidad, 22

TRIPS. *See* Trade Related Aspects of Intellectual Property Rights

tuberculosis, 27, 31, 38, 75, 80, 123, 133, 155, 168

Tunisia, 86

typhus, 75

U

Uganda, 53

Ukraine, 145

UN Development Program (UNDP), 3, 159

UN International Covenant on Economic, Social, and Cultural Rights, 170–71

underemployment, 25, 50

unemployment, 17, 25, 50, 70, 76–78, 126

UNICEF, 3, 28, 30–31, 45, 51–52, 82, 145

United Arab Emirates, 99

United Kingdom, 3, 91, 114–15

Universal Declaration of Human Rights, 170

Uruguay, 2, 81, 91

US National Security Council, 150

US Patent and Trademark Office, 150

US-South Africa Bi-national Commission, 150

US State Department aid policy, 12

US Trade and Development Act, 93

USAID (United States Agency for International Development), 30–31

USDA (US Department of Agriculture), 110–12

USTR (US Trade Representative), 148, 150–52

Utrik Island, 101

Uzbekistan, 99

V

vaccinations, 29–30, 51–52, 65, 75, 83, 141

Vatican, 30
Venezuela, 90–91, 93
Veotte, Lance, 121
Verdugo, Juan Carlos, 6, 57
vertical organizations, 24–25, 30–31, 40
Vieques Island, 169
Vietnam, 27, 97, 100, 168
Vivendi (corporation), 129

W
Waitzkin, Howard, 6, 69
Wall Street Journal, 110
War on Drugs, 97
War on Terror, 98
wars: in Africa, 140; in Central America, 141; Gulf Wars, 98–100; Spanish-American War, 47; Vietnam War, 97, 168; World War II, 17, 45, 96
Washington Consensus, 43, 48, 80, 161, 178
water: as a basic human right, 121–24, 128–30; Bolivia water war, 3, 91, 93, 129–30, 162–66; commodification of, 6, 79, 84, 88, 105, 119–29, 162–66; in South Africa, 54, 120–25, 128–29
Werner, David, 28
Where There Is No Doctor (Werner), 29
WHO (World Health Organization), 24, 31, 40
Wolfensohn, James, 124
women, 147
World Bank: and AIDS, 146, 153; creation of, 45, 81; debt and, 45–47, 52; government decisions undermined by, 54; on health reform, 4, 10, 30–34, 57–60, 63–65; HIPC Initiative and, 124; on mosquito net sales, 71; neoliberal policies of, 2–3, 33, 38, 95, 108, 116; privatization and, 10, 70–71, 86, 129–30; purposes, 43, 45; SAPs and, 48–54, 59, 69–71; "silent" policy-making, 71; South African water crisis and, 120, 124, 128–29, 138; SPHC programs and, 30–31; timeline, 90–93
World Economic Forum, 164
World Health Assembly (WHA), 31–32
World Social Forum (WSF), 164–65, 170
WTO (World Trade Organization): deregulation required by, 14–15; dispute resolution, 82, 85, 151; double standards of, 2, 83; intellectual property and, 112, 147, 156; neoliberal economic theory and, 2, 108; overturning government decisions, 14–15, 79, 82–85, 88–89, 113, 156; protests against, 3, 89, 93, 156, 159, 161; purpose of, 81–82, 92. *See also* GATS; GATT; Trade Related Aspects of Intellectual Property Rights

Y
Yamada, Seiji, 6, 95
Yamin, Alicia, 89
Yugoslavia, 99

Z
Zimbabwe, 50, 145

RELATED TITLES FROM SOUTH END PRESS

Globalization from Below: The Power of Solidarity
Jeremy Brecher, Tim Costello, Brendan Smith
$13
ISBN 0-89608-622-4 (paper)

Propaganda and the Public Mind: Conversations with Noam Chomsky
Interviews with David Barsamian
$16
ISBN 0-89608-634-8 (paper)

Panic Rules! Everything You Need to Know About the Global Economy
Robin Hahnel
$12
ISBN 0-89608-609-7 (paper)

Global AIDS: Myths and Facts, Tools for Fighting the AIDS Pandemic
Alexander Irwin, Joyce Millen, Dorothy Fallows
$19
ISBN 0-89608-673-9 (paper)

Cochabamba: Water Rebellion in Bolivia
(forthcoming November, 2004)
Oscar Olivera, in collaboration with Tom Lewis
$14
ISBN 0-89608-702-6 (paper)

Power Politics
Arundhati Roy
$12
ISBN 0-89608-668-2 (paper)

Biopiracy: The Plunder of Nature and Knowledge
Vandana Shiva
$13
ISBN 0-89608-555-4 (paper)

Stolen Harvest: The Hijacking of the Global Food Supply
Vandana Shiva
$14
ISBN 0-89608-607-0 (paper)

Water Wars: Privatization, Pollution, and Profit
Vandana Shiva
$14
ISBN 0-89608-650-X (paper)

Dangerous Intersections: Feminist Perspectives on Population, Environment, and Development
Edited by Jael Silliman and Ynestra King
$20
ISBN 0-89608-597-X (paper)

Undivided Rights: Women of Color Organizing for Reproductive Justice
Jael Silliman, Marlene Gerber Fried, Loretta Ross and Elena Guitierrez
(forthcoming, November 2004)
$20
ISBN 0-89608-729-8 (paper)

For ordering information, please call 1-800-533-8478 or visit <www.southendpress.org>.